My Canada

Edited by Glenn Keith Cowan

Royalties from this book will go to the Terry Fox Fund for cancer research, the Terry Fox Canadian Youth Centre, Ottawa, and the Roger Doucet Humanitarian Fund for cancer patients, Montreal.

IRWIN PUBLISHING

Toronto   Canada

Copyright © Irwin Publishing Inc., 1984

Canadian Cataloguing in Publication Data

My Canada

ISBN 0-7720-1444-2

1. Canada.   I. Cowan, Glenn Keith, 1917-

FC60.M9 1984   971   C84-098243-7
F1008.3.M9 1984

Typeset by Q Composition Inc.
Printed in Canada

1 2 3 4 5 6 7 8 WC 91 90 89 88 87 86 85 84

Published by Irwin Publishing Inc.

---✳︎---

Contents

2. "Go Canada!"

Gaetan Boucher
Ed Werenich
Dave King
Steve Podborski
Gilles Villeneuve
Guy Lafleur
John Magill
Alex Baumann
Phil Esposito
Guillaume Leblanc
Desai Williams
Gerry Dattilio
Russ Jackson
Hugh Campbell
Al Hackner
Philippe Chartrand
Mike Bossy
Gary Carter
Susan Nattrass

3. Artists' Impressions

Alex Colville
David Peregrine
Raymond Daveluy
Hugh MacLennan
Douglas Chamberlain
Veronica Tennant
Roger Lemelin
Ann Rohmer
Vanessa Harwood
Don Harron
Alden Nowlan
Annette av Paul

4. My Life

Russell W. Gowing
Ray Male
Mary Dover
William Mitchell
Dorothy Boan
Bill McNamara
Kay Reynolds
D.W. Darby
William Callahan
John Pierce

---------------- ✳ ----------------

Acknowledgements

My special thanks are due to all those who readily
contributed articles and to a number of persons who
gave encouragement, time, effort, and financial and
other forms of aid in the production process, among
them: author Bruce Hutchison of Victoria; Robert
Bonner of Vancouver; Dr. Davidson Dunton, Bill
Snarr, and Jean Piggott of Ottawa; Jim Osborne of
Regina; Montreal's Camil Desroches and Noel Perüse;
author Frederick B. Watt of Victoria; Cleo Mowers,
Lethbridge publisher, and Ray Male of New Jersey and
Prince Edward Island, for invaluable editorial
assistance; to Ken and Anne Fell of Oakville, Ontario,
for their help and provision of a home away from
home; and to my wonderfully supportive wife, Betty
Ann, for constructive editorial advice and for suffering
three years of household clutter from one table to
another as work progressed, following two previous
years of petition clutter.

Special thanks are due to publisher John Irwin for
his faith in the project, to editorial director John
Pearce, whose experienced judgement made
completion of the project possible, and to copy-editor
D.G. Bastian; with appreciation to Bev Johnston of
Victoria, for superb typing, cheerfully provided.

No less important is my grateful appreciation to the
hundreds of Canadians from every province who
voluntarily worked on the gathering of signatures for
the People to People Petition for Canadian Unity and
on its presentation to the people of Quebec from the
rest of Canada just before the 1980 Referendum,
which laid the foundation for this work, *My Canada*.

Glenn Keith Cowan

My
Canada

---------------------------- * ----------------------------

Introduction

What began in October 1977 on a troubled homeward walk along the sunset-bathed North River roads of Charlottetown, Prince Edward Island, past the ancient pillared mansion where Macdonald, Cartier, and the other Fathers of Confederation had dined and danced as they conceived a nation, has ended in early winter, 1984. I am setting down the final words for this book on the equally colourful shores of the Esquimalt Lagoon in Victoria, British Columbia, where I have come to live. Born in Rainy River, Ontario, of Canadian, Scottish, Irish, Welsh, and English ancestry, raised in industrial Hamilton, enriched by university years in Montreal, I have lived, worked, or travelled in all the provinces, and fought for Canada in war. I am in love with her, warts and all, and concerned for her future.

The Charlottetown walk happened during the most critical time in Canada's more than a century of existence. Bruce Hutchison, British Columbia's observant writer–historian earlier had warned that if Quebec chose to leave Canada in a referendum, the remaining scattered parts of Canada would prove impossible to hold together for long. Every part of the country would suffer. A magnificent experiment in freely conceived nationhood would end and the world would lose a widely admired model at a time of explosive divisions. A great healing effort was needed for our national malaise.

I could no longer push aside a persistent inner urge that had tugged at me for days, triggered by an an-

1

nouncement that the newly formed Pepin–Robarts Task Force on Canadian Unity would hold hearings in Charlottetown in less than a week: "Share your concerns with the task force. Holding Canadian citizenship carries a responsibility." I wrestled against these thoughts, for my life was totally filled with the urgencies of moving a home and family to British Columbia and forging a new career.

But conscience stirred up memory of a life-shaping decision made in battle as a volunteer Canadian on the open bridge of the British light cruiser, Black Prince, thirty-three years earlier in April 1944. White and yellow star shells eerily lit a black night sky as they floated down from the guns of Canadian, British, and German warships locked in high-speed battle inside enemy shipping lines off France's Ushant Peninsula. My eyes were riveted on three Canadian Tribal destroyers — the Haida (which is now sitting in Toronto harbour), the Huron, and the Athabasca (sunk in battle near the same spot two nights later) — and the British Ashanti. We had met, head on, six enemy destroyers and an unknown number of fast torpedo boats in a pre-invasion sweep of the French Coast. I felt and still cherish a pride in the skill and dash of my fellow Canadians on a task that had to be done.

Flames from a mortally wounded, sinking German destroyer added to the ghostly illumination of the sky. A daring seaman there was still firing his ship's last working gun. Suddenly his illuminated tracer shells curved directly towards our bridge. Excitement switched to fear. An officer in front of me instinctively raised the collar of his coat. Any sense of glamour war might have aroused in me was gone, although my sense of the need for adequate defence would remain.

I prayed; it was a prayer of commitment. "Should I return to Canada safely, I will devote my life's work to removing the hates, fears, and misunderstandings which divide people and races and give cause for wars." That commitment would return to memory in later times of crisis and decision. Thankfully we were not hit and the remaining Germans fled back to Saint-Malo, the birthplace of Canadian explorer Jacques Cartier.

I also found a renewed certainty in that instant: I was not alone. There was more to man and existence than blood and flesh, atoms and stone. There was meaning and purpose, order amidst chaos, a spiritual dimension. There was also the resultant of evil spread out dramatically on the sea in front of us. Man's age-old choices remained.

My steps on that Charlottetown walk quickened as I accepted the prompting to act. In speedy succession, my plea to the task force urging Canadians to express their hopes for a united country in letters mailed to friends in Quebec became a practical instrument, a petition that Canadians from every other province could sign for presentation to *all* the people of Quebec before their Referendum in 1980. Within two weeks, the People to People Petition for Canadian Unity had been written and the first signatures collected (see Appendix). The document was then read out by a dedicated minister, John Cameron, during an Armistice Day service in Charlottetown's old red-stone Kirk of St. James, where Fathers of Confederation had worshipped. The first signings followed.

Two months later, I turned over chairmanship of the first committee to an enthusiastic Islander, Rotarian James MacNutt, and my wife and I left for British Columbia and a new occupation, determined, *somehow*, to carry the petition to the other provinces.

By Referendum day, well over one million Canadians and a thousand civic councils had signed the document, and five separate presentations had been made to the people of Quebec, the last to Premier René Lévesque at his own request in front of the press four days before the Referendum.

It must be emphasized that the people of Quebec *themselves* worked at and decided the outcome of the Referendum — to remain Canadian. Canada owes a great debt of gratitude to them for their decision. The petition's primary task was to let them know how much other Canadians cared, in the midst of all the propaganda and broad media support for separation inside that province.

The idea for this book came as I reflected on two sets of experiences that gave me hope during the post-Referendum period of struggles over the Constitution, oil debates, the return of the Parti Québécois to power, and the rise of Western separatism. All seemed to be tearing Canada apart.

The first set of observations grew from visits to Africa, the Middle East, and India. We Canadians, even in difficult economic times, live in relative comfort and freedom compared with most of the world. It is equally clear that our massive resources of materials, capital, and skilled human beings make our chances of solving the problems of poverty and unemployment vastly better in a Canada kept together than in one broken into balkanized units.

A 1963 Act of Parliament forming the Economic Council of Canada set the nation's targets in this direction, calling for "the highest possible levels of employment and efficient production" so that "all Canadians may share in rising living standards"; and our new Constitution of 1982 speaks of "promoting equal opportunities for the well being of all Canadians", reducing "disparity in opportunities" through furthering economic development, and "providing essential public services of reasonable quality to all Canadians". The last is accomplished by the provision of revenues to each province from the federal government to guarantee that every area has "comparable levels of public services at reasonably comparable levels of taxation".

Our recent history supports the common sense of One Canada. When things were tough in one area, as in the Maritimes after World War I, individuals and families moved west to find jobs in Ontario industries. Out of the Prairies and British Columbia, over long periods of time, came brilliant and eager young men and women to work in the offices, factories, universities, and government bureaus of Eastern Canada where opportunities were greater. In the past few years, a flow of Easterners, French- and English-speaking, has moved to the West where jobs have been open. I vividly recall my mother's church groups in Hamilton, Ontario, making clothes and packaging materials to send to the parched Prairies in the troubled drought years of the 1930s. I remember watching with boyish enthusiasm the long harvester passenger trains heading west through Parry Sound, packed solid with thousands of assorted men from Ontario, Quebec, and the Maritimes, eager, before the days of huge farm machinery, to work and to help bring in the Prairies' grain.

The next boom area may well be the Maritimes, with excellent prospects for oil and gas, while Ontario, Quebec, and BC may advance in new technological sciences. As one area prospers, all of Canada is helped in the spin-off to other parts and to each citizen by jobs created in other industries and by sharing tax revenues through old-age pensions, unemployment insurance, health programmes, employment in federal work, the costs of defence, police, transportation, transfer payments, disaster relief, and the financing of necessary new developments. In our history, bonanzas have moved around, and they will in the future as resources in one area run out and new ones are discovered or developed elsewhere. We Canadians clearly need each other. Achieving Canada's legislated goals will depend on achieving a positive working relationship between politicians and other groups of the private sector with massive individual effort.

The second set of observations grew out of another heartening experience, one felt by so many of us who worked on the petition campaign: the evidence of a positive spirit ready to be tapped. Door-to-door campaigns, though difficult to organize, produced surprising proof of this spirit. Whether in Trail, BC, Briercrest, Saskatchewan, or Peterborough, Ontario, an average of almost nine out of ten persons asked to sign did so, once they understood the petition's purpose.

I joined the Trail door-to-door canvass at Mayor Charlie Lake's invitation. One concerned housewife reflected the thoughts of others: "I've been waiting for you to come. I've been terribly worried about Canada and haven't known what to do. I am glad of a chance to help."

No refusals to sign occurred on my allotted streets.

In Saskatchewan, Dorothy Boan, then aged eighty-five, and her husband, ninety-two, who drove her to every home in Briercrest, signed up almost the entire town. Their pioneer story of courage mirrors Canada's development and spirit (page 102). A Vancouver student, typical of many in other provinces, wrote asking for copies of the petition to use on street-corner signings.

How we would be received in Quebec was an unknown in that tense period. But in Trois Rivières, diners filling a banquet hall for the March 1980 annual meeting of the Chambre de Commerce rose in the presence of the mayor and other dignitaries in four, loud, standing ovations and, with a fervour I had never before witnessed, spontaneously broke out into "O Canada" *en français*. It was a response of the heart to an unannounced presentation of the first 10,000 signatures on the petition from their twin city of Sarnia, Ontario, by that city's mayor Andy Brandt and its chamber president — the only English speakers of the evening. The mayors write on pages 172 and 173.

Four weeks later, signatures reached 830,000. During the last days before the Referendum vote, petitions suddenly poured into collecting depots in unexpected volume from every direction. It represented an old truth: too often something of value isn't appreciated until there is danger of losing it. The idea that Canada might actually break apart took hold and people wanted to participate in preventative measures.

On April 11, under cold wet skies, a scattering of onlookers witnessed a startling spectacle at Montreal's Place Ville Marie. Families and mayors from each province carried their petitions forward and presented them to families from different parts of Quebec. Below the platform, two drum-banging, shouting parades, one English, one French, organized by the self-described "Marxist-Leninist Communist Party of Canada (in struggle)", drowned out our sound system but helped to achieve for the petition excellent press coverage. "Down with People to People," they howled in unison. Their actions contrasted totally with the wonderfully warm receptions given to the visitors from other provinces in the Montreal homes of their French Canadian hosts.

How did I feel about the interruptions, reporters asked.

"In Canada," I replied, "Communists have a right to present their views in an open public meeting — even if rude. But if we went to a Communist country, we would never be given the same chance." Indeed, a prison sentence or "treatment" in a psychiatric hospital would follow if we persisted.

I have no illusions about the difficulties in ongoing relationships between French- and English-speaking Canadians or about other Canadian issues, nor do I have serious doubts that we can find *working* solutions, if not perfect ones.

My own life experiences suggest that neglect, old-fashioned neglect, either benign, careless, or callous, helped fuel the fires of separatism in Quebec — and in the West.

I myself have had to learn the hard way. Although I learned to read French, nothing in my Ontario schooling of the 1930s or in my totally English environment helped me to know and respect French Canadian sensitivities. When I went to McGill University and later Presbyterian College in Montreal in 1936, I became totally absorbed in a unique English-speaking world. Somehow, French Quebec was out there on the fringe, mysterious and unknown. Not until my fourth year did I enter a French Canadian home to make a friendship.

In the post-war period, several years of work in the almost totally anglophone Montreal head office of a large Canadian company, whose plants were staffed with French-speaking workmen, gave me only a fleeting glimpse of resentments smouldering under the surface. The status quo could not remain for long. Thankfully, positive changes have taken place in many industries.

A period of living in a largely French community in Montreal gave our family the beginnings of warm friendships and insight into the richness of French family life and, as my perceptive young daughter Sandra so clearly observed, of the delightful vivacity of her French childhood playmates. And each somehow understood the other's language.

The rudest awakening came when I went to Ottawa

to join the National Productivity Council and became part of the civil service. I had hired, on advice from Quebec, a young, bilingual French Canadian with advanced educational qualifications to carry on our programme in Quebec. All of his mail came to us in French in spite of orders from a senior staff person to use English. My boss insisted I fire him. At some risk to my own position, I refused and instead tried to understand the problem over dinners with my Quebec associate in our home.

He had come to Ottawa to work in the civil service a few years before and found himself in a totally English working world where he could not use his native tongue and where the vast majority of the senior jobs and promotions went to qualified anglophones in the English mandarin community that was the federal civil service of the post-war years. He could not feel at home and returned to Quebec, embittered. He represented the new generation of highly qualified young Québécois coming out of their education explosion. Had I been in his shoes, I probably would have felt as he did. Thank God that scene is changing.

I grew up with a rosy glow about Western Canada, absorbed from my parents. It was a shock to learn how much resentment existed in the West towards Ontario and Quebec, some based in fact, much of it imagined. Many times in the West I was required to explain that for the nation's first one hundred years French Canada was unintentionally almost unrepresented in the management levels of Ottawa's civil service, and that much of the smoke and battle was merely the necessary correction of that situation, an investment that has paid huge dividends — keeping Canada together.

The allegation, widely propagated through English-speaking Canada by one or two English-speaking writers and spread by others, of the existence of a "conspiracy" by French Canadian leaders to make all of Canada French, is utterly without supporting evidence.

Some strident and excessive actions by the separatist party in Quebec have caused negative reactions in parts of English-speaking Canada. I have also seen distorted information in the French press. The booing by a small, noisy minority, of the singing in French of part of

"O Canada" at Toronto and Edmonton sports events when Quebec teams played got headlines in Quebec papers with no mention made of the majority of the audience's support of the singers, which I had witnessed.

All these concerns pointed to the need for a book. The heartening response to Terry Fox's run strengthened a growing resolve.

"Why not," a thought persisted, "invite a cross-section of convinced Canadians from every part of the country — such as those who helped with the petition — to write down their usually unexpressed convictions about Canada?" All of us could share them with the country and place value on the one thing we have in common — Canada itself. A book was born. It would, I decided, be non-political and non-governmental, expressing, like the petition, only personal views; a comprehensive though not all-inclusive volume, since no assurance could be made that every racial, geographic, occupational, or interest group would be included — just a sampling.

Writers contributed free of charge. No writer was asked to assent or agree to what others had written nor approve of the editor's views. They simply answered the question, "What does Canada mean to me?" A care for Canada was the only condition for participation. The ins and outs of the constitution, the pros and cons of federal versus provincial powers, the issue of Native claims, details of economic strategies, and so on, are left to other forums and to the press.

Only minor editing — to clarify meaning — has been applied to most of the submissions, and for that I assume responsibility. Regrettably, production costs prevented the inclusion of several excellent contributions and necessitated reduction in the size of others. The editor's royalties, after meeting necessary costs, go to the Terry Fox Fund for cancer research; the Terry Fox Canadian Youth Centre in Ottawa, to which young people from all parts of the country are brought to study and discuss Canada together; and the Roger Doucet Humanitarian Fund for cancer patients, Montreal.

I have great hopes for Canada. There is room for all of us, room to accommodate our differences, resources to

9

meet our needs, challenges to bring out the best in us. Most problems are manageable within the framework of our borders. None is of a magnitude that would require the break-up of the country.

Above all, I have found throughout the nation, in spite of annoyances, a basic common sense, a realization that what we have in common is far more important than the issues that divide us.

In the free democracy of Canada, necessary changes sometimes come slowly, but surely. All of us should be wary of those who would push extreme ideas, or divisive points of view, or support for a particular group to a point that endangers the nation itself. For keeping Canada united in body and spirit is everybody's task, as youthful students on a Calgary–Montreal exchange demonstrate in solving a race and language crisis (pages 168–172). A world at peace is an equally vital and equally challenging goal, a never ending effort.

Insights from the many writers on the pages ahead have increased my own appreciation of Canada. May readers of all ages and from all areas find the same.

Glenn Keith Cowan

1

---※---

Port Coquitlam to
St. John's

———————— * ————————

Terry's Driver Discovers Canada
Doug Alward

Terry Fox's driver and boyhood companion from Port Coquit-
lam, British Columbia, Doug Alward, took time off from school
and work in order to drive Terry's van on his historic run across
Canada, after helping him plan the trip.

My first impressions of Canada came from news stories
and word of mouth. Without ever travelling past the BC–
Alberta border, I came to visualize Canadians in other
provinces as quite different from us BC'ers. Newfoundlanders were simple fishermen who did odd things and
that was why we had Newfie jokes. Quebecers were a
bunch of separatists who screamed in a funny language
and would shoot an English-speaking person on sight;
the only thing good they had was Guy Lafleur. Ontarians
were people who suffered through snowstorms and heat-
waves, a mass of humanity that was crammed into a
bunch of Southern Ontario cities. The people of the Prairies were basically a bunch of farmers who had boring
scenery to look at and got pelted by snow as big as base-
balls during winter. Albertans swam in oil and money
and were eager to keep it all to themselves.

Driving across Canada with Terry one mile at a time —
staying at people's homes and viewing the countryside —
upset my impressions. Canadians we met from
Newfoundland through the Maritimes, Quebec, and
Ontario are a warm-hearted, friendly, caring, giving
people.

In Newfoundland we were given free meals and motel
rooms. Going across Canada we paid for only one meal
the whole five months. We slept in the van about two
weeks, and only because there were no motels for miles.
Every motel we stopped at, the owner wanted to give us
free room and meals. We even had a huge dinner waiting
for us in our motel rooms.

Car and truck drivers gave Terry a boost when they
tooted their horns. One truck driver stopped and pulled

12

the van out of a ditch when we got stuck in northern Ontario. The driver was eager to get Terry's autograph.

In Glovertown, Newfoundland, Caleb Ackerman came out on the highway with his car. He had great big Canadian flags on aerials on the hood of the car. He treated us like royalty. And this was when Terry was virtually unknown.

In Prince Edward Island, a woman came running out onto the highway in her nightgown and slippers at six o'clock Sunday morning to donate five dollars and offer us coffee.

In Quebec, drivers kept stopping to offer Terry a ride, not even aware of what he was doing, a result of inadequate publicity. Terry tried to tell them, but because he could not speak French and most of the Quebecers could not speak English, he had to learn "I am well" ("Je suis bien") so he could keep running and avoid getting into a confused conversation. Once a French girl came up and gave us seven dollars. She smiled and said, "For Cancer."

In Port Hawkesbury, Nova Scotia, the MacKeigan family came and greeted us on the highway, paid for our rooms, took us out to dinner, washed and vacuumed the van, and did our laundry. They then went to tell the radio station to start taking pledges for cancer. They got the local newspaper photographer out of bed at 5:00 a.m. to get some pictures to promote the run. The next morning at six they brought cookies out to us on the highway then drove twenty-five miles up the highway to pay for rooms and meals for us. They even went and told people who were taking pictures of Terry that it would cost them ten dollars a picture.

In Cap-Pelé, New Brunswick, a French-speaking Acadian area, the town raised a few thousand dollars for cancer, got all the school kids out on the highway to cheer Terry on, and got us free meals and rooms. The same warm and wonderful response occurred two weeks later in Grand Falls, New Brunswick, another Acadian area.

All over Ontario, response was incredible. People were willing to give even when they did not know what was happening. In the early morning, near Mississauga, I was out running a few hundred yards behind Terry in a massive traffic tie-up. Someone who was trapped in the traffic behind us saw everyone throwing money out car windows into our money buckets as they went by. The fellow stopped, pulled out a few dollars, and put them in the bucket. Then he asked what it was for. He must have thought we were running a toll booth!

Motorbike gangs even stopped and pulled out their money, often raising their fists saying, "Way to go man."

The Canadian police were super to us. The policemen who gave us escort service for some 2,000 miles of the 3,300 mile run risked their lives for us. They planted their cars fifty feet behind Terry with trucks and cars roaring sixty miles per hour at their backs. A CBC film truck doing that got smashed into by a truck going fifty miles per hour.

One policeman near Brantford, Ontario, even stopped cars and gave them a choice of a ticket for unsafe driving or a donation for Terry. Other police held their hats out the window so people could throw money into them as they went by.

As everyone knows, we never reached the Prairies. But I'm sure the people there would have proven as warm and caring as the rest of the Canadians we met on Terry's run. The slow drive across Canada made me realize that people were friendly in all places and changed my world view to look at ordinary Russians, Germans, Africans, and so on, in the same friendly way.

---------------------------------- ✳ ----------------------------------

Tributes to Terry Fox
Alootook Ipellie

Inuit writer and artist of Baffin Island and Ottawa; editor of *Inuit Today*.

On a sunny summer day I was walking along Bank Street

in Ottawa during the lunch hour. When I got to the Albert Street intersection, there were a couple of cops stationed on either side of Albert Street keeping the traffic from crossing while this young man with an artificial leg ran by.

"That's Terry Fox who's attempting to run across Canada for cancer," said someone close to me, his face lit with excitement. People around us were urging the young man on, clapping their hands.

Although there was a crowd around us, Terry and I were alone in thought. I felt his courage as I looked at his strained face, struggling in pain to lift that lifeless leg and then trying his best not to place it on the hard cement with a thump. Every step he took left a mark on his face. But he ignored the pain that he was suffering. It seemed the pains just spurted out of him with the sweat that came down his forehead.

That image of Terry remains etched in my mind to this day. His attempt at crossing the country came at a time when the nation sorely needed a national hero. At the height of Terry's run, seen from outer space, Canada undoubtedly had a sparkle of its own. It brought out my pride in being a Canadian.

To Terry
Lloyd Robertson

National newscaster, CTV network.

Terry Fox was propelled by a seemingly impossible dream: to set out from St. John's, Newfoundland, in April 1980 and run across Canada. His goal, now known by every Canadian and still pursued in annual Terry Fox runs, was to raise money for cancer research so that the disease that had taken away one leg at age twenty-two could be beaten back and conquered.

As he hopped painfully westward, the nation began to respond, seeing his dream take form, mile after mile, province after province. Near Thunder Bay, the run abruptly halted; cancer had returned this time to the lungs and a nation was stunned.

Quite by accident Terry Fox tapped the raw spirit of the country and found it to be warm and generous. Terry did us all a favour. He proved that we are much more than ten quibbling regions. He proved that we have the capacity to cry and feel as one people. He proved that as a country, we have a soul.

To Terry
David Suzuki

Scientist and science commentator, University of British Columbia and the CBC.

We are a self-deprecating people; too often that translates into a sense of inferiority: that if it's Canadian, it can't be first rate; that somehow pride in Canada is dangerous or unsophisticated.

What Terry Fox has made me do is think about the things that make me proud to be a Canadian. No country is without its warts, defects, and stupidities. But in our self-criticism, we must never forget the solid base of positive features.

As a third-generation Canadian, I felt the full force of panic, greed, and stupidity during World War II. I hope that the incarceration of the Japanese Canadians, which was forced upon all of us in my family, will stand as a powerful lesson in the fragility of democratic guarantees. Today, headlines announce the latest episodes of racism and violence that continue on. But for every report like that, I believe that hundreds, if not thousands, of instances of friendship, love, generosity, and kindness are extended across racial and ethnic lines.

I look at my youngest daughter, Severn Setsu, whose great-grandparents were from England and Japan, with a strong faith that the future holds endless opportunities for her in this country. The Canadian response to the plight of the boat people was astonishing for its intensity and generosity.

Canada is a unique experiment. Too often I am overcome by the negative features of our evolving society. Terry Fox reminded me of what I should be thankful for.

———————————— ✳ ————————————

From a Moving Window
Silk Questo

Creative designer and writer, Fulford Harbour, Saltspring Island, British Columbia.

I first saw Canada from a moving window. It was December 1970, but we two Americans knew little of the October Crisis and subsequent events that were tearing Quebec apart. We had left our California home to board the train in Vancouver bound for Christmas in New York via Montreal, and found ourselves surrounded by a coach full of festive people all riding the cheap seats back east for the holidays. It took nearly half an hour for the party to start.

There was a fresh-faced folk-singer bound for Camrose, Alberta; a Vancouver, Gastown socialite on her way to Saskatchewan; a big Indian from BC who played a hot blues comb; a crazy trombone player who performed barefoot at every station platform for spare change; a Hutterite family in their homemade clothes; and three FLQ sympathizers heading back to Montreal after an enforced vacation from politics. Someone passed some wine, someone else passed some food, and soon everyone was rifling their packs for something to share.

The music started before we'd passed through a dark and snowy Fraser Canyon. We had guitar, banjo, a brass section, an assortment of drums. Those who didn't have instruments sang, clapped, whistled, or stomped their feet, and by the time we hit the Prairies we were all convinced the train couldn't possibly make it to Montreal without our musical assistance. The coach was steamy and full of the human smell of three-day travellers; the outside was sparkling and bitter cold — mile upon mile of empty frozen landscape.

When we arrived in Montreal days later at 2:00 a.m., our Québécois travelling companions pressed the hospitality of their home on us. As they rallied their friends to a middle-of-the-night homecoming party, we fell asleep sitting up, to a background clatter of French; we left the next day to embraces.

We are now citizens and we've made Canada our home for thirteen years. I still believe our first impression of this country was right. Its vitality lies in its *unhomogenized* culture, a culture that values different identities, different languages, and strong individuals, unlike the pressures to conform that we had left behind in the U.S. The Canadian identity is continually evolving because of it, and that's creative. But the differences between us in Canada don't have to mean distances between us.

The sheer size of the country and the wide variety of cultures it accommodates sometimes allow Canadians to conceptualize their apartness too easily. Regional economic differences ought not to be confused with cultural differences; many of the perceived gulfs between us are great national mental blocks inherited from an age when the world wasn't so small.

On a person-to-person level, Canadians don't seem to mind sharing the same train.

———————————— ✳ ————————————

Renewal From the Sea

Mel Cooper

President of radio station C-FAX, Victoria, British Columbia.

Last summer I stood looking out to sea. It was a mild August day but none the less a chilly wind whipped around me. They say the wind always blows here. I was standing at Cape Spear, on Newfoundland's Avalon peninsula, the most easterly point of land in Canada. And as I watched the breakers in their clock-like precision smash against the rocks below, I felt a sense of awe, of freedom, of strength, of joy, of inspiration. I'd experienced the same emotional feelings many times before as a boy growing up in Newfoundland.

Just days later, I climbed the rocks and walked the soft sand beach at Point No Point on the south-western tip of Vancouver Island in my adopted province of British Columbia. Again I felt the same exhilaration as wave after wave of the more placid Pacific lapped at this the farthest western shore of Canada.

To me, the oceans that rim our eastern and western coasts symbolize Canada: its great natural wealth, wild beauty, vastness, unshackled freedom. And while storms may whip it to a fury from time to time, predictably, calm and quiet always follow.

I truly have experienced Canada from sea to shining sea, Signal Hill to Mt. Douglas, Quidi Vidi to the Gorge, Water Street to Government Street. And while like most Canadians I have kept feelings about my country inside, I now unashamedly admit a deep love for it. It is one of God's blessed countries, and we are bountifully blessed to live in it.

Whenever my confidence in Canada is assailed by damaging political and economic events, I find myself returning to the sea. There, my faith is renewed. There, by the majestic Pacific or Atlantic oceans, I feel the spirit, the vigour, the energy, the vitality of Canada.

---------------------------- * ----------------------------

"If You Come friendly"
Jean Paul Daneau

Foreman of a lumber yard in Langford, British Columbia.

My home town is Iberville, Quebec, where I grew up and went to school. I got my first job in the local bowling alley there when I was eight years old.

19

I always liked to travel. When I visited southern Vancouver Island in BC, I enjoyed the climate and decided to live there some day. But first I found a good job in Quebec with the Pirelli Company, which sent me to their home factory in Italy to learn cable splicing. I also worked for a while in Ontario. But in 1974 I decided to move here to Vancouver Island and take a chance on making a living. I found a job the first day I was here and have never been out of work since. If you want to work you can find something to do in this BC country, although it *is* tougher when business is bad.

My being a French Canadian who speaks English with an accent has never caused problems. If you come here with a bad attitude looking for problems, you'll find them. If you come friendly, you will find friendly people. I also like BC because of its lower taxes.

My parents still live in Iberville. I visit them often and they come here when they can. I enjoy my return trips to Quebec. My ancestors have been there for 300 years, and like many Quebecers I also have some Indian in my blood. I got a great kick out of meeting the Canadiens' Old Timer hockey team with Maurice Richard and the others when they played in Victoria.

We should never have different, separate nations in Canada, dividing families and stopping people from travelling without passports to find work in any part of the country they want.

Ten Gallon Hat
Ross Alger

Recent mayor of Calgary and long-time member and chairman of his city's Board of Education whose ten gallon hat caught press attention during the presentation of the People to People Petition in Montreal in April 1980.

I have always had an intense, passionate, almost audacious love affair with Canada. And yet when it comes to

20

putting into words exactly what it means to me, I some-how feel inadequate. Canada is an enigma, but inside I understand it all perfectly.

I was born in a little town on the Prairies during the harsh and desperate dust bowl years when it truly appeared that we were living in the land that God gave to Cain. In time I became the mayor of Calgary, a large, dynamic Western city, with all the rewards and trappings of high office. But nothing really changed. I was every bit as proud to be a Canadian when I walked to school carrying my little lunch bucket along the dusty roads of Saskatchewan as I was when I represented Calgary in high and mighty places around the world.

Being a Canadian transcends economic or social status. It is to be free to ride down a wild, winding West Coast river in a raft. It is to participate in the Quebec Winter Carnival, enter a fishing derby out of Halifax, or go trail riding in the Rockies. It is to have opportunity, education, tradition, and dreams. It is to be old or young, Dene or Inuit, French or English, Ukrainian or Irish. It is more than having the luck to have been born here or to have immigrated here and sworn an oath of allegiance. It is something that can take years to develop, or it can come upon you in an instant. But, even if you can't explain it, when you have it you know it.

Mostly, I suppose, it has to do with freedom. Being a Canadian is to have the freedom openly to criticize our governments and vote them in or out of office, take a job in Flin Flon or Toronto, or go panning for gold in the Cariboo. You can love or hate every minute of it and it doesn't matter. It might mean standing beside the Trans-Canada at Wawa waiting for a ride, being flat broke in Winnipeg, or riding a bathtub across Georgia Strait. Who really knows what it is?

Because we are a young nation, blessed with many resources, we are called upon to supply the world with the produce of our country, and in so doing there is a career for everyone who cares to work, except during temporary dislocation. Education is available to everyone at public expense. Our health care services rank with the best in the world. No nation offers its citizens the opportunities to succeed that are available to Canadians.

21

Canada has an added advantage over many other countries. In addition to a native population, and her immigrants from many countries, Canada enjoys two founding peoples, the English and French, each of which is rich in tradition and language. Part of Canada's charm is her French-speaking population in a North American sea of English-speaking people. Unfortunately, we do not avail ourselves of this heritage to the extent that we might, although efforts are being made to transcend language barriers and to understand one another's problems. Calgary is the sister city of Quebec City, and as mayor it was my pleasant duty to visit Quebec from time to time. No finer hospitality could be offered to Westerners than that proffered by our fellow citizens in Quebec. To their everlasting credit they rejected the notion of sovereignty association in the 1980 Referendum.

In my judgement, the alleged separatist views emanating from Western Canada are indicative, with a small number of exceptions, of nothing more than some deep dissatisfaction with one or another federal government policy. We are one nation, and we aim to keep it that way!

Even some young people who complain that Easterners are coming out West and taking their jobs have forgotten or don't know that since 1900 tens of thousands of college-trained, skilled, and other ambitious prairie youth went east to Ontario and Quebec where good jobs in offices, industry, and government were more available.

Most Canadians are aware of their great good fortune. If we have any problems, they are of our own making. Our difficulties arise more from prosperity than from poverty or hunger. As a nation, we shall have our differences, our growing pains, and our perceived difficulties. But as a Canadian I have great faith in the collective wisdom of our people to keep our nation progressive, prosperous, generous, thankful, and, most of all, united, strong, and free!

In a way, it is kind of reassuring to know that being Canadian defies description.

---- * ----

An Honour and a Privilege

Wayne Gretzky

Captain of the Edmonton Oilers hockey team, considered by many the best hockey player in the world; native of Brantford, Ontario.

I would like to tell you why we live in the greatest country in the world.

During my career as a hockey player I have travelled to many places and met people whose culture and way of life are different from our own. One thing remained the same wherever I went: Canadians are respected and admired everywhere.

Most of the people in the world know the opportunities that Canadians have. There are many of us who take for granted the privileges and rights which Canada offers to all.

Here we have schools for all, freedom of travel and speech, and the right to choose our own religion. We have an abundance of natural resources throughout the country. For those of us who love the outdoors we have fishing of all kinds, skiing, and hunting. Our free enterprise system allows those with ambition to achieve their goals.

All of this makes it an honour and privilege to be a Canadian!

Yellowknife Calling
Mike Ballantyne

Mayor of Yellowknife until his recent election as a Member of the Legislative Assembly of the Northwest Territories.

I have witnessed horrors of poverty, disease, oppression, and violence during the past fifteen years of extensive travel through Latin America, Africa, and Asia. The fundamental human rights we take so much for granted are seldom seen in most of the world.

Canadians are a favoured people living in a vast and beautiful land. It is always perplexing to listen to people who are determined to divide our country. The concept of Canada is a grand multicultural experience and our problems pale when compared with those of most other nations.

If, with our advantages, we cannot remain unified and take our rightful place in the world community, the future of mankind is indeed bleak.

First Lady of the Yukon
Ione J. Christensen

Mayor of Whitehorse, 1975–79, and commissioner of the Yukon, 1979.

My corner of Canada is the Yukon, up in the far northwest part of the Canadian map. We really are the western edge of the country rather than northern. Beaver Creek — and what better name for Canada's most westerly town — is on the border of the Yukon and Alaska.

My family first came to the Yukon in 1897 when my great-grandfather ventured north from Nova Scotia with his four sons. They never struck it rich. One son died in a typhoid epidemic, the father and two sons returned home South, but the fourth son, my grandfather, stayed and raised his family in Dawson City, centre of the gold rush. Mother in turn married her Mountie and I was raised in a very small village called Fort Selkirk on the Yukon River. My roots and fibre are Northern. I'm a Yukoner to the core, and yet as I have accepted additional responsibilities over the years, I have matured and broadened my perspective from the Yukon to all of Canada. The territories are Canada's future. We should not be in a great rush to exploit them. We have many resources and they should be evaluated and developed for future generations. Those who live in the North must benefit fairly from whatever happens. Provincial status will come eventually. Our politicians will have the long sought-after equality with their provincial peers, we will be grown up like all the other jurisdictions, but the North, the Yukon, will have lost its sweet mystery, the originality that has made it unique in Canada. Those of us who value that magic quality, the independent free spirit, will mourn its passing.

The roots of my patriotism go back to my very beginning. My father has served his country since 1921 when he first joined the army cadets. He is still serving at eighty-three as sergeant at arms for the Territorial Legislature. His dedication and pride of country were instilled in me from the day I was born. The sacredness of the flag, devotion to duty over all else — these were practised daily at the Royal Canadian Mounted Police post I called home. Father never took holidays, was never off duty and was never out of uniform in all the fifteen years I knew him as a member of the force.

My first act of patriotism happened at about six years of age. The little princesses, Elizabeth and Margaret, appeared on candy boxes, calendars, and school books, resplendent in white ermine capes. I was just learning to be a trapper then and when I caught my first ermine I just knew they would go to the princesses for a new cape. I spent days dressing those hides, rubbing the fur with corn meal to make it whiter. Then I took them to the Hudson's Bay store and gave very special instructions on their destination. In all future pictures of the royal family

I could always point to "my" velvet white pelts, right there in front!

Selkirk was a trading centre for a wide area and a large Indian population lived there. We all were close to the land, adapting so that we never felt isolated or deprived, although I am sure others thought we were. Common sense and good judgement were essential for survival; self-sufficiency and closeness of community made it a satisfying and happy time. The Indians lived in a cluster of cabins on the upstream side of town. The Whites lived in a long line of buildings, neatly fenced, downstream. I have often thought the Indians had the right philosophy: they lived in a community of people, homes all mixed together with no boundaries. We lived in a community of houses, with people fenced in. The Indians of the North are now negotiating Land Claims and I feel everyone must understand this fundamental difference if there is to be an appreciation of what the Claims are all about.

As a society, we have come to place great store in personal rights and freedoms. To keep them, each of us will need to be vigilant, to work, and to sacrifice. This cannot be accomplished by government alone, but only achieved through a united people, each corner of the land proud of its difference, each corner united with the other.

✳

Challenge to the West

Cleo Mowers

Recently retired publisher of *The Lethbridge Herald* who had previously performed editorial roles in Calgary and many public services for Canada.

Born in Alberta, educated in Saskatchewan, I "sat out" the war while most of my friends enlisted and some were killed. As a pre-theologue at university, I was an avowed pacifist and during the war a designated conscientious objector.

Now I have another battle of conscience. My friends

died to preserve their country, and now I am alive while their country, and mine, sometimes appears to be destroying herself. I cannot hide from my obligation, not only to their memory but also to their cause. My obligation is to Canada.

Every other race or nation that knows anything about Canada is jealous of our resources, our tradition of freedom, our opportunities, and of the beauty of the land. And yet Canada is a nation of complainers, and we Westerners, the most fortunate of all Canadians, bitch the loudest!

Western feelings of frustration, alienation, and separation are probably strongest of all in my own province of Alberta. Recent political events in which the West was poorly represented in the federal Cabinet have given much impetus to that feeling. The political process, if permitted time, will make its own amends in its own way, as past experience has shown. I am bothered, however, not so much by the arguments of the day as by the misreading of history, the misplacing of blame, the evasion of responsibility.

It is almost an article of faith among Western malcontents that the East historically, consistently, and deliberately has abused and exploited them. And I have found that it is considered by some impudent — even disloyal — to ask for proof of these allegations. "Doesn't everyone know that God is a Protestant and speaks English, that Jews are evil, Negroes inferior, and that Eastern Canada was created to exploit the West?" I have found that those who are most ignorant of Canadian history and most lacking in evidence are the most bitter and the most adamant that the West has no future as long as it is part of a country dominated, so they say, by Eastern voters.

My own feeling is that most of the grievances are imagined, even paranoid. Most of them are only malicious gossip, the exaggeration of childhood slights, or personal instances of exploitation magnified beyond common sense. On the other side, there are those who dismiss Western grievances out of hand because all they can see is Western affluence. And yet there are some very legitimate problems.

Somewhere, sometime, someone of competence should make a thorough, honest study of these alleged historical grievances. The long list of irritations must be examined one by one. Those not based on fact must be so labelled. The others must be identified, admitted, and resolved.

The most contentious issue in the West of course, and perhaps more legitimate than most, would have to be Canada's historic tariff policy, which was said to be a special tax on Westerners to build up the wealth of Ontario and Quebec. A closer examination will probably show that the building of a nation required a strong industrial base. As industry decentralizes, the advocates of both tariff protection and free trade possibly will shift their views.

The three most westerly provinces are the richest part of this rich country. It was not always that way, nor will it always be, but why does good fortune breed discontent and unhappiness? The psychologist or the moralist may have an answer; I do not.

Good fortune is transitory. It takes new forms and new habitations as technology advances. That it should be Alberta's to exploit and enjoy today at the expense of other parts of Canada, and Newfoundland's tomorrow, tears at the fabric of Canada.

Blame for Canada's ills must be spread evenly across the land. No group, province, or region is innocent. Just as the forces pulling her asunder come from every direction, so the forces that would save her — such as tolerance, understanding, and appreciation — must also come from every corner. Let every Canadian, everyone who feels he or she is first and last a Canadian, speak for Canada.

I cannot define Canada, or explain her, or even understand her, but one of the certainties in my being is that Canada can work. Canada has already long outgrown the calculations of her founders.

We need to see Canada as my friends now in war cemeteries saw it. Even if they had to stretch their imaginations a bit, Canada was very real to them, and very precious. Why can't it be that to us? If Canada fails, and it must not, how can the broader human brotherhood succeed?

—————————— ✳ ——————————

The Queen and I

Diane Jones-Konihowski

Commonwealth and international track and field champion;
resident of Saskatoon, Saskatchewan.

Many people ask me why I'm still in sport after fifteen
years on Canada's national track and field team. It's a
tough question because there is no one answer. It's a
combination of fifteen years of hard work, discipline,
success, failure, friendships, travel, education, maturing,
and desire. But if I were to single out one event that was
particularly special to me it would have to be the 1978
Commonwealth Games in Edmonton.

The theme song of the games exemplifies the spirit of
the competition and the words tell of the spirit among
the athletes:

The Games are for cheering
and we're gonna raise the rafters
Everyone in the crowd
is gonna be proud
of the skillful and the strong.
But there is a bigger and a better
prize we're after
and that is to stay together this way
for a long, long time.
We're gonna show the world! . . .
Tho' we come from different places
We're gonna show the world! . . .
that people of all races
can stay together — impossible?
Love makes it possible.

Everything seemed to go right for me in the competitions. The games were held in the city I was living in
at that time, which meant that husband, family, and close
friends could see me compete for the first time in person.
My sport was held in the newly constructed Commonwealth Stadium where my husband played football with

the Edmonton Eskimos. My only claim to fame over the awesome Eskimos is that I got to compete in their stadium before they did!

About two weeks prior to the opening ceremonies, the president of the Games Organizing Committee, Dr. Maury Van Vliet, asked me if I would carry the message to Her Majesty Queen Elizabeth to open the games officially. It was all hush-hush and no one was to know who the last runner was until he or she stepped onto the track. I was deeply honoured to be chosen from a group of fine Canadian athletes, but didn't realize the impact of the honour until I stepped out and was greeted by the roar of 45,000 cheering spectators — and a shocked Mom and Dad.

It was the longest 300 metres I'd ever run. Then, approaching the podium where Her Majesty was waiting to receive the message, my first thought was, "My gawd! what do I do now? I can't curtsy in shorts!" To this day I don't know what I did to acknowledge her. While she read the opening message, I remember Prince Andrew giving me a wink and a quick look me over. What could I say? His mother was right in front of me, and I was in front of 45,000 people.

The first day of the games dawned with sunshine, hot weather, and no wind. Ideal conditions for the pentathletes who were competing that day. It was an ideal day for me, too. Everything seemed to go right. The spectators never let me forget they were there helping me get over those few extra centimetres in the high jump. In my fifth and last event, the 800 metres, the crowd cheered me all around the track and drove me to a personal best performance that put me number one in the world that year.

What seemed like a perfect day ended on a royal note with Her Majesty the Queen presenting me with my gold medal, the first of the games. It was a moment to remember, with the sounds of "O Canada" blaring throughout the stadium and, I'm sure, to the skyscrapers in downtown Edmonton. Everyone in the stadium sang out. It's a day I will never forget because it's one of the few times that so many people in one place could experience pride in being Canadian. As the song says, "We're gonna show the world! . . . Love makes it possible."

---------------------------------- ✳ ----------------------------------

Not Only French and English

M.J. Kindrachuk

Saskatoon's superintendent of schools and a Ukrainian Canadian.

In listening to our radio, watching television, reading daily newspapers and general magazines, hearing our politicians as well as those from the intellectual sphere in our nation, one is left with the strong impression that all is not well in our country, that Canada is populated essentially by people of French and English descent and that it is even acceptable to speak of French Canada and English Canada as though they were distinct entities. One is frequently tempted to inquire where the Scottish, Italian, German, Ukrainian, or Scandinavian Canadas are. There is more to Canada than the French and the English and the West versus the East. It would appear that we have a nation in ignorance of itself and for that the national media may be largely responsible. Keeping a nation in ignorance of itself is, perhaps, one of the worst kinds of subversion.

Canadians should retrace the footsteps of our pioneers who came to this country with dreams, commitments, and spirit. Those were the days before the inventing of the generation gap, the rise of riots, the disaffection of youth, and the yield to the ever increasing demands for unlimited personal freedom — all "advances" of our liberated society.

Quite some time ago Horatio Alger (1834–99) authored more than one hundred books of boys' stories with the prevailing theme of acquiring success through exemplary living, heroic deeds, and a struggle against the odds.

Many generations of young people became enthusiastic readers of Alger's stories. They grew into adulthood with a philosophy that with a positive attitude and self-appreciation, success could be achieved, even for those starting with some disadvantage. It is this kind of attitude that should be nurtured in our country now.

Canada, a country of new dreams, is still basically a land of immigrants. So many of our grandparents and parents who came from their mother countries are still alive. So many of the present generation of Canadians are products of the multicultural upbringing in their homes and observe, with emotion, the many traditions and customs.

Our nation is indeed very young. In the one hundred years of its existence as a nation our pioneers seem to have "completed" Canada. They surveyed it from coast to coast, built highways, railroads, libraries, schools, courts, government buildings, and put in place so many of our laws. One may say that one hundred years is a long period of time, but if someone considers his own age and that of one of his parents or grandparents, the sum most likely would be close to one hundred years. A long period, but only one or two generations of people who completed Canada with bare hands, scoops, horses, shovels, and sheepskins.

How much commitment and faith the pioneers had in the future of our nation! Soon after Saskatchewan became a province, for example, the pioneers built the Legislative Assembly Building with quality material and design that to this day remains a source of pride. It is with that spirit and faith that we have to demonstrate our love for Canada.

We cannot be looking back exclusively or excessively or we may lose our stride. Our traditions must nourish us and support us, but must not hold us back.

There is strength in our nation in spite of the irritations. We have no less a commitment to Canada than our forefathers did. What will we add to Canada?

---- * ----

Unity: Town and Symbol

Leonard Boxell

Mayor of Unity, Saskatchewan, and farm implement dealer.

My parents immigrated to Canada from England to farm in the Senlac–Evesham area of Saskatchewan in the early years of this century. I often wonder what those young people's dreams were for the future. What did they envision for this vast country?

My father, George Boxell, who was raised in the big city of London and had a secure job in the printing business, was not one of the earliest settlers, having come in 1908. I think with amazement of my mother coming as a young girl to strange people, and to a strange country, at Senlac. As various district histories are now being recorded, we enjoy reading their stories. The people then seemed to enjoy life and persevered through many a hardship that society would not tolerate today.

I do not ever remember my parents complaining, even when raising a family in the "dirty thirties". Being of British stock they were very loyal to this country and to the Queen. I can remember my first train ride when the family came to Unity to see the King and Queen in 1939. What a day for the town of Unity. People came from miles around and lined the Canadian National Railway tracks for a mile. I still cherish the lovely snapshot I got, with my Brownie camera, of the King and Queen waving!

"Unity" is a word that has been kicked around a lot the past few years, but to this small rural town in Saskatchewan, it is a name and community to be proud of.

I'll never forget my trip, as mayor of Unity, to join with mayors from Victoria to St. John's, Newfoundland, to present petitions in the People to People Petition campaign personally to the Quebec people in Montreal. Joining with the other people from Saskatchewan, being hosted by French Canadian families, and meeting with other mayors from coast to coast and the North, reaffirmed my belief that we have the most wonderful, bountiful country.

I am proud that the journey made by my parents, and the people before them, has given us a great heritage in Canada. Possibly it is this same instinct that has driven me to take time and funds to do my little part in keeping Canada united.

———————————— ✳ ————————————

Multicultural Magic
Mary Elizabeth Bayer

Editor, writer, and Winnipeg Folklorama participant and enthusiast.

Where in the world can you sample, in one fell swoop, if you're wild enough to try, in a day or a week, beaver tail soup, tourtière, bubble and squeak, bannock, baklava, vina torta, vindaloo, graavad lox, gazpacho, guacamole, kasha, weiner schnitzel, won-ton, zabaglione, tempura, sachimi, piogi, paella, gnocchi, couscous, minestrone, and peking duck? In Winnipeg in a week in August, that's where.

Folklorama, a microcosm of Canada, is Manitoba's annual folk festival, the forerunner of Canada's great multicultural events. It's a fandango of food and dance, faith and culture, fun and wonder. Canadians of a multitude of national origins recall and celebrate their cultural heritage in a week-long fête that features some thirty pavilions dispersed over the city of Winnipeg and in other centres as well. Passports and buses assure access, and if there are waiting queues outside pavilions, they are a cheerful guarantee of the popularity of the programmes to be enjoyed.

In sparkling entertainment, fascinating exhibits, often borrowed from private homes, music from the host country, and delectable samples of *typico* cuisine, Folklorama becomes a mini United Nations, a splendid example of people proud of their heritage working together. It becomes a symbol of Canada. There are several features of Folklorama that are at once the key to its success and important to all Canadians. One is the hard work of hundreds of citizens who labour mightily for many months to organize and prepare for the festival. They are volunteers, of course, giving freely of their time and skills. The rewards are great, apparently; the same good souls return year after year, seeking improvement if not perfection. They bring enthusiasm, initiative, and enjoyment to the enterprise. Money could never buy this outpouring of pride, goodwill, and co-operation, all hallmarks of the event.

Folklorama mirrors the image Canadians have of themselves. Each of us is aware, whether vaguely or in detail, of his *roots*, conscious of belonging both to a tradition and culture many centuries old and to a nation new and growing and vibrant. The Greek pavilion, for example, harks back to the time of Pericles in decor, to the Plakka in food and drink; centuries are bridged with the balalaika and traditional arts and crafts.

And another feature of Folklorama is that it is enormous fun. There is an explosion of cheer as each pavilion opens, as hosts greet guests, as people wine and dine together, ooh and aah over the needlework or the painting, polka or jig or join in the chorus, enjoy the children at play, admire the lederhosen or moccasins or the mantilla. There are jokes and laughter, songs and cameraderie as families tour together, busloads debark, people of all ages run, walk, drive, roller-skate, or wheel their way to the "country" of their choice, have their passports stamped, and then gorge themselves with the delights of either discovery or reminiscence or both. In a world full of agony and anxiety, it is great to find genuine joy abounding. And there it is, at Folklorama, in Canada, every summer.

My Freedom
Sylvia Burka Lovell

World speed-skating champion in 1976–77, Canada's Female
Athlete of the Year in 1977. Winnipeg's Burka is also a bicycle
racer and small-business entrepreneur.

I have thought a lot about what Canada means to me.
My parents came from Latvia, a small country on the
Baltic Sea taken over by the Soviet Union at the end
of World War II. I grew up in Winnipeg hearing
their stories of the terrible times they had experienced
when the Russian troops marched into their town in 1944.
They were herded from place to place, finally slipping
through to Germany and the area controlled by the Western Allies, emigrating to Canada and Winnipeg shortly
afterward.

At an early age I loved skating and wanted to be a
speed skater. The loss of an eye in an accident was said
to be a handicap in racing, but I went ahead anyway,
working hard to reach my goal of representing Canada
in the Olympics and international competition.

At international sports meets, to which I have been
travelling for fourteen years, I began to meet competitors
of Eastern Europe from behind the Iron Curtain. I sought
them out, attended their parties, and tried to get to know
them. Sometimes I envied their expensive training
facilities. But the more I saw of them the more I recognized their lack of freedom. They were locked into a
tightly controlled government sports system, designed to
produce world-class athletes. My own freedom to choose
my sport, or leave it, select a career, and say what I
wanted when and where I wanted, became more precious
to me.

I especially like Canada's opportunities to make a living. When I married and settled in Ontario with my Toronto husband, I had to find suitable work. People in
Toronto's garment trade told me they were having trouble getting skilled people to work in their sewing shops.
Some were closing up. People had often asked me about

my wind suits, which were specially made for speed skating. They were designed with special materials to reduce wind resistance, to fit the body closely and give warmth. I knew how to sew, so I rented a machine and began taking orders for some wind suits for skiers. I was in business.

Canada gives me the freedom to be as rich as I can be or as poor as I want or somewhere in between and to make a choice. I would not want to live anywhere else.

---
*

My Ontario

Harry Boyle

Toronto-based broadcaster and writer, and former senior executive of the CBC and CRTC.

I was born in Ontario. When people ask me I'm inclined to say I was born near Goderich, in Huron County, and perhaps add that it's that area below where the Bruce Peninsula intersects Lake Huron and Georgian Bay.

The fact is, I grew up knowing full well that I was Canadian. Cousins, descendants of a great-uncle who stayed on after a winter in the Michigan lumber woods, were from Saginaw and they were Americans. When they came to visit in the summertime, I marvelled at the way they talked and dressed. But they also used to call themselves Michiganders. We didn't say we were Ontarians. We stuck up for Canada.

It's not that we haven't pride in Ontario. It has something to do with the size and make-up of the province. In actual fact, it's more of a kingdom than a province, embracing everything from fertile, garden land to moonscapes littered with the cruellest looking rocks you can imagine.

A great-uncle homesteaded in northern Ontario, in Algoma. He had to mount guard day and night to keep the wolves from attacking his stock. There wasn't anything as exciting as that in Huron County but it was named after Indians and I grew up not far from where Étienne Brûlé was disposed of when the Indians got fed up with his messing around with their squaws. This story was related to us in a much more refined way by a prissy schoolteacher forced to work in a rural school. Her lamentations about Toronto missed made us aware for the first time that it was really a part of Ontario and was big. Up to that point, sleepy London had represented my idea of a metropolis.

But this diversity and size is what Ontario is all about. While it detracts from a personal loyalty, such as a Prince Edward Islander might have for his tiny province, it is also a source of admiring wonderment.

Just think of the fresh water around and in Ontario. Hudson Bay and James Bay on the north. The Great Lakes forming a protective pouch around the southern part. Inside the boundaries thousands and thousands of lakes, and many have only been photographed from the air. They haven't been touched except I suppose by acid rain. And islands! Thousands of them freckle the lakes.

You'll also hear different accents. Ottawa Valley, Parry Sound, Sudbury basin! Ontario is a place where early settlers named their new locales after the places they had escaped from — such as Belfast, Donnybrook, Dublin, and Dungannon. You'll also find Indian names, such as Iroquois, Wawa, and Kapuskasing, and the names of explorers from Champlain, of missionaries such as St. Ignace.

Ontario is no more homogeneous than America. Canadians, in spite of the foolish pleading of Ottawa politicians, are not alike and interchangeable. Neither are the people of Ontario. To have a populace of instantly recognizeable Canadians or Ontarians would be a disaster. As to tensions and bickering — all healthy families have them!

We'll keep on identifying ourselves in Ontario as from the Ottawa Valley, Niagara-on-the-Lake, Huron County — or even as poet Al Purdy does, celebrating Ameliasburgh with hosannas, expecting others to know where it is, a part of Ontario, even if it is only a speck on the map.

But don't think of it as arrogance! There's a reason in the psyche of most people. We got this approach from our ancestors who fled the persecution and prejudice of those old countries and found safety and security in the communities of Ontario. They found freedom and instilled in us who came after, a deep sense that it really is the most important factor of living.

Ontario isn't any better than any other province. It's bigger than many. It's more diverse. Most importantly it gave our ancestors a chance. Canada did that. We know it and we cherish it and that's enough. That and the memories of Lochalsh, Bayfield or Goderich.

---- ✻ ----

Unabashed Canadian
Gordon Sinclair

Of Toronto; journalist, broadcaster, and member of Canadian TV's longest-running show, "Front Page Challenge".

I'm an unabashed Canadian nationalist. There aren't enough of us. That's why I have such an admiration for my Québécois friends. Most of them are more loyally Canadian than we English Canadians are and they felt that way long before we did.

Those loud but still few English-speaking Canadians who want to divide up Canada have no emotional blood in their veins. My devotion to this country covers the mountains, plains, lakes, forests, animals, and the people, too.

I am often asked — and ask — financial questions on television and radio. Here's one: What would be the price of breaking up Canada? Far more than any part of Canada would want to pay if they figured it out. And not only in financial terms.

✳

Regal Salute
Pauline McGibbon

Immediate past Lieutenant-Governor of Ontario, and present chairman of the National Arts Centre, Ottawa.

How do I feel about Canada? I love it. It's fun to travel to other countries, but it is wonderful to return to this great country which is home — where the cities are clean and the streets are safe.

As one who has travelled from the Yukon to Newfoundland I can say unequivocally that we who live in Canada are so fortunate. Whether you travel north or south, east or west, the beauty that is Canada's is always with you. In the midst of all this there is Quebec, which gives some of us the feeling of being away from home yet being at home. How fortunate we are to have the zest, the *joie de vivre* of our French Canadian compatriots. I wonder if they realize how much we appreciate them.

I do not need to say more. Canada is my country now and forever.

✳

A Love Affair
Huguette Plamondon

General vice-president, Canadian Labour Congress, and representative of the United Food and Commercial Workers Union; first woman to head the Montreal Labour Council.

I take pride in living in Canada, a country that respects my origin, my nationality, my culture — a land that respects, with dignity, my unique identity as a French Canadian. Canada offers to each of us, and for future generations, the possibility of building and initiating a society based on human values and the rights of the individual. I cannot think, even less admit, that one could partition Canada, a country that satisfies the social and economic needs, as well as the aspirations, of all Canadians from sea to sea.

The time has come for Canadians to show their appreciation of the advantages and benefits that Canada offers us. It is time we developed in our minds and in our hearts a patriotism, a loyalty, a love for Canada, this marvellous land of which we are not always worthy.

---

* ∗ *

A Hitchhiker Returns

Daniel Contant

An artistic young Québécois currently studying culinary arts in a Manpower Training Centre in Montreal.

I am very happy to be able to offer a few thoughts and feelings about my country. Maybe it will make someone feel as good as I do about it. I have lived in every major city in Canada but still prefer my home town of Montreal. Perhaps I am attracted by the dynamism created by the blend of two cultures that gives rise to a wealth of artists, musicians, and other creative people. In any case, I love this city and have always returned to it. Many people I have either known personally or met felt the same way, even when comparing Montreal with places outside North America.

But all of Canada is beautiful. In my travels across this vast country, I have observed varying geography of the land from the Maritimes to the St. Lawrence Valley, across the wilds of Northern Ontario along the shores of our Great Lakes over that sea of prairie grass to the majestic Rocky Mountains and further west yet to the lush vegetation of the coastal forest of British Columbia. The first time I travelled across the country, I hitchhiked, which allowed me to meet many Canadians and see much of the land in an intimate and unique way much unlike car or plane trips.

I have also observed, along with the changing of land-scapes, the varying life-styles of Canadians, from the steady pace and friendliness of the Maritimers to the fast pace of the big city, the boldness of the Prairie cowboy, the charm of the British Columbian — and all these variations of land and people within the common boundary of one big country! It is a rare thing indeed in a world so divided.

---- ✳ ----

Mon Pays, Mes Amours
Thérèse Casgrain

The late Hon. Thérèse Casgrain of Quebec, a Senator, combined her fight for social justice and women's rights with a strong love for her country.

As time goes by, I am prouder than ever to be a Canadian. In 1834, Sir George-Étienne Cartier, one of the Fathers of Confederation, who also was a musician, wrote a song entitled

O Canada
Mon pays, mes amours

As far back as I can remember, this melody was often heard in my home. So I grew up with a deep love for my country which only increased with time. It has been my privilege to travel around the world. Each time, I realized that people of different lands envied me to be a citizen of such a wonderful country as Canada. There is no doubt that our land is one of the most fortunate. It possesses wealth, education, cultural enrichment, and especially a great tradition of personal freedom.

In Canada, French philosophical humanism and British Parliamentary democracy are among the great accomplishments of civilized man. Canadians today have inherited these unique traditions.

I remember once our famous hockey team *les Canadiens* had just come back from the USSR where they had been playing. When they arrived in Dorval, some of them bent down and kissed the soil of their wonderful country, Canada. Their gesture, I can well understand, for each time I returned from any far-away trips, I felt exactly the same way.

----------------------- ✳ -----------------------

Tribute to Thérèse Casgrain

H.E. Jeanne Sauvé

Former Speaker of the House of Commons, Ottawa, during which term this tribute was written; Governor General Designate of Canada.

Senator Thérèse Casgrain was remarkable. She amazed those who knew her from the time she began her public activity as a young woman fighting for women's right to vote in Quebec, to her very last exceptional contribution to the Quebec Referendum in 1980.

She was an inspiration by her constantly renewed enthusiasm for the causes she supported. She could not have lived without a cause. The manner in which she worked at eighty-four years of age in the Referendum in Quebec amazed all those who had seen her in action before. Early in the campaign she was invited to appear before audiences. Because of the prestige she enjoyed in her native province, she soon became the star of all the rallies. She went everywhere, to Quebec City, Montreal, or even remote areas of Northern Quebec. One evening she turned up late at friends where we were having dinner, bone-tired, after making four speeches that day and journeying back on a bus.

She believed in Canada, in keeping it together as an entity, and in resolving, by patient dialogue, any differences in her province as well as in others. She felt we should work harder at developing a sense of nationhood to which as a young country we are perhaps not strongly enough committed. She herself was very careful not to limit herself to Quebec: she accepted as many speaking engagements in the rest of the country as in Quebec, and she was recognized by the whole country. She received a dozen honorary degrees from Canadian universities.

Senator Casgrain, from the time I first knew her, fought for a special cause that most people might not have been aware of. All her life she promoted the plea of the Indian woman who, under the provisions of the Indian Act, did not enjoy the same status as Indian men. She went from Indian chief to Indian chief trying to convince them that they were being unjust to their women, never tiring in her promotion of their rights. What was inspiring in her *démarche* was that she felt the frustrations of these women as if they were her own. This was her strength: a capacity to identify with other people's problems. What must be remembered also of Senator Casgrain was her dedication to social justice. She felt that harmony across the land had to be based on a society that shared its wealth.

Hers was a fulfilled life and one may correctly say that apart from the time she spent with her beautiful family and her friends, her energies were entirely devoted to the welfare of her compatriots. She has left us with a rich testimony of a person who cared about issues and did something about them.

A Student's Mirror
Richard R. Darrah

Recent graduate of Oromocto, New Brunswick, high school, where he was a student leader; now a student at Mount Allison University, New Brunswick.

In 1759, the French philosopher Voltaire wrote this about the war between France and England over Canada: "These two nations are at war for a few acres of snow, and they are spending for this fine war more than Canada is worth."

Some snow! Some expense! How wrong history has proven the great philosopher!

Optimism about Canada and its future may be overshadowed by activities of the past decade that frequently left feelings of frustration, restraint, and uncertainty. These, however, may be defined as signs of growth. In all ages of man, periods of social, economic, and political growth have been preceded by bleak and indefinite times.

To smother ourselves in apathy, to constantly find fault with every issue, to relegate our own nation to the level of mediocrity — these are characteristics of the defeatist.

Canadians have a great country, but few realize it. It is only when one has a fierce pride in something that the true strength is known. In the vastness of our Dominion there is so much from sea to sea that to fully appreciate the physical and the spiritual is the work of a lifetime.

Canada is a country, more than anywhere else, where young people can achieve their aims and goals. The country has excitement; it has heart.

Canada is a mirror to the future.

--------------------------------- ✳ ---------------------------------

The Middle Way—An Acadian View

Clarence Cormier

Former mayor of Dièppe, New Brunswick; currently Minister of Education for his province.

As an Acadian living in New Brunswick, why am I proud to be a Canadian?

We are living in an era in which the most contradictory doctrines appeal to us, and we are often quite uncertain of the direction we should turn: in favour of the trade union movement or that of the employer? Of federalism or separatism? Should the political attitude of Acadians aim at an *entente cordiale* or should we adopt the radical positions of our young militants?

In the past few years, a group of Acadians has been advocating the formation of a separate province here in

New Brunswick. I have to admit that instinctively, when confronted with two extremes, I am inclined to take the middle position. "In medio stat virtus," wrote Saint Thomas. It is the law of the pendulum which, even as it is forced to oscillate from one extremity to the other, always tends to regain its normal position and come to rest in the middle point.

Thus when the socialist takes an extreme position and fiercely demands equality for all, he takes the risk that it may result in abuses of power or even in dictatorship. On the other hand, the capitalist, in promoting free enterprise, is liable to commit all kinds of excesses against the common good of society.

Authority which is too powerful is dictatorship; if it is too weak it is anarchy . . . Open competition may lead to the exploitation of one social class by another; controls that are too rigid kill private initiative . . . There is always a happy medium between two extremes.

I would be wrong in becoming fanatical. I would be equally wrong in repudiating my origins. I am of French extraction, but since I am living in a country with an anglophone majority, I have to apply myself to harmonious collaboration with my fellow citizens. I am of Roman Catholic faith, but I want to respect the religious beliefs of all my countrymen. The general attitude I wish to develop for myself — and which I expect to find in others — is one of comprehension, tolerance, goodwill, and civility.

This having been said, I am admittedly a federalist. I love my country because it is vast, because it is rich in its very diversities. Its natural resources are varied. Its oceans and lakes provide numerous species of fish. The soil is fertile: here it is suitable for cattle breeding, there to potato farming; elsewhere mostly wheat is grown, or fruits. Forests are rich in resinous and leafy trees. Mines are plentiful.

More particularly, I like to live in New Brunswick, because here I find an ideal Canada in miniature. We have the ocean, the lakes, a fertile soil, a rich forest. Our provincial government is asserting itself as a defender of bilingualism and of the rights of the individual.

My town of Dièppe, of which I had the honour of being

the mayor, like the province, became officially bilingual in 1974. All our official documents are produced in both languages and we have made simultaneous interpretation available at all of our public meetings. It is a service that is not very costly. I hope more municipalities where both languages are spoken will follow.

Not only are our natural resources abundant and varied, but the social regime that has implanted itself in the country is ideal. In our land, there is no tyranny or dictatorship, as in some other lands where liberty is muzzled. Cases of violence are rare and not as spectacular as they are elsewhere. Our democratic system and our charter of human rights protect the individual.

Another point of satisfaction to me is the diversity of nationalities and cultures. The linguistic problem is at the source of these questions. In this domain, I believe that my country was right in promulgating two official languages, those of the two founding nations, into law. But I also believe that citizens of other ethnic groups who have chosen to come and live with us also have rights, and that they are bringing, in their cultures, a worthy contribution to the assets of the country.

It is for these fundamental reasons that I love my Canada: these diversities that are its wealth. But despite the more or less great distances between its regions, and their diversities, I should like to see a united Canada. A strong central government appears to me as the only kind capable of ensuring fair sharing and stability, communications, currency, defence, and the fundamental rights of citizens. It is with the achievement of this unity in mind that I am a federalist.

Each region certainly should benefit from its resources. But the principle of sharing must be applied to space as well as time. Let the East exchange goods and services with the West and vice versa, just as the generations of yesteryear have come to assist the generations of today and tomorrow.

I belong to one of the two founding peoples. The first, from France, arrived in 1604 and 1608, and have often been hurt, annoyed, attacked, and even conquered. Life was dreadful at times. It is especially in our region, Acadia, that the past was most tragic and the wounds deepest.

The expulsions of the Acadian peoples from their homesteads in the three Maritime provinces in 1755 and 1758 make up one of the saddest pages in Canadian history. But I do appreciate that by this time — 1984 — the wounds have been healed and we, and the others, have learned to live in harmony notwithstanding our diversities. That is what has made today's Acadian Renaissance so remarkable. That renaissance is very comforting, for us who have suffered and for our fellow citizens who recognize the fact!

Why do I feel so very much at home in Canada and in Acadia today? It is simply because my origins are so deep-rooted. Allow me to demonstrate how, in the tenth generation, I come to be a direct descendant from old stock, the first Cormier to arrive in Canada. I am Clarence Cormier, son of Willie, son of Josué, son of Laurent, son of François, son of Pierre, son of Pierre, son of Thomas, son of Robert. This Robert, the pioneer of this prolific tribe, came from France to Acadia in 1644 with his wife, Marie Péraud, and their very young son, Thomas, who was the second in my lineage.

In closing I should like to pay homage to one of my lineage who has most distinguished himself, Father Clement Cormier, c.s.c. He is my hero. He is the idol of my Acadian people. As the founder of the University of Moncton, his deed confirms forever the survival of the Acadian people in the world.

Home and Away

James MacNutt

Civic-minded Prince Edward Island lawyer from Charlottetown.

An unsettling fact of being Canadian is that one can feel like an alien when visiting in regions of Canada other than one's own. Mountains, vast plains, and towering cities are unknown to the daily life of a Prince Edward

Islander, as indeed are sand dunes, fishing villages, and the sea to Prairie residents. Our languages and cultures on PEI are British, French, and native Indian. Oriental and Central, Eastern, and Southern European languages and cultures are largely unknown to us. The sense of newness and lack of a traditional base of action found in many parts of Canada would be unknown to our deeply rooted Island traditions, values, and life-style. Each of these many differences distinguishes Islanders from other Canadians. We Islanders frequently look out from our secure insularity at distant parts of Canada with bewilderment, amusement, and caution, and yet with commitment as Canadians. If you are from off the Island you are classified as being "from away" by Islanders.

The size of our island has led us Islanders, particularly in this century, to being somewhat apologetic and retiring in asserting our place in Canada. We have been subjected to the prevailing notion in Canada that bigger is better, and that what does not meet that standard is necessarily inferior and of no consequence. As a result of our size, our provincial status has been a source of irritation and a cause of misconceptions to many Canadians. Why should a tiny island only 140 miles long with a population of 122,000 people have a separate and distinct legal status as a province? But many Canadians overlook the historical, cultural, and indeed political reasons for our provincial status. The building in which the Fathers of Confederation held the first of the meetings that led to Confederation had already been in use as a Provincial Legislature for forty years; Islanders have taken great pride and derive a great deal of their identity from their politics and independence.

Prince Edward Island has the highest density of population of any province in Canada; this results in a countryside dominated by humanity rather than land. Driving through the province with its prevalence of farms and communities is more like driving in England than in any province of Canada. With that concentration of population comes a sense of broader community — of being an Islander.

The living presence of history in our lives also gives depth and meaning to ethical and social values that have almost universal acceptance and observance. It must be remembered that the Island has been populated since the mid-1700s. My family arrived in 1781 and, with the exception of the inevitable emigrants in their ranks, have been living here since that time. Some of my fondest memories are of visiting a great-aunt and uncle in their home, the oldest part of which dates back to the eighteenth century. The sense of family and connections is always present and is an active means of reinforcing and strengthening that sense of community. This sense of living history is sometimes felt by persons moving to Prince Edward Island to be a detriment to their ever being fully accepted as "an Islander". In its more prevailing positive aspects, however, it provides a sense of place, identity, and security, and of a worth that seems so painfully lacking for so many Canadians.

Our culture and values, like those in the other Maritime provinces, set us apart from other Canadians. Yet, in spite of that distinctive identity and the lack of comprehension by Central and Western Canadians, and by Islanders of those same Canadians, we Islanders have by reason of our old-fashioned values and sense of history a profound belief in the worth and potential of a united and diverse Canada.

Our history has taught us that we, as a small island, are vulnerable in the larger world; that we and our offspring of each generation are enriched by having areas outside our boundaries but within our country offering challenge and opportunity to our restless and our unemployed; that our distinctiveness as a people in our political and cultural heritage has its greatest opportunity for fulfilment within our Canadian confederation; that our hope and opportunity for change and economic development can best be realized in Canada, rather than in a substantially weakened cluster of vulnerable entities.

A State of Grace

Alan Holman

A Charlottetown, Prince Edward Island, businessman and past
chairman, Fathers of Confederation Memorial Trust.

You ask me why I'm a Canadian and whether I like being
a Canadian. Well, as I was born on Prince Edward Island
and, except for World War II and a few holiday trips,
have not lived anywhere else, I guess I'm just naturally
a Canadian. This is a state of grace to which I have given
very little thought.

It grieves me that Canada is, in effect, being split into
racial, geographical, and economic regions. It grieves me
to hear WASPs and WASCs condemn the other peoples
living in Canada. It grieves me to have so many in our
so-called "founding races" (whatever that means) claim
a priority over the rights of the millions of immigrants
who have done so much to make Canada both a nation
and a great nation in which to live.

I know that many of these misunderstandings are due
to fears, both founded and unfounded, that one or other
of these "founding races" is going eventually to hold an
advantage in our nation. Unfortunately, the talk and the
actions can only lead to the fracturing of the fragile ties
that bind us together.

I sometimes think the best way to solve many of our
difficulties would be to take our political, social, religious,
union, and business leaders and lock them in a convention centre and inform them they would not be released
until they had hammered out a sensible and workable
agreement for the future of Canada. Negotiation can only
be successful if each side gives a little. What politician can stand up under the glare of the TV lights and in
front of the probing microphones and the press and say
that he has "given"? What we too often have is not
negotiation. It is confrontation!

Have we any assurance that if we continue our present
actions Canada will not fall apart? Certainly this disin-
tegration has happened to nations in the past, and most

assuredly to weak and stumbling nations with powerful neighbours. If this does happen, we have no one to blame but ourselves. Oh yes, the WASPs and the WASCs will blame Pierre Trudeau, René Lévesque, the French Canadian federal French Cabinet members. For their part, the French Canadians will blame the *Mauvais Anglais*. The other ethnic groups? I suppose they will blame the members of the "founding races".

However, it will be the responsibility of all of us — so we better start now to get together — to try to understand both the fears and aspirations of all of us and, without the politicians and political parties, attempt to work out our differences so that Canada can go forward as a united nation, a nation that will continue to be a leader for peace and prosperity in this world!

---------------- ∗ ----------------

A Quality of Gentleness
Robert Stanfield

Premier of Nova Scotia 1956–67; Member of Parliament and leader of the Progressive Conservative Party 1967–76.

My feelings towards Canada are admittedly prejudiced. Canada is where I was born and grew up; where I lived with my mother and father and family; where I married and brought up a family of my own; where I have lived, worked, played, and struggled to realize myself. Canada is therefore very much a part of me.

I like gardens and rolling fields, forests and streams and lakes, mountains and oceans. Like music, these move me. I like to visit other countries, but I like to return home to familiar and evocative associations.

It is a wonderful land, a country with room — lots of room for me, lots of room for all of us. We are lucky to have all that room. But it does create some problems. Because Canada covers so much space and is peopled by men and women from many lands, she is not an easy country to govern. Space and diversity bring great gifts, but they do not make easy the unity in diversity envisaged by the Fathers of Confederation. This requires tolerance and understanding and a willingness to see the other fellow's point of view. The majority in any democracy, and the government it elects, must respect the views of minorities, and this is especially true in our spacious and diverse country. Sometimes we forget this.

Our roominess also affects our self-confidence as a nation, because we are not sure that we are making the most of all that space, or that we have as much in common as Canadians as we should have. Self-doubts are in a sense a weakness in a country, but they have some advantages, too. People who are sure of themselves and sure they are right are not always pleasant to live with; and they are often intolerant and wrong. Those, on the other hand, who have some doubts are more inclined to listen and consider other points of view. We need some of this in Canada if we are to understand each other and work together.

We have many faults, but as a people we have some virtues and a lot of luck. We are perhaps not the most enterprising or daring of peoples. We are apparently not at the forefront of the arts or technology. We have perhaps an exaggerated idea of what our living standards should be. We are sometimes inclined to take the easy course. But as a people we are not all bad. Some of us are rough and others want their way regardless, but as a people we Canadians are fundamentally decent. We have a quality of gentleness. This is not softness or weakness or lack of courage. It is strength. And it is why it is easy to feel at home here. Canadians are decent, in part at least because we realize we are enormously lucky to live in this rich land with all this room.

No Matter How Small
Manning MacDonald

Cape Bretoner and mayor of Sydney, Nova Scotia.

Someone once asked me if I was a "Cape Bretoner". Naturally I responded in the affirmative, and was proud of it. Then I hastily added that I was also a Nova Scotian and a *Canadian*.

If I could be permitted, I would like to mention just a few of these "Cape Bretoners" who have made their mark on our country. The Deputy Prime Minister, Hon. Allen J. MacEachen, and Nova Scotia Premier, Hon. John Buchanan, are both from Cape Breton as is Flora MacDonald, M.P., for Kingston, Ontario, and Al MacNeil, a Stanley Cup winning Coach of the Montreal Canadians, is a native of Sydney. The greatness of this country is that no matter how remote the location, or how small the population, its sons and daughters can make their mark as great Canadians.

The Genuine Article
Brian Blackmore

A Grand Falls, Newfoundland, lawyer and participant in civic and provincial affairs.

When I first went away from home in Grand Falls, Newfoundland, to complete high school in Kitchener, Ontario, I always told my new schoolmates that the part of Newfoundland I came from wasn't really the true Newfoundland. I came from the woods of Newfoundland. If you really wanted to see and speak to a real Newfoundlander, I told them, I wasn't the best example. You had to find one who came from a coastal, fishing community. There would be the genuine article.

Since my original "leaving home", I have travelled widely and come to the conclusion that I really was a genuine Newfoundlander. The question "who is a true Newfoundlander" leaves the real question unasked: "Who is a true Canadian?" I now believe that there is no true Canadian, just as there was no true Newfoundlander. As a country we are into our second century and have expansively drawn into our mosaic a much wider spectrum of peoples, cultures, and languages than the French and the English.

We should not be anxious because the differences between the two founding cultures are so often and so clearly evident. As my image of the true Newfoundlander was broken, I believe the image that the true Canadian is one with French or English roots must also be broken. All of us, no matter what our province of birth or residence, heritage of culture or language, are true Canadians. Let us get on with moulding a positive, multiplicitous future.

---------------------- ✳ ----------------------

Proud and Grateful

Joseph Roberts Smallwood

First premier of the newest Canadian province, Newfoundland; known as "the only living Father of Confederation".

We have been here in Newfoundland, on this Island, we Newfoundlanders, for just under 500 years. We were the first people from any part of the continent of Europe to come across the Atlantic and settle. We are the original settlers in the New World.

And so, we're very proud of that, intensely proud of our Island home.

But we've been Canadians now for a bit more than thirty years, and we are in an excellent, an unusual, an extraordinary, perhaps a unique position to be able to make a comparison: We can compare Newfoundland today as a province of Canada, with Newfoundland as she was before she was a province.

It's not that we're getting any more out of Confederation than the other nine provinces, but that we're getting it more recently. We can compare our lot with what our lot was before. And that has to fill our hearts and minds in Newfoundland with gratitude.

It was a terrible decision that we had to make. For thousands of us, it seemed as if we were turning our backs on our tradition, on our heritage, on our history, and that we were betraying our country, throwing in our lot with another country that was not our country.

Today, if this were put to the test, disregarding as you must do all foolish talk, and boastful talk, silly talk, from occasional persons (including an occasional politician), excluding them, one hundred per cent of the people of Newfoundland, not less loyal to Newfoundland than they ever were, not loving Newfoundland less than they ever did, are loyal Canadians, loyal, and proud, and grateful.

If there are no other proud Canadians, they are here.

If there are no other grateful Canadians, they are in Newfoundland.

And I am one of them.

2

---*---

"Go Canada!"

---------------- ✳ ----------------

Skating to Win
Gaetan Boucher

Speed skater from Ste. Foy and Ste. Hubert, Quebec. This piece
was prepared some time before he won gold medals in the
1,000 m. and 1,500 m. races in the 1984 Winter Olympic
Games at Sarajevo. He now holds more Olympic medals than
any Canadian in history.

Have you ever wondered what the rest of the world is
like? How often, after travelling in other countries, do
you come back saying: "It was just beautiful. I would
love to live there"?

Perhaps you don't fully realize what you are saying.
Of course, there are interesting cultures and nice scenery
in other parts of the world. But how long were you gone?
Two weeks? One month? Two months? What have they
got that we don't have? Just think about that.

Having to compete mostly in strange lands, I have
learned to appreciate what is under my feet. Canada
is a big country. We do not encounter the stress so frequent in most other countries. We are free to do as we
please. There is not a law for each and every move we
make. We also have the resources: water, electricity, land,
agriculture, and gas are all within reach.

Being the world's second largest country, our field of
possible activities is unlimited. We have many parks. You
want to play golf, tennis, or just go fishing? Nobody is
going to stop you and you will not have to wait your
turn.

But probably the biggest advantage is the security to
walk at night in most of our cities. No place is perfect
but you better inquire before leaving your hotel late, after
sundown, when you live in a foreign land.

I have learned to appreciate my country, and after
travelling the five or six months of my competitive season, the best way I know to relax is to go home and think
of the freedom, peace, and quiet of our land, Canada.

---- ✳ ----

When Bagpipes Play
Ed Werenich

A Scarborough, Ontario, fireman; member of Don Mills Curling Club, skip of Canada's 1983 world championship curling team, and runner-up, Canadian Brier, 1984.

The feeling first grabbed me when they handed us our Canada sweaters. Bagpipe players were lining up to lead the curling teams from all over the world into the Regina Arena. Canada would come in last and competition would then begin. Paul Savage had put his "Canada" sweater on right away. We stared at it in a kind of wonder. We had always worn a local club sweater.

Then we marched in. The roar of thousands of Canadians giving us a standing ovation made my backbone go all numb with tingling. Here we were in the heart of curling country, representing Canada after years of training and trying, and months of competition from our local club championships to the Brier. Ours is the toughest route of any country for getting into the world event; you have to win every meet from the start to get there.

A week later we captured the title and I had that feeling all over again. I was standing on the platform with the team during the presentation ceremonies. Our flag slowly went up and everybody began to sing "O Canada". I couldn't sing a note. I didn't dare. I would have broken down, with all those national television cameras on me. A few minutes later when they asked me to speak, I finally did. But I had to stop my words, collect myself, finish quickly, and get off the platform.

Our team really was Canadian. I came from a farm at Benito, Manitoba, where my Ukrainian parents had settled. I began curling at eleven and moved to Toronto at eighteen. John Kawajo was born in Quebec. His father is Nova Scotian and Lebanese in ancestry, his mother, Scottish from Prince Edward Island. He learned curling as a kid in Newcastle, New Brunswick. Paul Savage is all Toronto, start to finish. Neil Harrison first curled in high school at Peterborough, Ontario.

But the route that got us there doesn't matter. We were four very proud Canadians in that very special moment of our lives in Regina, Canada.

✳

World and Olympic Hockey
Dave King

University of Saskatchewan hockey coach and coach of Canada's world champion junior hockey team of 1982, and of Canada's Olympic and World hockey team.

Thinking over the tremendous effort made by our hockey team at the recent 1984 Winter Olympic Games, I was reminded of winning the world junior hockey championship on January 3, 1982. That was a significant event for hockey in Canada. People from all over sent telegrams of congratulations.

What did it take to win? It required twenty young Canadians to pull together, to put personal egos aside and share in the workload. The players, from seven different provinces in Canada, displayed excellent technique, poise, and discipline. These are important aspects of why we did not lose a game, beating the Soviets, the Americans, the Swedes, the Swiss, the Finns, and the Germans and tying the Czechs for the title!

My greatest satisfaction came from seeing players from East and West, English and French Canadians, all working in unison. There was never any thought of where a player came from or his cultural heritage. They felt a responsibility to represent Canada in a class manner in an attempt to regain prestige for Canadian hockey. I can say the same for the 1984 Olympic Team at Sarajevo. We can all be proud of them.

Skiing Home

Steve Podborski

First Canadian to win the World downhill ski title, in 1982; a native of Toronto.

I was speaking at a film presentation the other day and was asked where, of all the places in the world I have visited, I would prefer to live. That question has many implications and I was fortunate to have had the chance to consider it.

I have been to some eleven countries in my travels, from dictatorships to monarchies to democracies and everything in between. In many of these countries there is very little money for the average person; in fact there is none. In other countries there is more money but less freedom to use it . . .

One way or the other it ends up that Canada is the best place for me to live. There is a high standard of living and an open enough government policy to allow free enterprise. There is also a diversity of cultures to stimulate a sometimes too complacent Canadian. This complacent Canadian sometimes needs a little more prodding than he may like, but I feel that a lesson learned hard is a lesson long remembered.

I am very fortunate to have had the opportunity to travel around the world and it has only made my pride in our country and my love for it, in all its diversity and troubles, stronger.

Only When We Are Separated

Gilles Villeneuve

The late Gilles Villeneuve, Canada's first world-class Formula One racing driver, prepared his thoughts on Canada not long before his death in a fiery racing crash.

Sometimes it is only when we are separated from something that we can appreciate it to the full. In effect, my non-resident status has made me prouder than ever to be Canadian; I am so much more aware of what Canada has to offer now that I live abroad. Life is different all over the world and I constantly find myself making comparisons.

I feel most intensely Canadian when I have just won a race and they are playing "O Canada". I cannot help thinking that our national anthem is the best in the world; as far as I know, it is the only one that actually begins with the name of the country. It conjures up vivid memories and, without fail, my thoughts turn to the beauty of home. I grow very sentimental every time I hear it.

I am made to feel welcome wherever I go. Perhaps it is because of the part Canada played in World War II, I don't really know, but even people who don't know I am a Formula One driver are friendly as soon as they find out I am Canadian. Canadians are well liked all over the world.

I am automatically looked upon as Canada's representative in international car racing. This is inevitable since I am the only Canadian driver in Formula One racing. However, I do not represent Canada officially like the members of our national teams.

Living in Monaco and travelling so much has made me appreciate just how good North American life really is. Everything is so easy and there is space enough for everyone. Even in our cities, which by their very nature are more confining, there is still room to move around freely.

I can now see how fortunate we Canadians are to have four distinct seasons. I love snow. When everything is blanketed in white, the country seems more magnificent and more powerful than ever. The changing seasons give a feeling of renewal and rebirth that is difficult to find anywhere else.

When I visit my father in Berthierville, Quebec, I look out at the fields stretching as far as the eye can see and I say to myself, "This is truly a beautiful country."

I love Canada, and, naturally, Quebec holds a special place in my heart. Its two cultures make it very special. I am not nationalistic and have no strong feelings about federalism or an independent Quebec. It is true that we have a language problem but it is not devastating. I have come to realize that every country has its differences when it comes to language. Just look at Belgium and Switzerland.

I think it is only after living abroad that one can fully appreciate our way of life as we know it, or comprehend its greatness and freedom. The land of our birth takes on a totally new dimension once we have left it. Just ask Canadians who live abroad.

---

*

Tributes to Gilles Villeneuve
Guy Lafleur

Star right winger of the Montreal Canadiens hockey club. Lafleur writes here of his friend, the late auto racing star Gilles Villeneuve.

I always had great admiration for Gilles. When I learned of his death, I had the impression I was dreaming. It does not make sense and I still haven't got over it. A true and marvellous champion, Gilles Villeneuve spent his whole life in the constant pursuit of excellence. I'm sure it was his highest ideal.

His courage and fearlessness were those of the greatest athletes. The perfect model that he always chose to be for sportsmen will make a legend of him. Canada has lost its greatest representative around the world.

To Gilles

John Magill

President of the Canadian Automobile Sports Club.

Gilles Villeneuve at thirty years of age was thought by his peers and by experienced observers of motorsport to have been the fastest Formula One driver on the Grand Prix circuit, and perhaps one of the most talented of all time. He was killed in an accident on the race track during a qualifying run for the Belgian Grand Prix in May 1982. He died trying to do more.

How typical of Gilles to slow down long enough to write for a book on Canada dedicated to Terry Fox and others. Despite his success and fame, he never lost that special common touch, yet no one who knew him as I did or watched him ever doubted his courage, determination, or fighting spirit against what must have seemed overwhelming odds. It was his life. He always gave everything he had. How similar Terry Fox and Gilles Villeneuve now seem, each in his own way, and so *Canadian*.

Surely it must have been such men who built this country and then stood fast through thick and thin to make it great. We have lost these two in their prime and yet we are all the richer for having known them. May God grant us the strength to keep the faith and the spirit that these men personified.

———————————— ✳ ————————————

Tattoo for My Country
Alex Baumann

Swimmer, winner of two gold medals, World University Games, Edmonton 1983, and world record holder in Medley swimming event; native of Sudbury, Ontario.

When I get up every morning at half-past five to start my training routine, I sometimes think of all that has happened to me.

I came to Canada with my parents from Czechoslovakia in 1969 when I was five years old. I was too young to understand the difference in the social and political structures between the country we had left and the land of our choice. But in the course of time, on the basis of new experience and with the help of my parents and new Canadian friends, my ideas grew more concrete and exact.

It became evident to me that the basis of a real democratic country is the freedom of expression: the independence to hold different points of view and the liberty to express them. I now see Canada as a land of enormous opportunity. I have stayed in many countries and seen many cultures and life-styles, but to me, Canada, as a country, is the greatest.

Opportunity in Canada has meant that I could follow a sport or a career of my choice. For a lifetime career, I am focusing on studies that will help me qualify to represent Canada in the diplomatic service.

In sports, I chose, freely, swimming. When I was nine-and-a-half years old, I began to swim for fun and recreation at the Laurentian University Swimming Club in Sudbury. The club's magnificent swimming coach, Dr. Jeno Tihanyi, a refugee from Communist Hungary, encouraged me to swim in competitions.

At age ten, I began training for racing and in two years had advanced to a twice-a-day routine. The first two-hour swim starts in the pool at 6:00 a.m., the second at 4:00 p.m., ending at 6:00. Another forty-five minutes goes into weight lifting. In between comes school, family, and recreation. My specialty race, in which I was fortunate enough to gain a World Record at the Commonwealth Games, is the Medley, which demands four different swimming strokes in succession — the Butterfly, Backstroke, Breaststroke, and Freestyle — and perfection in each. It's hard work, but worth it. My goal is an Olympic medal.

I wear my pride in being a Canadian not on my sleeve, but on my chest, with a small tattooed Maple Leaf.

———————————— * ————————————

Terrific Times
Phil Esposito

Hockey superstar with Boston Bruins and New York Rangers, known for prolific goal scoring and dedication to international competitions, and now a colour commentator on Rangers' broadcasts.

It's hard for me to describe one great moment in my career. Like most athletes, I suppose I have quite a few terrific times, since I started to play hockey when I was four or five years old. One was when I was eighteen and I was playing hockey in my home town of Sault Ste. Marie. We had just won the Ontario Juvenile Championship, and I was the captain of the team. This was one of my greatest thrills. It was the last time I played hockey without pay, and this is why it stands out in my mind.

I guess my second greatest thrill was when we won the first Stanley Cup in Boston. It sure was a thrill when Bobby Orr scored that overtime goal.

My third greatest moment had to be for my country, when we were playing against the Russians in 1972, when Henderson scored the goal in the dying seconds of the game and I was fortunate enough to assist on the goal.

Right now, the United States is promoting an educational series for children to get high on themselves, to prevent them from getting into drugs. The hockey series in which I participated in 1972 was as high as I could get, no matter what, and I think this typifies what they are trying to get across. I got high on myself, and my country, and I didn't need any drugs or anything else. I didn't think anything or anyone else could get that high, but I sure reached that level.

As you can tell from all of my greatest moments above, they are all team oriented. Don't get me wrong, I am not trying to say that I am totally a team guy all of the time. Individual awards meant a lot to me, too. I certainly did receive my share of individual awards and commending statistics, which I will not go into now. But hockey has given me more things than I can say. Hockey has given me a great life.

I guess Canada has allowed me to do these things. I suppose if I had grown up in the U.S., I would have concentrated on baseball or football or some other sport, but God gave me the talent to be a hockey player, and living in Canada I had the opportunity to develop that talent. That is why I like it when I say I am a Canadian and Canada is a great country. Sure, Canada has its problems, but so do other countries. As my life progresses, I find it necessary to live in the U.S. I don't think it is that much different; they have problems, too. But as life goes on, you find people in general are very much alike. I like the U.S., but I suppose it would have been a lot nicer if I could have had my career in Canada and could have retired to a half decent job there. But, I can't be a hypocrite, I like the U.S., and I enjoy living here. But Canada is always in my heart.

---------------------------------- ✳ ----------------------------------

I Walk to Win
Guillaume Leblanc

Of Sept.-Îles, Quebec; winner of the gold medal for the 10,000 km. walk, World University Games, Edmonton 1983, and an engineering student, University of Montreal.

I was eleven years old when I first learned that walking was my athletic event. I went into a walking race in school at Sept-Îles, Quebec, in 1973, and beat everybody, even the older boys. I decided to give up other kinds of races and jumping and train myself to walk.

In winter I also trained by racing long distances on skis and snow-shoes. In the past two years I have been planning for the Olympic Games and I walk twenty miles every day, ten each morning and ten each afternoon at different racing paces under the care of my skilful coach, Pierre Léculyer of Montreal.

I have raced in British Columbia, Alberta, and Newfoundland, as well as Quebec. The people of English Canada have given me good support, as do the fans in my own province. I could not speak English at first and it was hard. Now I have many friends in the other provinces and I get along okay in English.

The track and field team of Canada has a very friendly spirit, like a good hockey team. I believe sport unites Canadians.

---------------------------------- ✳ ----------------------------------

"Does Everybody Smoke?"
Desai Williams

Toronto-based world class sprinter, who immigrated to Canada as a boy of twelve from St. Kitts in the Caribbean.

I well remember arriving with my family in Toronto, as an immigrant, a Black boy of twelve from the green and warm Caribbean island of St. Kitts. It was December 28,

1972. Suddenly all of the boys I wanted to play with were White instead of Black. And when I looked out a window later on, I wondered, "Does everybody here smoke? All the air is white." I had never seen snow before. It freaked me out.

I was quickly accepted among my new White friends at school, as fully as I had been among my Black chums on St. Kitts. There, I had a few White friends, but we were just kids. We never classified each other as White or Black. I can honestly say that I have not met any prejudice towards me since I came to Canada, although I know there must be some here.

It was not long before I asked for a pair of skates to replace the soccer ball that I had used all the time in St. Kitts. I also had never heard of football or hockey. When I first saw these guys knocking each other down all over the place, I thought, "What the heck are they doing?" I soon found out. When I got to North View Heights Secondary School, coach Fred Burford had me playing wide receiver on the football team, because I was fast. I also turned out for soccer. But when soccer collapsed, I went over to the track team partly because when I had nothing to do my mother had encouraged me to go out and practise with my brother who was in track.

During 1977, my first year of hard training, I won four gold medals at the Canada Summer Games in Newfoundland. The 100- and 200-metres became my specialty. Canadian and Commonwealth championships followed.

Recently I won the 300 metres indoor in the fourth fastest time ever run. I was also a member of the Scarboro Optimist Club relay team when we set a world record at the 1983 indoor games in Sherbrooke, Quebec. These records have given me hope for a chance to reach my main goal, a gold medal for Canada at the Olympic Games. To achieve this, my coach at York University, Charlie Francis, has me practising six hours a day, six days a week.

I like Canada. I would choose it first as a place to live, because of our high standard of living and our freedoms of choice.

I am now studying physical education at York and plan to enter coaching so I can give other kids the same kind of concern, skill, and extra effort that Charlie Francis and other coaches have put into my own sport career and those of other athletes.

---

*

Canadians Can Play Quarterback
Gerry Dattilio

Recently a quarterback with the Calgary Stampeders football club and previously with Montreal Alouettes; now back in Montreal, with the Concordes.

Being Canadian is something special to me. My grandfather came to Canada from Italy. This country has provided a good life for my family and relatives ever since. I was brought up in Laval, Quebec, where I played with French, English, Italian, and other kids. We were friends and never thought of each other as foreigners. As a kid, I spoke French before I spoke English. My Mom is French and I am proud of both my ethnic backgrounds.

As I prepare these words in Calgary, my baby boy is six days old. Christiane and I will bring him up a Canadian all the way. Christiane immigrated to Canada from Germany as a little girl, adding another ethnic background to our new Canadian.

My early football was played with the Laval West city team and the Chomedy Protestant High School, always as a quarterback. We won the Montreal city championship in my second year.

My capability was improved at Northern Colorado College where we only lost seven games in four years and won three division championships.

I wanted to play in Canada and sure was pleased when the Alouettes — and then the Calgary Stampeders — gave me a chance as quarterback, to prove a Canadian can play this complex position.

I have been worried and sorry about those Quebecers and Westerners who talk about dividing Canada. I am one hundred per cent opposed to this idea. The people of Calgary have been wonderful to me and my family even when the press has been down on the team. It makes you feel good.

I have close family ties in Quebec and Toronto and warm friends all over Canada whom I have met in football. I especially like Canada because it gives you room to move around and do what you want to do. No way should we be separated by foreign borders.

A Quarterback Remembers

Russ Jackson

Principal of P.L. Kennedy High School in Mississauga, Ontario; formerly quarterback with the Ottawa Roughriders football club which he led to three Grey Cups, coach, and TV broadcaster.

Having had both the opportunity to play professional football in nine Canadian cities and the pleasure of visiting many other Canadian cities through this association, I have come to sense the magnitude and the complexities of our country.

If you live in Western Canada, it is not always easy to understand the problems related directly to the Maritimes. If you are struggling to make ends meet in Eastern Canada, it is not always easy to be sympathetic to the West's concerns.

And yet, regardless of these problems, I have always been acutely aware of the unification of our people during my many discussions and debates about Canadian football. Being close to our American neighbours, we sometimes have been reticent to sing our own praises. But we have never wavered in our unified support for the sport as a national game. Canadian people everywhere have their own choices and support their favourite team, but they also indirectly relish the spirit of competition among the cities of this land.

We are a friendly, competitive people. Let us hope the differences that attempt to divide our country will not overshadow this grand feeling and friendliness that permeates a national sports crowd. I am proud that I have had the many opportunities to share these feelings with so many fellow Canadians in all parts of our country. I am most proud to say I am a Canadian.

———————————— * ————————————

Coach's Comment
Hugh Campbell

Currently coaching in the National Football League, Campbell led the Edmonton Eskimos football club to five successive Grey Cup wins.

How fortunate Canadians are to be part of a country that combines great area with small population. Add to this the fact that Canada is so young in comparison with other developed countries. Canada's life is the future ahead, not buried or established in the past. Most of the population is only now manifesting what it is no longer to have their roots across the sea but, rather, to be establishing them for future generations as Canadians.

———————————— * ————————————

The People's Game
Al Hackner

Of Thunder Bay, Ontario; skip of Canada's 1982 world champion curling team.

My Dad taught me how to throw a curling stone when I was thirteen. We lived in Nipigeon in Northern Ontario and I played on his team. The next year we won the club championship. In the third year I skipped my own team and won the title. Curling was in my blood.

When I reached eighteen we moved to Thunder Bay and I joined up with some curlers I had met in other

Northern Ontario bonspiels. Our great ambition was to win the Canadian Championship. It took nine more years. My greatest thrill was when that finally happened two years ago at the Labatt Brier in Brandon, Manitoba. In both of the two previous years we had reached the Canadian final but lost. Winning took off all the pressures. On to the world championship — the Air Canada Silver Broom in Germany. We were relaxed and eager.

A real change hit me when we got into the world tournament. In all my previous competitions I had played for the personal satisfaction of winning and for the team. As we played country after country, I realized that I was no longer playing for myself and our team. I was playing for Canada. It was a new and strange feeling.

The number of Canadians in the stands amazed us. If there were 5,000 spectators present, there seemed to be 1,000 Canadians. Maple leafs were everywhere. Every day these Canadians would come up and encourage us to play our best for Canada and tell us how well we played. They helped us keep up our determination.

I thought about Canada afterwards and the privilege of living here. I find that curling is a wealthy person's game in most other countries. Joining their curling clubs is very expensive and taking time off to play very costly. In Canada almost every town with a thousand people or more has a curling rink and the ordinary person can play. About two million Canadians curl at least once a year, one million of them regularly. It is Canada's greatest winter participation sport — perhaps it fills a need in helping us cope with our long winters. As in most Canadian sports, like hockey and golf, and in work and career opportunities, Canadians of every income level have a chance to succeed.

Curling officials tell me that curling in other countries is improving fast. We found every world game tough. Even a newcomer, Italy, beat us in the first round. To keep our chances of winning world titles, Canada must continue to use the best team available from the whole country.

I hope more Canadians in every province and territory learn the game at an early age. Canadian bonspiels and championship Briers are very competitive, but the competitors are friends. We socialize and visit with each other when travelling to Halifax, Calgary, Brandon, or Montreal.

All these opportunities make me grateful to live in this country, which has provided them.

---------------- * ----------------

From the High Bar
Philippe Chartrand

Gold medal winner on the gymnastic high bar at the 1983 World University Games in Edmonton; now a physical education student at the University of Montreal.

My gymnastics training may have started when I was born; I arrived at home, healthy and kicking, before my mother had time to get to a hospital.

One day at College Laval, my high school, I was playing badminton in the gymnasium and noticed nearby on the floor some intriguing gymnastic equipment I had never seen before. A friend asked me to try it. I did and have never stopped.

When I had learned the different gymnastic events, someone I knew invited my present coach, Michele Vanne, to come watch. Afterwards he said, "You are a little too big and maybe not flexible enough but you are very willing. I will train you." He entered me in the Quebec Championship in 1977 and I won my first gold medal.

Several years of training, six hours a day, resulted in going to Edmonton, and the World University Games Championship. I am now adding new routines that have never been done before for the Olympics and other international meets. We expect that the Chinese will be our toughest competition on the bars. But I am confident.

It's a good thing that all the provinces in Canada get together for international competitions. Without the best athletes from every part of the country, we could not do as well as we are now doing — and we will do better in the future.

I want to say thanks for the wonderful support of the Canadian crowds in Edmonton. This helps the athlete.

There is a good spirit in Canada, no matter where we have competed. Canadian people are very warm and friendly. It's unbelievable.

Canada is certainly a nice piece of the world.

———————————— ✳ ————————————

Backyards to Stanley Cup

Mike Bossy

Of Laval, Quebec; a star on the New York Islanders hockey club, four-time winners of the Stanley Cup.

It's pretty easy to guess that I love hockey. I also have strong affections for my family, my country, and my province of Quebec. I learned to play hockey in the backyards and rinks of Ahunsic near Montreal. From there, I moved along in the minor hockey leagues of Montreal and with junior hockey in Laval until the New York Islanders drafted me when I was twenty.

Luckily, I was always on a championship team and got a real taste for winning while I was learning the skills of the game from good coaching and lots of hard work.

My greatest thrills in hockey so far have come during the past four years. First, some personal achievements — winning three Most Valuable Player awards two years ago, first on Team Canada, then at the All Star Game, and finally during the Stanley Cup, the year before scoring fifty goals in fifty games, and this year reaching 400 goals. But I find I am just as pleased with team achievements and the satisfaction of team work, playing for Team Canada, and winning the Stanley Cup four times with the Islanders.

I come from an English-speaking home, where my mother is English and my father is Ukrainian. When I started to play hockey, I played with both French- and English-speaking kids on all the teams. So I learned a little French, just enough to get by. But it never mattered what language you spoke. You were respected for your hockey skills, and we all got along fine. It has been the same since I joined the Islanders, where Denny Potvin is a close team-mate. When I first met my French Canadian wife, neither of us spoke the other's language. Now we are bilingual and are bringing up our little girl to be the same. I have even MC'd a radio programme in French.

When I got to play with Team Canada in the Canada Cup, that unity and respect were the same, but now we were all playing for our country. It was strange, in a way. Most of the Team Canada players were from other NHL teams, and I had played hard to beat them in league games. Yet here we were playing for Canada and enjoying the teamwork. All of us had this strong feeling for our country. One of my greatest ambitions is to play on a winning Team Canada. We are getting better at international play. It should not be long.

We enjoy our winters and our American friends on Long Island, New York. In the summers, as we intend to do when I leave hockey, we return to our beloved Canada and Quebec, where we feel at home.

---------------------------------- ✳ ----------------------------------

Behind Home Plate

Gary Carter

Player on the Montreal Expos baseball team; considered by many the finest catcher in the game.

Professional athletes are often viewed in awe. Sometimes it is very easy for athletes to become caught up in this admiration and lose sight of the fact that only because God has blessed us with a special ability in one specific area do we have this great opportunity. You cannot lose sight of the fact that there are other things in life of far greater significance. But at the same time you owe it to yourself to make the maximum use of whatever talents you have.

Terry Fox's run was one of the greatest examples of this dedication and faith I have ever seen. His effort rates as the ultimate of any athletic endeavour. He character- ized all the things that make a person a great athlete and a great human being. This is but one image of Canadians that I have had as an American playing baseball in Can- ada. I also admire the honesty and friendliness of the people. I have had the opportunity of visiting many parts of Canada. Each area has its own strengths and weak- nesses, and sometimes one part of Canada may see itself as being better or worse off than another.

But as an outsider I have had the opportunity to see how as one country Canada can take all its talents and work to become one of the greatest places to live in the world.

——————————————— ✳ ———————————————

"Never Old Hat"

Susan Nattrass

Native of Edmonton, Alberta, and six times world champion in trap-shooting.

There is a flagpole behind you when you take your place on the winners' podium after winning a world cham- pionship. When the gold medal is placed around your neck, you turn to face the pole and, as the first notes of "O Canada" sound, the maple leaf flag starts its steady rise to the top.

I have had the experience of watching that flag from the winners' podium six times and find it difficult to describe how moving it is every time. There is invariably a lump in my throat and I try to keep back tears, but never quite succeed. I feel immensely proud to be who I am, where I am, and representing the country I do.

In day-to-day life I don't think every time I take a practice shot, "I'm doing this for my country." But during competition, I am very aware of the letters spelling Canada across my back and feel both the pride and responsibility of being a Canadian.

A friend of mine — a member of the Italian trap-shooting team — teases me about my obvious emotion during award ceremonies. "Nattrass, it should be old hat to you," he says.

Let me tell you, it never could be.

3

*

Artists' Impressions

---
*

Choice for a Lifetime

Alex Colville

Internationally recognized painter from Wolfville, Nova Scotia, and chancellor of Acadia University.

In 1967, my wife and I moved to California for a year; I was a kind of visiting artist at the University of California at Santa Cruz. The university was very good, we had many friends, we lived in an award-winning building, the salary was generous. At the end of the year, the provost of the college of which I was a fellow pressed me to stay on; he was a man I liked and respected. I mention this because for the first time in my life I had to seriously consider *not* being a Canadian.

I decided to return to Canada. In trying to explain my decision, I told the provost that for him (an Englishman who had taught for years, first at Cal. Tech., then at Harvard), it was easy to move from one cosmopolitan milieu to another — in a sense he was a world citizen. But for a Canadian (as, I think, for an Israeli, a Swede, a Swiss), the change would be from a micro culture to a macro culture. My point was that a citizen in a smaller nation has a kind of national feeling that is perhaps essentially provincial; this word has, for me, more good than bad connotations.

I remember thinking at the time of other qualities of Canada that I valued: Canada is less coherent than the U.S., less of a melting pot, more a "community of communities". Thus in Canada it is possible to belong both to the country as a whole and at the same time to a unique segment of it, as I belong in particular to the Maritimes.

Canada is also a developing country — in a sense an underdeveloped country. Its future is likely to be greater than its past, and I prefer to live in a country that is still labouring to form its culture.

I believe Canada is essentially a conservative country, cautious about preserving what values it has from its past, with a strong sense of order, an absence of reckless-ness. We are fortunate, I think, to have the U.S. as a neigh-bour because, while we share many qualities, we can better realize our uniqueness by comparing ourselves with our great neighbour; we *are* different, and I like the differences.

———————————— ✳ ————————————

Capturing a World Title
David Peregrine

A principal dancer of the Royal Winnipeg Ballet.

On July 16, 1980, my partner, Evelyn Hart, and I performed the "Belong" *pas de deux* on the last night of the Tenth International Ballet Competition in Varna, Bulgaria.

The performance went well, despite a last minute dis-agreement over lighting. While we performed, the au-dience was absolutely quiet, almost eerily so, because every night for the past three weeks they had applauded or whistled at every chance.

The performance took place in the outdoor Arts Am-phitheatre at the edge of the Black Sea. I still remember the gulls calling overhead, the sound of the wind in the trees that surrounded the theatre, and the smell and feel of the wooden boards of the stage that we lay upon, waiting for the lights and music to begin.

When we finished, the audience remained silent for several seconds longer than usual, leaving us feeling in limbo in that delicate moment after the music stops and before the applause begins. Then they began, letting go all the enthusiasm of the past three weeks, because this was it, the end of the competition, where two terrified children from Canada, totally unknown, had seemed to win the hearts of the audience. The applause went on and on, surprising us all, because we knew that, regardless of the crowd, the clinical eyes of the jury would see all the flaws in our little team and award the major prizes to the Russians.

We didn't want the night to end because the following day the results would be announced, the Russians would win, and the previous night's memories would become dim. So, after the performance, we walked around and talked to the dancers from so many countries who had all been so kind to us. A Bulgarian critic, who had been supportive from the start, pronounced us his adopted son and daughter, and even the Russians congratulated us.

The next day, the impossible happened. The "Belong" *pas de deux* won the gold medal for choreography as the most appealing piece of the competition. Among the men, I was the only non-Russian to be awarded a medal — a bronze. Evelyn won the coveted gold medal and the award for artistry. Our pianist, Earl Stafford, was named best accompanist.

What made it all happen, what tipped the final balance, was that last night's performance of "Belong". The Bulgarians, Russians, French, and even the Americans had, for the most part, never seen anything like it before, because "Belong" was not Bulgarian, Russian, or American, but Canadian — as distinctly Canadian as maple sugar or Inuit sculpture. The choreography was by Norbert Vesak from Vancouver, as well as the costumes and lighting. The music was by John Mill Cockell, formerly of the group Syrinx from Toronto. The two dancers, myself from Ottawa and Evelyn from London, Ontario, were both members of the Royal Winnipeg Ballet, where the director, Arnold Spohr, had originally invited Norbert to create the ballet from which "Belong" is taken.

Now, each time I wait during the brief silences before "Belong" starts, or after it ends, I think of when I lay there on those wooden boards, when something special was about to happen, and I remember . . .

---------------------------- ✷ ----------------------------

Climate for the Arts
Raymond Daveluy

Renowned organist of the St. Joseph Oratory in Montreal, and a composer, and a teacher at the faculties of the Montreal, Trois Rivières, and McGill University Conservatories.

Coming from two old French and English North American families — my first ancestor who was born in Canada, Jean-Baptiste Daveluy, married in Montreal in 1701, while Marie Françoise French was carried off by French soldiers to the town of Darfield, Massachusetts, and my mother, born a Dunn, belonged to an old Scottish family from the eastern townships — I can quite properly think of myself as a Canadian representing the diversity of origins in our population.

Thus Canada constitutes for me a very authentic homeland, but it is especially as a career musician that I have been called to attest to its exceptional value.

Preoccupied with exploiting material wealth, with reuniting the parts of a very diverse population, with building a politically active and viable federation, with setting up a social order in which the individual liberty of citizens would be respected and their well-being and security assured, Canada could have found plausible reasons to detach itself from cultural matters. But, on the contrary, it desired a very strong place in spiritual and artistic life.

In the Council of Arts and Culture, Canada has created an institutional patron that never ceases to sustain activity in all artistic fields. It manifests and assures, in international artistic endeavours, an increasingly more noticeable presence, by sending its artists and intellectuals to the most renowned concert halls, the finest museums, the most learned assemblies.

It is from outside that one best realizes the position our country occupies and the admiration it inspires as one hears artists from other countries marvelling at the importance Canada accords those who represent her.

Canada constitutes a privileged environment for artists and there are very few among the artistic community who do not feel pride in contributing their work to the edification of its spiritual treasure.

———————————— ✳ ————————————

No Nation So Favoured

Hugh MacLennan

Eminent Canadian author and professor of English at McGill University, whose post-war novel *Two Solitudes* is a Canadian classic.

Until my twenty-eighth year, I knew virtually nothing of Canada. Having been born in Cape Breton, Nova Scotia, within half a mile of the Atlantic, having grown up in Halifax, I then studied in England, travelled over most of Europe, and later lived for three years in the United States. Finally in my twenty-eighth year I came to Montreal for a Depression job and have lived there ever since. So it happened that most of my adult life has been occupied in the adventure of discovering for myself the Canadian land and — more important by far — the nature of the Canadian people and the Canadian society. Therefore, what Canada means to me comes close to being the meaning of my entire professional life.

Canada is a country unlike any other I have ever encountered in history. Her population is derived almost entirely from people whose causes had been lost elsewhere. The Québécois were abandoned by their motherland more than two centuries ago. The Loyalists were driven out of the thirteen American colonies by their own brothers. The Scottish Highlanders were enclosed and forced overseas in starvation ships by their own chiefs. Most of the Irish were starved out of their ancient home, and, since World War II, a flood of immigrants have come in from the wreckages of Europe and Asia. Canada has given all of us a home, and her true nature is all the more mysterious because none of the stereotypes come near to her human reality.

We are more respected by others, I believe, than we are respected by ourselves. Students who have travelled in Europe tell me they have encountered American students with Canadian flags stitched onto their backpacks. "These Europeans hate our guts," one of them said, "but you guys they really like."

Yes, as Pericles said of Athens, Canada is certainly better than the report she gives of herself. When I see our bickering politicians stirring up trouble and hatred where there is no need or cause for either, I remember Clarendon's comment on England after the Puritan agitators had talked the public into a terrible civil war. "Oh too fortunate, if only they had understood how fortunate they were!"

✳

My Stage
Douglas Chamberlain

Radio, television, and stage actor in Charlottetown, Prince Edward Island festivals and other Canadian productions.

Relaxed, tanned, and salted from the sea, I sit on the shore of Rustico Island, PEI, pondering the question of what Canada means to me. In my thirty or so years as an actor in Canada, I have had the good fortune of performing in all ten provinces in all seasons of the year. I've had the chance to see various audiences differ in response as radically as the mountains differ from the prairies.

I've played in theatres that no longer exist, with companies that are now only memories, with actors who have come and gone. But I have seen those ten provinces grow in population, culture, and industry. I have seen those very audiences burst into standing ovations, and I have seen the mountains, the prairies, the forests, and the sea's coasts join as one to remind the world that this is Canada.

With the building of new cultural centres and theatre stages, with the continued artistic growth of theatre companies in all major Canadian cities, with the ever-increasing encouragement and recognition of our actors and actresses, we in professional theatre are now able to stay in Canada and pursue our individual goals.

This means I can remain in my own country in a profession that has for so long given in to the draw of the U.S. and England. This means I can work in a successful, world-recognized Canadian Musical here, on beautiful Prince Edward Island. This means that here, on this isolated beach on the eastern coast of Canada, I am relaxed, I am cared for, and I am home.

———————————— ✳ ————————————

Land of My Choice
Veronica Tennant

A principal dancer with the National Ballet of Canada in Toronto.

Canada is my land. I came here from England as a child, and even now I live here not by circumstance but by very deliberate choice. I remember visiting Paris as a teenager and the thrill of having a taxi driver welcome me as a "cousine" (canadienne); speaking my most conscientious French, there was, I felt, no need to redefine myself as an English Canadian.

I am deeply committed to my country, and that love is reaffirmed each time I return from being away.

---- ✳ ----

"I Owe Everything . . ."

Roger Lemelin

Author of the popular television series "The Plouffe Family" and current best-selling novel *Le Crime d'Ovide Plouffe*, and former editor of *La Presse* in Montreal.

I owe everything to my country. Born in Quebec in a working-class milieu, I was brought up in an atmosphere of freedom. As a writer, I have been showered by Canadians of both languages with their generous feeling for my work. Several times in the course of my career, I have had to travel for extended stays in Europe or the United States — it was never my idea.

My Cap-Rouge, my Quebec, my Canada — these are my country and that of my children and grandchildren, that of my forefathers for the last 350 years. I suffer its troubles, I rejoice in its successes. Whenever I feel the spirit of enterprise is threatened or that individual liberties are violated, I arise, ready to fight the dangers.

My literary sources have come from far and wide, but it is on the soil of Quebec that they have been able to germinate into all my works.

I am proud to be French, to be a Canadian citizen, and to be a writer.

The Children Never Knew
Ann Rohmer

Co-host of Global television show "That's Life" in Toronto.

The people I interview daily on television give me my image of Canada. They are as diverse as the nation and intensely proud of their differing backgrounds and races. To my surprise, the one common link between them is their pride in being Canadian.

I have also been amazed when I travel outside Canada with our TV crew at how wonderfully people respond when they learn we are from Canada.

I am especially proud to be broadcasting in Canada. Our television industry is no longer in the shadows of Big Brother U.S.A. It has made a name for itself. In fact, American networks now buy a number of Canadian shows. More than any country I know, Canada's TV industry has given young Canadians like myself a chance to try their wings. I am thankful that this has allowed me to turn down U.S. offers in order to work in my own country.

During a recent stay in Israel to interview children of that country, I was saddened to realize that these youngsters did not know what it's like to live in a peaceful land where no one wonders when the next bomb might explode or where the next bullets will fly. War and death are second nature to Israel's children. They could hardly believe me when I told them that Canadians walk around freely, without fear. Now I know how lucky we are to live here. Sometimes I wonder whether it would be fair for me to bring a child into today's world. If it happened in a place like Canada, I would have no hesitation.

My father, Richard Rohmer, is an ardent nationalist and influenced me a lot when I was a child. Now that I am standing on my own two feet, I have come to agree with his deep affection for Canada. Maybe some day I'll take over where he left off.

---
*

Strength From the Audience
Vanessa Harwood

A principal dancer with the Canadian National Ballet in Toronto.

I have travelled from coast to coast in Canada with the National Ballet of Canada since 1965, performing repeatedly in each province, in every large city, and in many smaller communities. I feel I have come to know Canada and Canadians. I've experienced the warmth and hospitality of the East and the boisterous generosity of the West. I particularly enjoy the cosmopolitan atmosphere of such places as Vancouver, Toronto, and Montreal. We have much to give to one another in this country. We can be a strong nation, but petty differences threaten to tear us apart. It is unfortunate that the politics surrounding language rights are separating Canadians.

When touring throughout Canada as a ballerina, I see people everywhere united in enjoying the performing arts. Dance is not political. It has universal appeal; it is a universal language. Whether performing in Saint John, Vancouver, Montreal, or Saskatoon, I dance for the audience and for myself, not for their politics or for mine. There is a sense of unity in dance, a bond of dedication to excellence and common goals that transcend personal differences, insecurities, and politics. Canada would become stronger if these same principles were applied to pulling this country together.

---
*

All the Identity I Need

Don Harron

Also known as Charlie Farquharson; familiar radio and television broadcaster, actor, playwright, and author living in Toronto.

People are always asking me why I stay in this country. They don't realize I spent about fifteen years away from home, working at my trade in London, New York, and Hollywood. My first sojourn outside my country lasted for two years and was an accident. My first night in London, I was cast in a West End play and signed up to write a comedy series for the BBC. With luck like that, what was the point of coming back to Canada? I returned by way of a six-month tour of U.S. theatres in a British play. I came back when television began in Canada and stayed to take part in the first Stratford Festival.

But I always kept going away to test myself in foreign waters, and, in so doing, I began to think about the people I left behind and of how to portray them; eventually I began to write about them. I tried writing in other countries but it didn't seem to mean much, to them or to me.

What brought me back? To be specific, it was a little orphan with red hair and freckles. "Anne of Green Gables" was a television adaptation I wrote just before becoming a resident alien in the U.S. Every time I came back to visit, I would take something Canadian back with me —books about Emily Carr, for example — and try to turn them into something for the theatre or television. The success of "Anne" at Charlottetown made me realize that if I wanted to say something meaningful for me as well as any audience, it would have to be here at home.

I made this decision in 1966. I have never had reason to change it. I cannot speak for others but Canada has given my life, particularly my creative life, meaning. The fact that I wanted my children to grow up here rather than any place else is beside the point. Canada gives me all the identity I need.

---- ✳ ----

"Go Into the Pubs"
Alden Nowlan

One of Canada's best-known writers and poets, who died while poet in residence, University of New Brunswick, in June 1983.

Some time before he died, I phoned Alden Nowlan, asking if he would write his appreciation of Canada and express for us all what so many feel but cannot put into words. He instantly agreed. "Go into the pubs anywhere," he crackled, spitting out his feelings over the phone. "You'll find out. The ordinary guy knows damn well that this is *his* country. He can't describe it. He doesn't talk about it. But he doesn't have any doubt. Just knows it as a fact."

Alden Nowlan died before he could put his contribution into writing. Canada has lost a great Canadian. — Editor.

---- ✳ ----

Ambassador for Humanity
Annette av Paul

A principal dancer with Les Grands Ballets Canadiens in Montreal.

As a dancer, I wish to be an ambassador for humanity and reach and touch the lives of the people, to bring them joy and hope. I wish to share with them my love for life and for this world in which we live, and for this very special country, Canada. Here's what Canada means to me:

Vast spaces
Endless sky
Profoundly inspiring mountains
Catch the milky way at night

91

Autumn leaves in Newfoundland
Whales playing in the water
A double rainbow over Nova Scotia
A cat crying in the snow
40 below in Prince George

Our touring bus full of energy
French and English Canadian
(Swedish and Philippine, too)
And the universal language of dance
That we share

Theatres, theatres, theatres, large and small
Thousands of people
Young and old
Wanting to be touched through our craft

Identity? It's already there!
A tapestry of fears, joys and dreams
   oh so similar
Endless potential, riches, and great things to share

Vast spaces

I hope we all care

4

---- * ----

My Life

Capturing a Dream
Russell W. Gowing

Head of French language and French immersion courses on British Columbia's Saanich Peninsula; immigrated to Canada on advice of POW comrades from World War II.

There I sat in the BOAC plane finally descending to land in Canada in April 1952. Alone, with a plastic briefcase and an expired one-way BOAC airline ticket, I had finally left England and Europe with all its memories and miseries of 1939–45. My young English wife with a daughter of six and a son of nine months were to follow me by boat as soon as I had found a job.

My airline ticket took me from Dorval to Toronto. From there I managed by bus to get to a little town called Simcoe in Southern Ontario. I had been invited to stay with Ike Hewitt, a former Prisoner of War comrade of the RCAF. My recollection of the time spent in Simcoe is vague. Everything in this new land was so different. I felt alone, and it was sometimes difficult to make the adjustment. I tried to remember the four years of long evenings in POW camps in Germany where a number of young Canadian soldiers and airmen imprisoned with us would talk about the beauty, breadth, and opportunities that were in Canada for those who wanted to work for it.

Those young Canadians were proud and positive, and so different one from the other. Gautier, the gold miner with a strong French accent, Ken Laing from Moose Jaw with self-reliance and a farmer's hands, Lofty Hodgins, a radio announcer from Winnipeg, and many more. All had a deep and quiet affection for this vast northern land and wanted you to share it with them. It had to be a good place to bring my tiny family to grow after the war, I decided.

After a brief stint in a furniture store in Simcoe, I was invited to Toronto to talk to Gordon Wright in the education department of the Ontario Ministry of Education. We discovered that my English qualifications were not adequate to teach immediately in Ontario. I had to have employment in order to feed my family. Gordon Wright went to some trouble to introduce me to Dick Gordon, then principal of St. Johns Ravencourt School at Fort Garry in Winnipeg. I was offered a position as residential teacher at the school. I had at least found shelter for my family. By that time my wife and family had arrived and we bid farewell to our old friends in Simcoe. With our few "landed immigrant" packages we boarded a bus bound for Winnipeg. I must admit to being surprised to find that the shortest route from Simcoe to Winnipeg was through the States, but that's another story.

Our stay from 1952 to 1954 in Winnipeg was a delight. We loved the fierce black and white climate of the prairies. It was a different country; the good folk of Wildwood Park, the suburb at Fort Garry in which the school was located, treated us well, as my service buddies had said they would. They themselves had undergone a disastrous flood the year before and had overcome the discomforts. They were not going to let a lonely little immigrant family feel unwanted or left out.

Despite the fact that we now had a good place to live and solid friends around us, we didn't feel as though we were part of the country by teaching in the somewhat separate atmosphere of a private school. So, after two years, we decided to move on again once more, further west, we hoped.

Teachers were in short supply at that time right across the country. *The Globe and Mail* ran columns of vacancies. We ran an eye down the columns seeking a position anywhere in the West that provided a teacherage. "Ucluelet" seemed like an interesting place on the West Coast of Vancouver Island. I suppose we thought it would look something like Brighton in England! I telephoned from Winnipeg to Ucluelet, accepted the position, and then tried to find out exactly where it was. We were able to obtain misleading and sometimes disturbing information from airmen who had flown out of Tofino. Nobody seemed sure where it was or in fact what it was.

Once again we put our meagre belongings together and packed up the kids. This time we would take the train. What can be said about a train journey across the wide prairies up the foothills and through the awesome canyons of the Rocky Mountains? This journey has been documented many, many times. For an English family accustomed to the patchwork fields of England, it is a journey that remains forever in the memory. We eventually found our way to Vancouver and then by ferry to Vancouver Island. Still dragging our "landed immigrant" boxes, we made our way to Port Alberni. It seemed we could go no further. A local sage told us that we should go to the end of a wharf very early in the morning and a boat, the Uchuk I, would be there to pick us up and take us down the Alberni Inlet and on to Ucluelet.

Two marvellous years followed in Ucluelet: teaching in the winter and salmon fishing in the summer. For us it was a wilderness experience, with interesting people to live with and yet a still secluded Long Beach as our playground. We were soon part of the local village life that circled around the arrival and departure of the Uchuk. Coming to Victoria from time to time to attend the university soon told us that this was the place that we would put down our roots and raise the family.

Since 1958 we have been living in the Victoria area. It was a struggle at first but very worthwhile. The children have grown up and taken their separate ways as Canadians. They know nothing of Europe. My son, now thirty-two years of age, is a teacher in the Cariboo and wouldn't trade his life there for a kingdom. I settled down to teach history and French in the high schools of this area.

Some fifteen years or so ago we had saved enough for a trip we had promised ourselves: a visit to Quebec, a province we did not yet know. What a delightful experience! Since that first visit we have been back a number of times. We were excited that we could now, as Canadians and still within the borders of the country, experience another culture that is European yet *tout à fait* Canadian. It was a joy for us to travel without the problems of passports. My wife could be in Montreal, the most cosmopolitan city in the world, and I could wander around the walled city of Quebec and watch in my imagination the sailing ships coming up the St. Lawrence.

For some time now I have taught French to young Canadians. I now had a real reason. This could be my small contribution to the country for which I proudly hold citizenship. I worked for a change from prescribed French texts in BC to texts with Canadian content. I took summer courses in Montreal and made friends with some very fine French Canadians, in particular Pierre Calus, now of the University of Ottawa and the author of *Le Français International*, one of the texts used in BC. In the past two years I have been involved with early French immersion teaching, which I consider an extraordinary opportunity for young Canadians. Requests for admission outpace space available, in spite of a loud but small minority of voices raised against the teaching of the other Canadian language. I find it difficult to understand why so obvious an educational advantage can be immersed in emotional and irrational political argument.

As I look back now at the age of sixty-five I know I was right to uproot my family from Europe so that my children could become Canadians. My young friends in the POW camps had been correct. We have lived in peace and prosperity for more than thirty years, and can look to the future without fear.

———————————— ✳ ————————————

Through an American Eye
Ray Male

A resident of Newark, New Jersey, and Prince Edward Island; former commissioner of labor in New Jersey and mayor of Princeton, NJ, sees Canada through ''The Island'' and an incident with John Diefenbaker.

Twelve summers ago, on a blistering hot smoggy morning, much in need of rest and renewal after a demanding work-life in the turbulent cities of the U.S. Eastern Seaboard, I packed my wife and children into the station wagon and set out from Princeton, New Jersey, to vacation at a Prince Edward Island seaside cottage. We were drawn by a colourful description painted in words by the editor of this book, whom we had met at a National Labour Relations conference in Canada.

Two car-weary days later we caught the last ferry at Cape Tormentine, NB, and drove off into Borden, PEI, in total stormy darkness headed for nearby Argyle Shore. Later we would own a small inland farmhouse at New Argyle, which I like to call Rear Argyle, as it was named in an 1830 atlas. There we have summered each year, always finding renewal.

In the midnight darkness of our first hour on PEI, we followed instructions and regretfully wakened an elderly farmer, John Downs MacPhail, who met us with a wide, warm smile and gave us a caring that we would experience time after time.

Bringing the key, he took us to the shoreline of his farm on Northumberland Strait, opened the cottage door, and set about cheerfully explaining the mysteries of lighting a strange new stove. To this day, though John Downs MacPhail now rests in a cemetery along the road, David, my son, still asks; ''Dad, did you ever see a sweeter smile on any face? I can never forget him.''

Should your car break down in the countryside of PEI, almost every car will stop and give a hand. Should a farmhouse or barn burn, the neighbours gather and feed, clothe and house the victims, and frequently help in building a replacement. We have found among PEI's country Canadians, refreshment for body and mind and a rebirth of faith in people.

When John Diefenbaker was Canada's Prime Minister, I was mayor of Princeton, New Jersey. The Honourable John had come to my city to receive an Honorary Degree from venerable Princeton University, and I was seated beside him on the platform. Each participant had been informed by letter that unbroken traditions of 200 years prohibited speeches by honorary degree candidates. A Nobel Prize winner was first to be introduced and hooded; then Canada's First Minister was introduced and called. Rising ramrod straight, he walked briskly to the podium, listened to the eulogy intently and then bent a craggy face to receive his hood. To everyone's astonishment, the Prime Minister reached inside his jacket, pulled out several pages of a speech, and proceeded to read them in a ringing voice.

Princeton's young president, in seeming shock, rose

and moved forward menacingly as if to tackle the great man, but pulled back, had words with a wiser and older official, and slumped into his seat. Students, faculty, and guests stared dumbfounded.

John Diefenbaker had come to make a speech, and an important one as I realized later in reading it over, but one that received stony silence from everyone present. When he sat down, I turned to whisper appreciation and found piercing eyes and a severe frown surveying an unresponsive audience. A loud "Humph" ended the incident.

Somehow it spelled out for me another side of Canadian life, the determination of the pioneer, the overcoming of obstacles and traditions, and an unbowed demeanour, all important assets in a turbulent world.

This is how one American sees your country.

———————————————— ✳ ————————————————

Daughter of the North-west
Mary Dover

A lifelong participant in public service, granddaughter of Col. James F. MacLeod, leader of the Great March West of the North West Mounted Police which united Canada in 1874 without an angry shot, and daughter of the founder of the Calgary Stampede.

As the years go by, Canada's birthday, July 1, brings for many a picnic or a celebration beside a public building or in the park. Perhaps we feel a little swelling pride, we barbequers. There are all sorts of people. Who are they? Do you know their story? Do you wish to? What are their visions of Canada? Do they share ours or yours?

For me, I remember my mother's father. He was a man of history and perhaps in his later years he knew himself to be a man of destiny.

Canada had been settled in Ontario and Quebec and the Maritimes. But a flood of immigrants across the Great Lakes and west, up the rivers from Fort Churchill and York Factory and over the boundary of the 49th parallel, necessitated the bringing of law and order. The Hudson's Bay Company, which had brought to the West people, trade, homesteaders, was no longer capable of handling political and community problems.

Fortunately, leaders in Ottawa, after the Red River Rebellion of 1869, saw the need of a permanent police force and, acting speedily, recruited, equipped, and dispatched a body of men. The departure of the North West Mounted Police is in the history books, but little is known of the Great March. It was across the prairies always facing west; each day brought adventures and hazards as they marched the unknown land, crossing hill after hill between the plains like the waves of the ocean.

The sounds of leather, the wild cacophony of Red River Carts, wheels ungreased, protesting; disturbed cows and oxen attached behind carts murmuring complaints; birds all about, flying in their thousands; and the voices of men sometimes joking, laughing, or shouting commands at dangerous crossings. This was the making of Canadian adventure without parallel; at its completion, with great ceremony, the flag was raised. Without a shot being fired in anger, effective government was installed from coast to coast.

That was 1874, the March of the North West Mounted Police from St. Boniface, Manitoba, to Fort MacLeod west of present day Lethbridge in sight of the Rockies, beginning on June 7 and completed in October with the building of the fort beside the Old Man River.

My grandfather was Col. James F. MacLeod, second in command to Commissioner French during the first part of the march, but becoming commissioner himself to lead the force into the far west. He and Chief Crowfoot negotiated Treaty No. 7 between the "Whites" and the Indians, which was signed September 22, 1877. During those three years a friendship was founded based on mutual trust, respect, and sincere admiration for each other.

My own father also had an important part in the making of the West. Born in Montreal in early 1861, A.E. Cross took care to prepare himself for frontier life by learning bookkeeping, agriculture, and veterinary surgery before serving at the Cochrane Ranch west of Calgary in 1884. He took up a homestead in 1886 west of

Nanton, Alberta, and married my mother, Helen Rothnie, in 1894. In 1892, having decided to build a brewery in Calgary, he studied the arts of brewing at an institute in Chicago. Through the years my father joined his associates in the oil and electricity business, and in starting up the Calgary Exhibition Stampede, fish and wildlife care, and conservation programmes. He was an MLA in the NWT legislature and never ceased to interest himself with great generosity in the care and welfare of his fellow man.

In 1914 he built a house on the A.7 Ranch to which he gave the name of Braehead, chosen because his forebears had come from a farm of that name in Lanarkshire, Scotland, in the early 1800s. During the building of the house, arrangements were made with the CPR for a flagpole to be shipped from BC. It was of such a size that this undertaking took two flatcars; undoubtedly there would have been some strenuous manoeuvering to haul it with horses over the fifteen miles from Nanton. On July 1, 1914, the great pole, which still stands, was in place and the flag run up.

In my own time I have seen many flags through the good fortune of travel. During wartime years, the daily raising was insisted on as an important part of service life. In peace, the gradual transition of the Union Jack, the Red ensign, to the Red Maple Leaf has left its impact. For the day of the proclamation of the Red Maple Leaf I had somehow managed to obtain a copy of the new emblem. I felt I could not run it up on my own home's flagpole standing alone. So I telephoned about the countryside and found that it would be possible for one or two busloads of neighbourhood school children to assist me.

We got nearly every child in the district to help pull down the old flag, and then put up the new. The old ensign was carefully folded for the last time for safekeeping. Then, at attention, we sang "God Save the Queen" and "O Canada".

What is it that makes us Canadians? It is not the symbol itself. I see it as the whole tapestry of our lives full of splendid colours in all shades surrounding our own inner convictions.

---***---

Grandma Mitchell's Advice
William Mitchell

Presbyterian minister who has ministered in the Prairie towns
of Assiniboia and Star View, in Saskatchewan, and the Ontario
towns of Dundas, Kincardine, and Durham.

In 1913 father, mother, sister, and I were hurriedly getting ready to immigrate to Canada from Falkirk, Scotland.
It would be a new life in a new world. Grandmother
Mitchell, a staunch figure indeed, called us all together
to meet her in the "big house".

Addressing my father, Gran, as we called her, commanded him: "Now Robert, you are going to Canada."
Raising her voice, she added, "Remember, when you
arrive, *be a Canadian.*"

I was twelve then and never forgot her admonition.
Canada was good to us. Dad soon found work and we
never looked back.

---***---

Sod Hut Pioneer
Dorothy Boan

A resident of Briercrest, Saskatchewan, who came from England at the turn of the century as one of the settlers brought
to farm still unopened prairie lands by the British clergyman,
Isaac M. Barr.

In view of the fact that very few of the original Barr
Colonists will still be living I would like to write down
some of the things I remember of those days while I am
still able. First of all I want to make it very clear that
these memories have not been added to, nor enhanced
by imagination, but are just the plain facts as I recall
them. I can only recall certain things, leaving big gaps in
which I do not seem to remember any details. This, I

think, can be accounted for by the fact that children take life very much for granted and are not impressed by events unless they are unusual and startling.

In the spring of 1902 my parents, Robert and Catherine Holtby, my two brothers, Oliver and Robert (Bob), my sister, Bessie, and I, age eight, travelled by train from Leeds, Yorkshire, our home, to Liverpool the day before we were to set sail. We stayed overnight in a hotel. Next day, amidst great excitement and confusion — so much noise and so many people — we went on board our ship, the Lake Manitoba, and set sail for our new home in Canada.

I remember the large crowd of people standing on deck waving handkerchiefs and crying, and a similar large crowd on the pier doing the same as the land slowly receded and we were on our way. My mother and sister and I were fortunate, for we had a cabin. My father and brothers were in the hold with a number of other men.

We landed at Saint John, NB, on April 10, my brother Bob's nineteenth birthday, and proceeded westward by train. I don't remember much about the train ride except that my mother had a difficult time getting our meals prepared with too many people trying to work around a small stove in the railway car all at the same time. Finally, we arrived at Saskatoon, a small town at the end of the rail, with wooden sidewalks and hitching posts for tying up horses in front of the few stores. My father bought two tents and these were to be our home for many weeks to come. Tents sprang up more or less in rows on the outskirts of the town, all alike — very confusing for a little girl trying to find her way "home" after play.

During this time purchases were made of things necessary for our 200-mile westward trek and for our use after we arrived at our homestead. My father, who was a good judge of horses, bought a beautiful team, and also a covered wagon, plough, campstove, and food to take on our trip. The other settlers were doing the same and day by day they started out, several together for company and mutual aid. Some had cows tied on behind.

Progress was slow, at a walking pace, and not many miles were covered in a day. My mother, sister, and I walked a good part of the time because it was not as monotonous as riding. Various incidents broke the monotony — most of them unpleasant. One terrifying experience was descending the steep Eagle Hills and fording the swift stream below. Many of the settlers tied the front and back wheels of their wagons together to act as a brake and slow them down. To make it all the more dangerous there were huge stones hidden from view beneath the water. We saw some of the wagons overturned and the contents dumped into the water; other wagons were smashed, but most people managed to cross safely, ourselves among them.

For one whole day of our journey the ground was seething with snakes everywhere you looked. The trail was sodden and greasy with their bodies, crushed by the horses' hooves and wagon wheels. We stayed on the wagon all day, not stopping for lunch. By night we came to the end of them and were able to pitch our tents and relax. Next day and for several days after we travelled through country blackened by prairie fires, the charred grass crunched beneath our feet giving off an acrid odor. The smell of burnt grass still brings back memories.

Marquees, provided by the government for the use of the settlers were put up about twenty miles apart along the trail. Each had a large stove and plenty of firewood and was divided into compartments to give a certain amount of privacy. We did not use them much but stayed in our own tents. My mother cooked tasty meals on the tin camp stove after we stopped for the night. Quite often we dined on prairie chicken or wild duck shot by my brothers. Game was plentiful and not at all gun shy.

After a while, travelling this way day after day became a way of life to me so that I was astonished and bewildered when the wagon came to a halt and we were told to climb down — we had arrived! This was *home*? I looked around and saw nothing — no house, no garden, no fence — nothing! But the men were sure this was the place; they had found the corner posts. So we prepared to make it our home. First thing was to pitch the two tents and dig a well. Good water was found not too far from the surface, for which we were very thankful. Next job was to plough up some land and plant potatoes. This was new to my father and brothers but they made nice straight furrows with the walking plough we had brought from Saskatoon, turning over the rich virgin sod and placing the seed potatoes underneath. No further cultivation was done and the crop turned out well.

More plowing was done and the sod was used to build a house. A framework was made of poles cut from our own land and the sod was built up around it, with thick walls to keep out the cold. Lumber to make the floor, a door, and glass for a window were obtained from Lloydminster, seven miles away, a town springing up — mostly tents so far — and fast becoming the centre of the new colony. Supplies were necessarily expensive having to be freighted in from Saskatoon 200 miles away. Sod was placed on the roof in place of shingles and our new home was ready. More lumber was bought to make a few pieces of furniture — beds, table, chairs, and a few shelves.

Summer came to an end and autumn brought shorter days and colder nights. Our supply of money was disappearing fast so my father decided to go to Toronto, where he had several cousins, and look for work. Another decision was made — to sell our team of horses and buy oxen and a driving horse and buggy. My brother, Bob, drove my father back to Saskatoon with the team and wagon and brought back a horse and buggy. He also brought a cat, in a gunny sack. This cat was a valuable addition to our household, both as a pet and a mouser. She was snow white and followed me no matter how far I roamed. People would come from miles around to borrow her to keep down the mice as this appeared to be the only cat in the colony, until finally, she became confused as to which was home and wandered from one place to another.

The winter of 1903–04 was an unusually severe one but we were well prepared. Before my father left, a large amount of firewood had been gathered and piled up, teepee fashion, beside our door. And we had a good supply of groceries. So my brother, Bob, decided to look for work in a lumber camp, leaving us in Oliver's care. All went well for a time. Although the stove was small and the house large, Oliver became expert at getting the most heat out of our firewood, banking the fire at night with green logs which would last longer than dry ones. We found, to our dismay, however, that a gap was appearing between the sod walls and the roof, letting out our precious heat. This was caused by the walls settling while the roof remained stationary, being held up by posts. Nothing could be done about this in the dead of winter except to bank up the fire even more than before and add more fuel at intervals during the night. Each morning we awoke to find our eye lashes frozen together and hair frozen to the pillow. Everything in the way of food was frozen stiff and had to be thawed before we could eat breakfast. But we had very happy evenings. Oliver read to us each night by flickering lamplight out of such books as we had found room for in our baggage, including Shakespeare and, what I enjoyed most of all, the *Boys' Own Annual*. He played his violin for us, too, and we gave him our rapt attention.

However, this more or less comfortable situation came to an end. Walking home from Lloydminster one day, Oliver froze his foot badly. It did not heal and he became ill.

My sister and I, with great effort, were able to man the bucksaw and keep the stove going, but we couldn't keep ahead of it. We had to bring the sawhorse into the house and drag in the logs one by one because it was too cold for us outside. I don't know how long this continued but I do know that my mother was very worried, partly by the illness of my brother and partly because we were running out of supplies. We had nothing left to eat but beans and tea. Finally, in desperation she bundled us up in extra clothes and sent us off, through deep snow, across country, to get help from a neighbour two miles away. We couldn't see his house for the bluffs and trees in between but she showed us the general direction. But before we got out of sight she called us back, otherwise this story would have had a different ending. This must have been a difficult time for her. There was nothing else she could do but pray and this she did. Her prayer was answered, speedily, for the next day a man by the name of Mr. Slater arrived at our door, on horseback. He had been working with his team of horses on the CNR railroad. One of his horses died and he was seeking a replacement at Lloydminster, striking across country to save time. He offered to pay mother for the meagre dinner but all she wanted was to get word to a doctor.

Dr. Amos came the next day and diagnosed Oliver's ailment as scurvy caused by an inadequate diet. Gangrene had developed in his frozen toes, one of which was later amputated. The doctor prescribed lime juice. This had to be freighted in by heated wagon and sold for five dollars a bottle. Next day a big sleigh arrived to move us all into Lloydminster where we were housed in a big Marquee divided into compartments for the use of several families. This served as our home until the immigration building, then under construction, was ready for occupancy. By this time spring had arrived and, with it, Bob from the lumber camp. Oliver's health continued to improve and mother, with us two girls, joined my father in Toronto.

Soon after this we were joined by my other sister, Kitty, who had remained in England. Two years later we were back in Saskatchewan and have lived here ever since.

The next few years were spent in catching up on my education. In those days a grade 10 certificate and a few weeks of Normal School permitted one to teach for a year under the supervision of the Inspector, and then it was back to high school and further Normal training. Following this course, I found myself in charge of a country school with forty-nine pupils in eight grades. Attendance was less in the summer months when the big boys were on the land. After several years I married the son of a Scottish family, Alex Boan. We farmed at Claybank for several years then moved to Briercrest in 1928 with our family of three, two boys and a girl. Before the year was out another little girl was added, Zaida.

As everyone knows, 1929 saw the start of the Great Depression when money was scarce and jobs non-existent. To make the situation twice as difficult, it also was the start, for the farmers of Southern Saskatchewan, of the long drought. People still associate the Depression with dust-laden winds.

I well remember how grateful I was when the wife of

the hotel keeper gave me a pail of soft water two or three times a week with which to bathe my baby. The hotel had a large cistern beneath it; no one else had any soft water. I also remember that we set our tables for meals with the plates upside down to keep them free of dust until we were ready to eat. This was during the worst dust storms. Alex was away at this time gravelling the highways, a government project to provide jobs. I also remember the boxcars that came from Eastern Canada with gifts of fruit and vegetables. These were distributed as fairly as possible by the village council.

Feed for cattle was shipped in from Northern Saskatchewan, but that proved to be impractical and after that the cattle were shipped out by train to where feed was more plentiful. I felt sorry for them — so thin and weak as they dragged themselves along Main Street to the railway.

In the fall of 1932 the local telephone company advertised for an operator, to take the place of Miss Allen who was leaving. The board of managers, for which I was secretary, told me to destroy all applications that offered to fill the position in exchange for shelter. There were many! In the finish, they persuaded me to take the job at forty dollars a month including the work as secretary. In 1942, at the age of fifty-five my husband took on the job of telephone lineman. He knew very little about the work but learned fast and built some beautiful lines.

We look back on those days with mixed feelings. The shortage of money was a challenge and brought neighbours together. We all made use of the versatile flour bag for dish towels, pillow cases, even sheets — four joined together with a fifth split down the middle and added at the bottom. Aprons made out of them were beautiful, with embroidery and sometimes handmade lace for trimming. Some went so far as to use them for underwear. One woman burst into tears when a friend proudly showed her a very neat garment made of flour bags which by chance showed a bold Robin Hood in all his bright colors!

In looking over my diary of those days I see a notation that my daughter, Jean, who did the shopping, came home with the weekly roast, four-and-a-half pounds of top quality beef, for forty-five cents! The farmers often brought their produce direct to us, meat, milk, cream, eggs to pay their telephone bills. The young people had to stay home and make their own fun. One winter, under the leadership of Rev. Wes Harland, United Church minister, they put on an excellent concert. It took all winter to prepare, and they worked hard. Catholics, Protestants (United and Presbyterians) and others were all included. Great excitement and secrecy followed as they were in competition — the boys against the girls. When the night arrived the judges declared it was a tie and everyone was happy. They also served a lunch and baked the cakes themselves.

In 1939 when war was declared against Germany, conditions began to improve and money to circulate as jobs were available. Our own two boys, Jack and Dave, joined the air force and were sent away for training. Meanwhile, in 1938 another little son, Bruce, had arrived. Dry weather still prevailed on the Prairies. The year 1937 was the driest and hottest on record. Not even Russian Thistles grew. But by 1940–42, conditions improved for the farmer and money began to circulate normally.

In 1980 my memories and feelings of love for Canada were gathered together through working on the People to People Petition for Canadian Unity. I was driven about town house-to-house, gathering signatures, by my husband, aged ninety-two. After sending in my list of signatures I turned my attention to other things. Imagine my surprise then when I received a phone call asking me if I would like to go to Montreal, with a companion, expenses paid from voluntary donations, to attend the presentation of the signatures to Quebec. I was given four hours to decide. The answer, of course, was yes.

My husband was not able to go so I took, as my companion, my sister-in-law from Moose Jaw, Mrs. Myrtle Boan, better known as "Scotty". We were delighted to find upon arriving in Montreal that a French Canadian family was waiting for us and would be our hosts — Mr. and Mrs. Paul Thibault.

Next day we met in different rooms of the Queen Elizabeth Hotel where we stood around getting our bearings and talking to many others from every part of Canada

before moving out to make our presentation at Place Ville
Marie.

We were taught a little song to be used later as the
signatures were presented:

Dear Québécois, now is our turn
To come and speak to you of love.

As I look back on our trip to Montreal and the warmth
and kindliness of our newly made friends as they made
sure that we were not "left out", I knew that although
we could not understand all that was said at the dinner
table here was something very lovely that we must cherish. Why did I help? I can think of no better reason than
I gave in Montreal — because I love Canada and do not
want to see it broken up.

And here we are, today, concerned about Canada and
the troubles that threaten her. I have discovered as the
years have rolled by that, in a way of speaking, I own
Canada and Canada owns me! Everything there is, of
beauty and grandeur, belongs to me, the awesome mountains, beautiful lakes and rivers, the gorgeous sunsets,
mysterious Northern Lights, the wide open spaces of the
Prairies. They all belong to each one of us, to enjoy while
we are here, and to be responsible for!

We reap today what we sowed yesterday, and we continue to sow, whether we realize it or not, for tomorrow.
We hand the reins over to our children and just hope
that they will be equal to the task.

Salt Spray
Bill McNamara

A fisherman from Catalina, Newfoundland.

I grew up here in Catalina, Newfoundland, enjoying my
boyhood years of living close by the sea. As soon as I was
old enough I was out in the boats and learned to love

the sea with its different moods: gentle breezes and glass calm in summer, then winter storms with the sea in turmoil. In my early teens I left school to go fishing with my father to help earn a living for our family (I had six sisters). We fished summertimes and in winter worked the woods to get firewood to heat our home. Then in early spring when the northern ice floes drifted close to our shores, I would get a feeling of awe and excitement in my heart as it would soon be time to start fishing again.

Fishing was hard work then. We kept long hours, from before light until after dark with only a kerosene oil torch for light. The cod would have to be dressed and salted, washed out, and spread to dry in the sun. But I loved this life; I would not have changed it for any other job. I felt free. You did what you wanted to with no boss telling you what to do. The time never seemed long enough. You just did the best you could. The time just flew by.

This was before 1949 when we joined with Canada and became the tenth province, just nineteen years after my birth. After we came under Confederation, things began to get better. New things began to happen. We were getting fresh fish plants. At the end of the day we would know how much money we had made for that day. With the salt-dry fish you hardly ever knew — maybe when you straightened up at the end of the season with so many grades, five or six, you would know. It was almost impossible to get first grade. But now with the fresh fish, as long as you got it to the plant fresh and clean, you would get top price.

Then we began getting better boats and mechanical haulers — before, everything was done by hand — and sounders, radar, radio telephone. The hard work was gone. You still had to put in long hours but it was a lot easier. And now with our federal and provincial ministers centralizing the fishery and the 200-mile limit that Canada controls and manages, we have our own fishermen's union with part of the executive also fishermen. The fisherman takes part in meetings and serves on committees. In the earlier days, before Confederation, the fisherman caught the fish, the merchant gave him a price —

that was it, like it or leave it. Now the fisherman has a say in all those things that concern the fishery. And it's getting better. I'm glad I am a Canadian fisherman.

---------------------------------- ✳ ----------------------------------

Wheelchair Canadian

Kay Reynolds

Of Charlottetown, Prince Edward Island; active in associations for the handicapped.

I am Kay Reynolds, "Islander of the Year" for 1981, a great honour. This in itself makes me pleased to be a Canadian.

Living in many parts of Canada throughout one's lifetime is commonplace for Canadians. I was born in Dartmouth, Nova Scotia, and went with my parents to the Ontario cities of St. Catharines, Welland, and Niagara Falls. I also spent time in Ottawa.

As a young woman, I attended PEI's Prince of Wales College. I taught school for eight months until I was old enough to train for a nurse and graduated in 1945 from the PEI School of Nursing. I am now teaching St. John Ambulance Home Nursing and Wheelchair Training from a wheelchair.

I was married and had two children. I now have four grandchildren. It was 1939 when I developed Multiple Sclerosis ending my ability to walk.

I joined a number of interested people to form the PEI Multiple Sclerosis Chapter of the MS Society of Canada in 1955. I was also the chairperson for the PEI Committee for the International Year of the Disabled Person and am the provincial representative of the Coalition of the Provincial Organization of the Handicapped (COPOH), as well as a member of the CN Marine Task Force. The freedom of speech in these organizations and in this country makes me feel very proud to be a citizen.

My affiliation with COPOH has enabled me to see Canada from Vancouver to Newfoundland. I especially favour PEI for the beauty of its red clay, green fields, and beautiful beaches.

Today with the many crises in the world, we Canadians are indeed very privileged.

---- ✳ ----

Half Way Between
D.W. Darby

A farmer and businessman from Uxbridge, Ontario, and Victoria, British Columbia.

"What is a Canadian?" People on other continents often ask me this when I'm travelling. "We are slower than our American cousins and faster than our British cousins," I always reply — and they seem to understand.

---- ✳ ----

Salute to Alain Frecker
William Callahan

Publisher of *The Daily News* in St. John's, Newfoundland; Callahan pays tribute to Canada and to his province's eminent citizen, the late George Alain Frecker.

The first time I saw Canada, it was autumn 1950, with the vast deciduous stands aflame with colour and early morning frost glittering on stubble fields as the train swept into the Eastern Townships of Quebec.

There were, it seemed to me coming from the then independent nation of Newfoundland, two Canadas. First, the Canada of the dank, foggy, port of North Sydney where the Newfoundland ferry docked (and Canadian Customs and Immigration officials did their duty), and the nearby depressed coal mining towns of Cape Breton. Second, the Canada of Dominion Square, Montreal, on a brilliant September day.

Emerging from the railway station into the din and bustle of Ste. Catherine Street, a world of endless streams of people, speeding traffic, police whistles, newspaper vendors, two languages, the powerful smells of a mighty metropolis, I thought: "This is the real Canada. This is the way it should be!"

I was two months short of my seventeenth birthday, but well old enough to be aware of, and to engage in, the great debate over the future of Newfoundland, the only province that was an independent country before it became a province: a separate, proud, Old Colony, the first one, in existence close to 350 years.

Would we continue on our own? Could we? Or would we join up with Canada? My mind was suddenly made up, at least to this extent: if we joined, it must be to become part of the wealthy, modern, proud Canada of Dominion Square, Montreal, and other parts of Canada I learned to know. Dominion Square and, a stone's throw away, the modern skyscraper edifice of Place Ville Marie.

How prophetic that the first stirrings of affection for Canada should flame, thirty years later, into the People to People Petition presentation at Place Ville Marie, encouraging Quebecers not to reverse, for their province, the decision made by Newfoundlanders three decades before.

My own involvement in the work of the petition came about at the urging of a man for whom I had boundless respect, George Alain Frecker, a public servant, educator, cabinet colleague, and friend, perhaps the most respected person in all of Newfoundland. He was then in his eighties enjoying his busy role as chancellor of Memorial University and other voluntary chores. Without hesitation, he devoted his total concern, indeed the final days of his life, to an intense, determined effort to gather support for this coast-to-coast expression of love and fealty for Canada.

It had been my privilege to be at his side, and to receive the torch from his hand when he passed away, probably caused by strain from these extra efforts. I was asked to hold it high as he did, at once a beacon signalling safe

harbour, and a glowing signal of our unity, in this land
we call home.

---------------------- ✳ ----------------------

Goodbye Rocking Chair
John Pierce

Ontario Land Surveyor from Peterborough.

Across this great country of ours a million alarm clocks
will bring a halt to a million sweet dreams and snap
millions of Canadians into reality. Some will coax the
kids into eating their breakfast and shove off for school;
husbands or wives will be pushed on their way, too. And
while all that commotion is going on, I will be listening
to gentle music, quietly sipping my coffee and settling in
for a leisurely read of the morning paper. I have just
retired! At last I can turn a deaf ear to the strident clamour
of the marketplace.

A deaf ear to the clamour of the marketplace? Okay,
but what about that little question that sticks in the memory? The one that says: "How much will you do for
Canada?" That is a mean question. It is reminding me
that our Canadian way has made it possible for me to sip
my cup of coffee and tune out those strident noises. Damn
that inner self. It also knows that our nation needs lots
of help to keep it together and much much more building
and healing before it can be seen and recognized as the
finest nation in all the world.

Oh, for God's sake. Haven't I done enough? I did spend
almost four years wallowing in the mud of England, Italy,
France, Holland, and Germany during the last war. I have
stayed out of jail, paid my taxes, raised my family, op-
erated my business, and taken part in many community
projects. I even played a major role in organizing the
People to People's Petition for Canadian Unity. Before
that I helped in Peterborough to send out thousands of
Christmas cards for several Christmas seasons to people

in Quebec whom we had never even heard of, to demonstrate goodwill and help strengthen Canada. Surely it is someone else's turn. But the questions really are: "How much will you do for Canada?" and "What should I do?"

I know that many things in Canada are good, but even today inequities exist. In the past, many of our native people were exploited and policies then put into place that did not allow them access to opportunity. The seeds of animosity and even defeat flourish in too many places. There is work to be done. The conflict between our English and French Canadians should not and need not be. The two cultures have found a way for goodwill and understanding in many places such as Wakefield, Quebec, and I'm sure there are truly many Wakefields throughout Canada. Let us hope we can yet find a way to live in harmony with each other.

Across the pages of history stride great men and women all bearing one common commodity — a dream of a Canada united, proud of its heritage and its many people, prouder still of its high regard for law and order and justice for all, a nation of people working harmoniously together, not just for self but for fellow humans anywhere in the world. Not a bad dream!

Goodbye old rocking chair. You haven't got me yet. It looks as though my retirement is over!

5

---*---

Great Achievements
and Growing Pains

History by Canoe

Ralph Brine

A Gabriola Island, British Columbia, sheep farmer and canoeist.

I am one of four Westerners who learned in Montreal that a deep and long-standing bond exists between Canada's East and West and all the land between. We had just completed a three-and-a-half-month trans-Canada canoe expedition from Pacific to Atlantic tidewater. It was July 15, 1967. Journey's end was the marina at Expo 67, Montreal.

Congratulations poured from those on hand to welcome us as we paddled, tired but happy, into the Expo waterways to receive the long-awaited caresses of our families. One final duty remained. We lifted out of the canoe four sealed canvas bags that contained 2,000 letters we had transported as "canoe mail" from New Westminster, BC. It was to be delivered to the postal authorities in Montreal for sorting and mailing.

The letters had been with us the entire 4,200 miles, on our backs when portaging and in the canoe when on water. We never cheated an inch. It was an authentic duplication of the way dispatches were carried across Canada by the voyageurs of another generation, before the coming of the railway.

We were driven to the central post office and taken upstairs to a large concrete-floored sorting room. It was a cavernous receiving area. We dropped the bags on the floor. The manager called the several dozen or so workers on hand to gather around. As we stood in the centre of their circle, he addressed the staff, saying simply, "These men have brought the mail to us from the Pacific in the manner of our forefathers — by canoe."

The response was electric. No one spoke. Instead these people from Montreal just stood there and clapped and clapped until tears came to our eyes. The air was vibrant. They knew what we had done and exactly why we had wanted to do it. For them it was history come to life.

Many with names such as Lalonde, Gagnon, Fraser,

Quesnel, Trudeau, would have had great-great grand-fathers who had paddled the watery canoe routes that laid the framework of Canada. It was they who had shown us the way.

For us, it was a unique and never to be forgotten experience to witness this immediate response to an older century's unity of purpose, a purpose that had pulled men from towns, farms, and Indian villages along the St. Lawrence valley and had led them across a continent on the lakes and rivers of Canada that connect Montreal, Quebec, with New Westminster, BC.

--------------------------- ✳ ---------------------------

The New Nationality

Jacques Monet, s.j.

Native of St.-Jean, Quebec, formerly professor of history at Sherbrooke and Ottawa Universities, and now president of Regis College, Toronto; prolific writer on Canadian historical subjects.

"Le Bon Dieu est Canadien!" ("The good Lord is Canadian!"). This was the expression French Canadians in times past often used when they wanted to express their faith in our country's future. And so it was frequently on their lips in the middle of the nineteenth century, when Sir George-Étienne Cartier was busy turning into a political and social reality the great dream first expressed 200 years earlier by Samuel de Champlain: the establishment of a vast and wealthy kingdom in which men and women of different cultures would work together in harmony to achieve and share the power, the beauty, and the glory of their service to each other and to mankind. The kingdom of Canada would extend from the shores of the Atlantic westward, in the words of the Charter of the Company of One Hundred Associates (also known as the Company of New France) in 1627, "as far and forward as the glory and name of His Majesty could be proclaimed".

Cartier, Sir John A. Macdonald, and the other Fathers

of Confederation gave this dream a name. They called it "the New Nationality". They were bold men of daring and courage. Across the border was madness and murder, as the American republic was locked in the world's bloodiest war to force unity onto its own population. Further away, the French Empire was imposing foreign domination on Mexico, while, elsewhere again, in Europe, Germans were coming together "by blood and iron" and Italians were killing each other in the name of unity. But at Quebec, in 1864, and earlier in Charlottetown, it was by peaceful exchanges, by human dialogue, that the Canadian Fathers worked out their understanding.

They were founding a new country but, even more so, they wanted a new kind of country, a way of life that would be enriched by diversity, in which freedom would grow through the sharing of riches and the joyful acceptance of service. Canada would come together around an ideal which, in the words of Prime Minister Pierre Elliott Trudeau, "was full of understanding and generosity, nobler and more inspired by love than could be citizenship based on language and blood relationships".

This ideal was not, in fact, new. It was Champlain's faith carried forward into a new Canadian future. The dream had been renewed and strengthened by the generosity, excitement, and challenge of the great voyageurs who had been driven ever forward, ever westward into the open horizons of freedom; by heroes such as Alexander Mackenzie, making his way from Montreal unrelentingly foot by foot across the blown fields of the rich Prairies, on through the passes of the Rockies, as far and forward as he could (dream fulfilled!) to inscribe on the shore of the Pacific his celebrated landmark: "Alex Mackenzie from Canada by land 22nd July 1793"; or Joseph-Elzéar Bernier sailing ever forward from Quebec through the ice floes of the Arctic on through the gradually opening vistas of the Northwest Passage as far and forward as he could to reach the very end of the world and, he too, thereon to plant a Canadian flag. Bold, free, courageous, and ever undefeated, they knew dominion from sea to sea, and from the great river to the ends of the earth.

In the 1840s Champlain's faith bloomed with fresh

bursting in the ideal of sharing wealth and culture. "Canada is our Country," wrote the young French Canadian leader Louis-Hippolyte LaFontaine in 1840, "as it is also that of the many peoples who come from all parts of the globe to help develop our vast forests and to settle here ultimately." It was LaFontaine's insight, toleration, and courage, and those of such other frock-coated parliamentarians as Pierre Bédard, Robert Baldwin, and Joseph Howe, that reconciled in peace the ugly and frustrating clash of order and freedom.

Our great democracy would then rise above the differences of blood, language, and religion. Born without violence or destruction, it would mature, as LaFontaine wrote, "in a spirit of union, friendship, and harmony".

I am proud to be a citizen in a country sustained by values such as these. These, and many other qualities, I find embodied since the beginning of our history in our Canadian monarchy. Placed above and beyond the rivalries, collisions, and conflicts that inevitably mark the course of a democratic society, the Crown has always personified the principle of unity. It witnesses to our faith in our common future, and to the continuity, in time, of that ideal of harmony and understanding, of sharing and service, first proclaimed by Champlain.

The Crown's witness is one of the fundamental and permanent facts of our Canadian experience. It has well withstood the test of time; and today the office of Governor General is the only institution in Canada whose uninterrupted service goes back to the first coming here of our earliest ancestors.

The representatives of the Crown are charged with fairly precisely-defined constitutional responsibilities. These have evolved across the years, according to circumstance, just as did our Constitution and the shape of our country. But the Crown's essential duty remains always unchanged: to be, in tangible presence at the head of the State, the living and faithful witness, in the words of Her Majesty the Queen, "of all that is best and most admired in the Canadian ideal". Today, it is to the Queen and to the Governor General that the task has been entrusted. They continue into our own generation Champlain's great dream: of toleration and diversity, of sharing and ever-widening horizons. They call us to the renewal of our brotherhood. And thus they open up for us new times.

---------------------------------- * ----------------------------------

Give and Take
Tommy Douglas

Premier of Saskatchewan, 1944–61; leader of the federal New Democratic Party and Member of Parliament, 1961–71.

Today Canada presents a discouraging picture to those who have *never* taken the trouble to look beneath the surface to the roots of our national life. Some see a distinct possibility of Quebec separating to form a French-speaking republic. Others view the demands for a greater measure of independence by certain groups in Western Canada as a prelude to the eventual economic and political absorption by the United States. In my view the apprehension we feel and the energy we expend in combating these divisive concepts would be better mobilized to propel Canada towards the great future the Fathers of Confederation dreamed and worked for in 1867.

Many of us make the mistake of thinking that Confederation was brought about by a group of dear old gentlemen, known as the Fathers of Confederation, who were motivated by noble sentiments and who radiated feelings of mutual goodwill. Nothing could be further from the truth. They fought like cats and dogs, in fact some of their pre-Confederation conferences make our federal–provincial gatherings look very tame indeed.

It was not mutual affection or noble sentiments that brought the Fathers of Confederation together. It was the fear of absorption by the United States. At the end of the Civil War there were more than a million armed men in the United States and voices were raised suggesting the appropriation of British provinces north of the 49th parallel. It became increasingly clear that survival depended upon uniting the British possessions in North

America into a self-governing nation under the British Crown. Consequently, those who gathered to discuss this possibility held widely divergent views to which they clung tenaciously during the many conferences preceding Confederation.

The debates that took place were bitter and contentious. At times it looked as though the prospect of bringing forth a new nation on this continent was completely hopeless. There is no doubt that in the final analysis it was the patience and genius of Sir John A. Macdonald and his vision of a nation that finally found some common ground upon which the representatives of the various independent provinces could agree. Even then they did not all enter Confederation in 1867; some came in later in the century, while Newfoundland did not join Canada until 1949.

In the 1860s it took foresight and courage to believe that this mish-mash of provinces, composed of French, English, and other nationalities, with strongly held religious convictions and widely divergent ideologies, could some day be welded into a united Canada.

What, in addition to the fear of eventual absorption into the United States, were the factors that made the formation of Canada possible? The first factor was the recognition by those involved that unity does not necessarily demand unanimity. They knew the truth of the old saying: ''Where everyone thinks alike, no one thinks very much.'' They recognized quite properly that differences of opinion are inevitable in a free society. They conceded that the right to hold and express different viewpoints is the very essence of democracy — but only if we are prepared to grant the same right to others.

Our forefathers knew from bitter experience that the real tragedy of life is *not* to live in a land where there are sharp differences of opinion but rather to dwell in those countries where differences of opinion are forbidden. They knew only too well that unity of thought by compulsion rapidly creates a police state. Many early Canadians came to this country to escape that fate and wanted no part of it for their new nation.

The second factor making the formation of Canada possible was the gradual recognition that democracy is a give-and-take process by which we get some of the things we want in exchange for accommodating the more pressing needs of other groups in our society. In a democracy no segment of the population can get everything it wants; to do so would mean that other groups would get little or nothing. That each segment of the population eventually gets some of its requirements met is the best protection we have against a concentration of power in the hands of a few, with all the social injustice that flows from special privilege.

The ultimate heresy is not to challenge the status quo but to refuse to recognize that co-operation and accommodation to the needs of others is basic to our national survival. I can understand and appreciate those who argue vehemently for the claims of their respective regions or ethnic groups. It is out of these competing and often conflicting demands that social justice finally emerges. What I cannot condone are those who threaten to withdraw from the Canadian Confederation every time they fail to get what they demand. In a true democracy we cannot all get everything we ask, because if we do, others will get short shrift. Compromise and accommodation to the needs of other regions was the genius of Confederation; to this time they have assured our national survival.

The third factor in the emergence of Canada's federal system is that while diversity of race, language, and ethnic origin creates problems, this diversity also provides the stimulus that comes from the exchange of ideas and a cross-fertilization of cultures. Nearly all the great civilizations of the past arose out of the merging of different countries, and religious and political systems. Those of us who speak proudly of the contribution towards world progress made by Great Britain should never forget that the British people themselves are an amalgam of English, Scottish, Irish, and Welsh, with a considerable amount of Scandinavian blood contributed by the Vikings.

Canada has not attempted to be a melting pot like our great neighbour to the south. Instead we have encouraged ethnic groups to preserve their culture because we believe our social and cultural life is made richer by the cross-fertilization arising from the free association of people from many lands.

It is worth noting that the largest concentration of French-speaking people outside of France is to be found in Quebec. Equally noteworthy is the fact that the city of Toronto has the largest Italian population outside of Italy, while the three Prairie provinces have more citizens of Ukranian descent that can be found in the capital of the Ukraine.

I can remember when the mere thought of this national diversity appalled some of our native-born Canadians. Today they are coming to recognize that our country is stronger and our social life enriched by this intermingling of people having different national backgrounds and outlooks.

Let no one think that our diversity of population weakens our national will or our capacity for national effort. In the two World Wars Canadians closed ranks to play an important role in defence of the basic freedoms we believed to be at stake. We Canadians differ, and sometimes quite strongly, on a wide variety of issues; but when the ideals and institutions we cherish are threatened, our people forget their differences and unite to meet a national crisis.

"Canada is not an easy country to govern," Sir John A. Macdonald is quoted as having said. That is still true today. We are a people holding widely divergent views and representing conflicting economic interests. So was the nation the Fathers of Confederation brought into being in 1867, a nation brought into being because they believed that the things that unite us are infinitely more important than those that divide us. Time has proven that they were right.

It remains to be seen whether we, in our day and generation, will have the same keen insight and an equally powerful urge for national survival to cope with the problems of the 1980s and beyond as did our forefathers at the birth of Canada. I believe we will.

---
*

Ancestry — Proud Heritage

R. Wendell Phinney

Mayor of Kentville, Nova Scotia, and small-business proprietor.

In Nova Scotia we look back with pride when we think of Canada's history and of our forefathers who founded this great country. Many of the folk in the Annapolis Valley are able to trace their ancestors back to the United Empire Loyalists, the Acadians, and the New England Planters. My family is able to trace its forefathers back to those hardy folk who landed at Plymouth Rock on board the Mayflower and who eventually immigrated to Nova Scotia as New England Planters. Perhaps a person automatically inherits a pride in the country that has grown from the seeds sown by his ancestors.

As the years pass on and our towns and cities blossom and glisten with towering edifices of glass and steel, the original habitats of our forefathers become even more precious. It is hard to express the feelings I have when I am given the opportunity of strolling around the lower city in Quebec or through the redeveloped waterfronts of Halifax, St. John's, or Charlottetown. A feeling of excitement grows, as I am transported back into the eighteenth century. This is where my country started. This is my country!

A great number of us had the privilege of serving Canada during times of conflict. Perhaps our sense of loyalty to both our country and to our Queen was strengthened by this experience. I find even now when I have the opportunity of meeting the Queen, the Queen Mother, the Prince of Wales, and other members of our Royal Family that a sense of family relationship and of belonging comes over me.

Every so often I have the opportunity of attending Citizenship Court and witnessing a number of "new Canadians" taking the Oath of Allegiance. When I view the expression on their faces, when I chat with them and discover how their love and appreciation of Canada has grown, I no longer have a need to ask why I love my country. Another group of people now have the advantages of being citizens of our great country. I hope they soon will join with me and proclaim, "I am a Canadian, and proud of it."

---

*

By St. John's Shores
Dorothy Wyatt

Nurse-educator and recently mayor of St. John's, Newfoundland. She accompanied Terry Fox on the first mile of his run, and presented, in her colourful mayor's robes, her province's unity petitions in Monteal.

Canada was born from a sense of adventure. The struggle and adversity encountered were accepted as meaningful challenges to be met as our forefathers pursued the unknown with fierce dedication to building a Canada where there was room to absorb the ideals, realities, and differences of the participants. The tools employed in the job of building this great nation were their hands, their heads, but mostly their hearts. They had a reason to make it work in their village or in their town.

Luxury was neither expected nor obtained but hardships and tragedies were expected and endured as brave men and women provided food and fought diseases without the assistance of current instant foods or modern medicine. In a milieu where birth, marriage, and death were significant milestones in the drama of life, they found time, after work, to relax in celebration in dance, art, poetry, and costume. Canada was still emerging.

In the development of transportation, whether rail, sea, road, or air, they understood. The development of realistic communication was between people before radio, television, or cable, because they relied on the newspaper, which was only a message sheet, hand delivered in those days. Also, there was the signal received by Marconi at Signal Hill in 1901, and even the business houses in St. John's flew historic flags indicating the arrival of their ships. Alcock and Brown started from St. John's in the first successful flight crossing the Atlantic.

As our country grew larger and more sophisticated, our forefathers delegated representatives through the most unique system of government any nation has yet developed. They looked at the models then existing and incorporated all the essentials in a meaningful way, ensuring the freedom to select our special government, the right to practise our religion, the right to freedom of the press, and the right to an education.

In sharing with the rest of Canada this gratitude for our forefathers and the pride of all citizens of St. John's, the oldest city in North America, I thank all people who have selected Canada as their home, who have decided to take up the new challenges as we continue to emerge.

---------------------------- ✳ ----------------------------

History Restored — The Manitoba French
Georges Forest

St. Boniface, Manitoba, insurance agent, and World War II air force veteran, whose court appeal over an English-only parking ticket led to a Supreme Court ruling upholding French rights in the original Manitoba Constitution.

Like most Canadians, the stream of my life has many tributaries. In 1623, my ancestor, Jessie DeForest, a Huguenot, born in Avesnes, France, landed on Manhattan Island (New York) as head of 300 immigrants from the Flanders region of France. They named their Huguenot Protestant community New Avesnes. Across the Hudson River, the Dutch founded New Amsterdam. When the British finally took over they called it all New York.

My own father, Ambriose Gabriel (by this time the family was Roman Catholic), was born in Bonaventure, Quebec, and came to Manitoba in 1912. He was a ninth-generation Canadian. His first Canadian ancestor, Michelle Forest, a descendant of the founder of New Avesnes, was brought to Port Royal, Nova Scotia, in 1659, by Thomas Temple, the British governor of both Acadia and Boston.

On my mother's side, Grandfather Joseph Desgagnés married Celina Charètte of Métis ancestry from the Cree Indian nation. My first schooling was English.

All of these social and cultural strains have enriched me and made me truly a Canadian. A unique "awareness" — probably a product of my native ancestors, a French enthusiasm and an English perseverance — has served me well in the extremely difficult tasks I have voluntarily undertaken in Manitoba.

The law required that I attend an English school in Manitoba for my primary education. But at home, I would be sent to bed without my supper if I spoke English, not French, to members of the family.

An understanding of the larger question of French language in Canada began, however, in nearby St. Norbert, where I was sent for secondary schooling, since much of the schooling there was undertaken in French. But the act of hiding our French textbooks whenever the Manitoba school inspector visited the classroom left me perplexed. To read them was against the law. I began to feel alienated from my English class-mates.

Grandmother Desgagnés, with whom I lived in St. Norbert, had once hidden Louis Riel behind a large kitchen cupboard. She would take me to "La barriere" in the town where Riel had resisted federal troops. I listened, fascinated, to her tales of Riel and the Red River uprising, caused by unnecessary injustice inflicted on the Métis settlers. She told me how Riel and his Provisional Government had won agreement from Canada for certain educational and other rights which were then written into the Federal Constitutional Act forming the province of Manitoba. Later, a Manitoba legislature took these away. That was why I had to hide my French textbooks she explained. I wanted to cry out, "What happened to the rights secured by Riel?"

War came in 1939, threatening Canada's freedom. I

joined the air force. Afterwards I attended university and normal school and began a career in teaching. But underneath, I was smouldering. Disunity between French and English Canadians grew with sharpened intensity, and in 1948 I decided to establish an insurance agency in St. Boniface, a French Canadian community where I hoped to find a vital, growing French Canadian culture that English Canadians would be eager to share. Instead I found resignation to unlawful acts and a passive acceptance of assimilation into the English cultural world.

Within a year I had formulated my basic belief in Canadian identity: English-speaking Canada, either native or of immigrant descent, has had an opportunity to share or at least recognize the French Canadian language culture of modern Canada, as had been agreed in 1867 at Confederation. At the same time, French Canadians would naturally embrace the dominant language and culture of the North American continent. Such a sharing would give all Canadians a distinct identity, founded on dualism but producing . . . Canadians.

Canada must be Canadian, neither English nor French. But we must also be aware of our past history.

French has been spoken in Canada for more than 400 years. Voyageurs and French explorers brought civilization to Western Canada, down the Mississippi, and across the American Midwest. British-born explorers and traders followed and further opened up the new world. Every treaty and entente in Canada has recognized the values of these two great cultural entities.

Huge immigrations of races other than French and English followed, including the Ukrainian, German, Icelandic, and Scandinavian groups, with today's immigrations from Vietnam, Eastern Europe, the West Indies, Hong Kong, India, and many other areas. In Saskatchewan, for example, a majority of the people are from cultures other than French or English. The Canadian culture I foresee, therefore, is one in which not only the two official languages are commonly used but in which our ethnic mosaic encourages the learning of a third, fourth, even a fifth language.

I see each culture making a contribution as we learn and respect each other's gifts. Canada cannot be either a French or an English melting pot. That is why I fought — with success, I am grateful to say — to have the laws of Manitoba protecting French culture that were given to us by Canada, brought into effect again. That is why I am opposed to certain parts of Bill 101 in Quebec that would take away basic rights of English-speaking Quebecers.

Seventeen years ago, one René Lésvesque visited the French Canadian communities in the West. They are "dead ducks", he charged on return to Quebec, "rendered negligible and expendable because of assimilation". How wrong he was.

I can report to the people of Quebec that we are very much alive and French Canadian culture is thriving, not as a leftover memory of the past but as an ongoing, developing movement determined to make a positive contribution to Canada.

I have never sought, and never will, bilingualism for each English-speaking citizen of Manitoba or any other part of Canada, as some extremists have charged. That would be untenable, unattainable, and damaging. Four years ago in May 1980, before my Supreme Court case was heard, I publicly stated my views, at Red River Community College. "If all French-speaking Manitobans and their children realized that their language rights were fully respected, then they would carry on to develop their culture instead of waging a continual struggle against assimilation of the slight culture they possess. At that time, willing English-speaking Manitobans (and this would apply in other parts of Canada) would be able to truly share French Canadian life and culture instead of just conducting a second language exercise."

I want to report that never before has there been such an interest in French education and culture in Manitoba and throughout the West. Classes for French immersion in our schools are full and the waiting lists of English- as well as French-speaking parents who wish to send their children to immersion schools from the first grade on, increases steadily. And French parents in communities have French-speaking schools.

Despite a recent setback, the law permitting the use of French in courts and in the legislature is gradually coming into effect. There will be a settling down in Manitoba of the passions and fears that change brings. It is also unthinkable to me that the province of my roots, Quebec, would desert Canada.

How proud I am that Canada gave me the freedom in law to bring about justice based upon that section of the Canadian constitution creating Manitoba. The new Constitution offers similar protection to others.

Now we must cement the bonds of Canada by attending to the spirit that unites. Canadian literary critic and scholar Northrop Frye has spelled out the challenge far better than I could: "Real Unity tolerates dissent and rejoices in variety of outlook and tradition [and] recognizes that it is man's destiny to unite and not divide. . . . Unity so understood is the extra dimension that raises the sense of belonging into genuine human life."

---———————————— ✳ ————————————---

Common Goals

Robert Thompson

Member of Parliament for Red Deer, Alberta, and head of the National Social Credit Party 1962–68, in association with Réal Caouette of Quebec, and now a professor of political science, Trinity Western College, Fort Langley, BC.

Canada has started and continued her existence in defiance of the laws of economics, which is almost a cardinal sin in our materialistic age, which worships the comfort and gadgetry of modern living beyond nearly any other value on earth. Our nation was formed at a time of economic crisis and has remained in a difficult position ever since. We have made our tariff policy divert trade from its natural north–south channels and forced it to flow from east to west. We pushed through the Canadian Pacific Railway, an act of sublime faith to some and of supreme folly to others. Since then, we have added a second transcontinental railway, the Trans-Canada Highway, airlines, and vast broadcasting and television networks, all for the purpose of uniting our country.

The greatest need of Canada continues to be unity. However, true unity is not found automatically in a confederated union. Neither is it to be found in uniformity. True unity will come only if we set our hearts and minds and our wills to achieve that spirit of unity found only between partners who are working together towards a common goal. Canada, created in defiance of the natural laws of geography, history, economics, and politics, is not a nation that will survive by herself.

Canada is a nation built upon an ideal. The marvel is not that this is done badly but that it is done at all, that a nation with such unpromising beginnings can yet live at peace within itself and take a proper place in the world family of nations. Yet we have gone beyond this. It is a fact of history that no other nation has progressed so far in so short a period.

Canada is the pioneer of the emerging former colonies that now crowd the world stage. For us it is of desperate importance that this experiment of Canada be made to work. If we succeed, there is indeed hope for a peaceful living together of the nations of the world.

I never cease to marvel at the part of our history that relates to the Confederation and at the spirit that actually brought Canada together as a nation. As I read and re-read the records of the pre-Confederation years, I have come to realize that Canada became a nation because the Fathers of Confederation had come to a point of agreement. They were willing to set aside the things that divided them, standing together on areas of mutual concern and conviction.

At the Quebec Conference in October 1864 the final decision was made to go ahead with the drafting of the Constitution, which on July 1, 1867, became the British North America Act. Sir Leonard Tilley, the Governor of New Brunswick, reading in his morning devotions prior to the opening of the day's session, was impressed with what the Psalmist recorded in the eighth verse of Psalm 72. He became convinced that, if the Fathers were really to succeed in their objective, Canada would have to be a nation under God. When Sir Leonard came down to the Conference session, he convinced his fellow politicians to adopt a motto for this new nation. As one enters under the east arch of the Peace Tower of the Parliament Buildings in Ottawa, there it is inscribed in stone above the arch: "He shall have dominion from sea to sea." And over the west arch: "Where there is no vision the people perish." The work they accomplished has not perished, nor will it perish if Canadians will but understand that it is this spiritual strength that has made Canada unique among nations.

Individual men and collective society, including governments, must remain spiritually strong or there will not be any future justice and freedom, public or private. The resulting moral standards are a guide in life, like the North Star. As a pilot I quickly learned that every navigator determines his position by that star. It tells him where he is and where he must go if he would have a safe arrival.

Such guidance is necessary for society as a whole, even as it is for the individual, as it governs and guides human behaviour. As Canadians this is our heritage.

---

   *

Tribute to John Fisher, "Mr. Canada"
Harry Boyle

The Ontario broadcaster and writer pays tribute to John Wiggins Fisher, "Mr. Canada".

The myth of American homogeneity has plagued us in Canada. Our media and political forces continue to campaign for the pious fraud of national unanimity. We are, in fact, a nation of natural divisions, familial squabbles, and divided opinions, depending on our interests.

Our culture, and we do have one, has been influenced by geography and space. We glory in the whole, proud that it is open for us to explore and move through freely, ours to enjoy, and yet our deepest emotions are reserved for a place or a region. It may be a birthplace or it may have ties of immediate family and work, yet it is a conquering sense.

It was the genius of the late John Wiggins Fisher — "Mr. Canada" — that he knew this fact about us. He never forgot that he was born in Frosty Hollow, NB, of United Empire Loyalists who chose Canada. Born November 12, 1912, he graduated in law, practised as a newspaperman, had a fling in politics, and in 1943 came to broadcasting.

His first item on CBC News Roundup concerned the wartime story of a small girl on the Halifax docks saying goodbye to her serviceman father. It was fashioned with evocative words, teetering on the edge of the heart-touching emotion that permeated the scene. To some it would be considered extravagant, as would his subsequent broadcasts, but Fisher always led with his heart. He spoke in terms that average Canadians accepted and, more often than not, wished they could articulate themselves.

Few people find their proper niches. Fisher did. He took the commonplace of people and occupations and their localities and stitched them into broadcasts and speeches that celebrated the Canadian experience. They were intimate, individually, but in their totality they produced reactions usually only engendered by poets. But then, although he spoke in glowing prose, he had the instincts of a poet.

By one of those strange flukes of good sense John Fisher became, in 1963, commissioner for the centennial celebration of 1967. Here his natural empathy, reinforced by the thousands of letters he received as a broadcaster, his proclivity for travelling to every nook and corner of the country, and his ability to communicate with all Canadians, reinforced his own sensitivity. We know what 1967 did for Canadians. We know that Expo 67 awakened in all of us inner wells of pride and even astonishment. Fisher was honoured with the Order of Canada, awards, citations, and honorary degrees. Average Canadians understood him. To this day they strenuously defend him as "Mr. Canada" and will suffer no substitutes.

On February 17, 1981, the House of Commons in Ottawa paid full tribute to him in death. It is a measure of our time that no one stood on the occasion to spell out some adequate measure of the man. It could have even been John's own tribute to a fellow New Brunswicker, Sir Charles G.D. Roberts: "He lunched with presidents, travelled with princes, was toasted by the great, but the simple things of life inspired him."

If Roberts was the Bard of Tantramar, then John Fisher was the Bard of Frosty Hollow, and of all the thousands of places that we hold dear as keystones of our firm feeling for the heritage of freedom with which we have been endowed.

It was the particular quality of Fisher that he knew, understood, and championed what Charles Dickens meant when he said, "In the love of home the love of country has its rise."

∗

Return to the Canadian Fact

Bruce Hutchison

Victoria, British Columbia, writer and historian. Editor emeritus of *The Vancouver Sun*, and author of *Canada, the Unknown Country*.

To an old citizen who knew Canada before its population had reached half the present numbers, knew it as a frontier of dusty little towns and a few distant cities, of general poverty (then reckoned as abundant wealth), of simple politics, no economics, no statistics worth reading, and a lonely silence broken only by the railway's haunting whistle — to such a man the nation's contemporary mood seems strange, even depressing.

Of course all nations are troubled these days, for that is the nature of our age, the symptom of a human revolution without precedent or map to guide us. Yet among the nations, everything considered, ours must surely be the most fortunate.

That any Canadian should think of dismembering it and destroying the work of more than three centuries is unbelievable to those who lived through pioneering times. A few angry men are tempted by national suicide and enjoy some brief masochism, but not many. Like all peoples, we may be confused but we are not crazy.

Within the family, however, the diverse and ever-growing family spread across half a continent, between three oceans, we can speak candidly. And to tell the truth we have been making, in recent times, a sorry botch of our joint affairs.

Governments and people alike mismanage them and for an obvious reason: we demand from a governing system quick solutions to intractable, long-term problems. From an industrial apparatus of huge capacity we expect more than it can produce. Piling up debt, foreign and domestic, for our children to pay, we eat the seed corn of the future, a folly that no frontier folk dared risk.

We survived, without breaking under it, the grinding toil of the early days, then the miseries of Depression and the bloodshed of war, emerging from our shared experience with an identity and distinct character that no one has been able to articulate in words.

But in the family, in the heart of things, we understand our own special lifeway, the words unneeded, the reality enough, the secret treasure beyond price. Of Canada's nature, a certain shrewdness, a common sense, and a tolerance for differing views have always been the essential elements, the invisible glue, the unspoken but operative Canadian Fact, embracing all others.

Now all that is questioned, as never in the past. What else could be expected at a time of world-wide disorder? But amidst the clamour of politics, economics, and Constitutional debate (the superficial mechanism, not the inner life of a people), the unbalanced budgets, the taxes, regional disputes, inflated prices, and social inequities of all sorts, let us remember the Canadian Fact and return to it.

There, in our old instincts of thrift, patience, and neighbourly compromise, we can find our guiding North Star, our safe trail, as our fathers found theirs, through a wilderness which, though different on the surface, in essentials is the same. And remember, too, that our transcontinental estate is still whole and lavish, a single organism indivisible, that the Atlantic still washes our eastern shore, the St. Lawrence Valley nourishes its crops and industries, the central plains turn green in springtime and gold in autumn wheat, the Rockies haven't moved, the western forest surges to the Pacific, and the great rivers run, changeless, to the Arctic — a fine country that needs nothing but our will to make it finer yet.

✳

The "We/They" Frontier
Arnold Smith

Immediate past Lester B. Pearson Professor of International Affairs, Carleton University, Ottawa, Smith has served extensively in Canada's Department of External Affairs, from ambassador to Moscow to elected secretary-general of the Commonwealth. Author of *Stitches in Time*.

My studies of history and my experience in many countries of the world have led me to the firm conclusion that one of the boldest acts of creative statesmanship in Canadian history was the original and basic decision to establish a bilingual state. Today some people are suggesting that such multinational states are abnormal. Nonsense. What we Canadians did in 1867, unusual though it seemed at the time, was the necessary wave of the future for most of the world. Ninety per cent of countries that have gained independence since 1945 have done so as multicultural, multilingual states.

Learning how to build and maintain a free political society out of several cultural and national groups with two or more official languages is relatively new and forms one of the most important political challenges of our age. These modern political societies of many cultures and languages do not want to become melting pots. The peoples of India, for example, do not wish to lose the rich cultural heritage of the Punjabis, or the Tamils, or the Bengalis, or the dozens of other ethnic units. They insist on preserving and developing the cultural wealth of their various national communities. At the same time they want and need an effective political unit that is larger than any one racial group.

When I was closely involved with the leaders of so many newly formed plural societies, heads of state or government of these new countries frequently told me that their most difficult and important task is, as the Africans put it, "nation-building". The Asians have a different word. But roughly it means, for instance, making Kenyans think and act politically as Kenyans for certain purposes, instead of always as tribal Kikuyus or Luos or Masais. And the challenge is to do so without losing their own rich cultural artistic and linguistic heritages, while providing at the same time an opportunity of learning to enjoy something of their fellow neighbours' culture. In most cases, there has been good success in building cohesion and co-operation. Not in all.

I could give many detailed reasons for the bust-up in Pakistan, Cyprus, or Lebanon. The common element in bust-ups has invariably been a lack of enough spiritual generosity: sometimes on the part of the majority, sometimes of a minority, sometimes of both towards each other. The key issue is where people draw the line between those they think of as "we" and those they think of as "they". This "we/they" frontier is, in my experience, the most critical problem in world politics.

The separatist challenge both in Quebec and, to a lesser extent, in Western Canada has been the greatest threat in Canadian history, a threat all the graver because it is almost entirely self-created, the product of our own inadequacies. What can men and women of goodwill do?

First of all we must try facing up to facts. For instance, Canada is the only plural or multinational society I know with no federal input whatsoever into the content of education in the subject of history. Most federations in the world have both central *and* state or provincial ministries, as we Canadians have in agriculture. This was a remarkably unimaginative omission on the part of our Fathers of Confederation. And so grave differences and gaps in perception are produced by our ten provincial history teaching systems. It will take conscious effort by our Ministers of Education, and generosity, to overcome them.

There are also legitimate grievances in East and West. The West lacks political power at the centre of national government. And in Quebec ten or fifteen years ago it was a fact that most of the larger businesses were in English-speaking hands. Promotions to middle management and to top management did not come easily if your mother tongue was French. Thirty years ago this was also apt to be the case in the federal civil service in Ottawa. Thankfully, there has been a big change in recent years. Promotion rates in many of the bright national firms are better now in some cases if you are French-speaking than if you are English-speaking, in order to make up for past discrimination the other way.

There are also recent injustices in Quebec against the English language that should be resolved. Resentments have understandably developed in Quebec, because the English-speaking minority has been much better treated since Confederation in education and other exclusively provincial fields, than Francophone minorities in other provinces.

I was also shocked, since my return to live in Ottawa, to learn that Grade 13 French, or the equivalent, was no longer required for university entrance in Ontario and is therefore less extensively taught in schools, although a move has been made in the right direction, making it once again a requirement for a high school certificate. I am told that this change was not the result of any conscious decision to downgrade French but was a more or less unforeseen by-product of the silly decisions to abandon core curricula in high schools, and to finance universities by a grant formulas calculated to encourage each college and department to admit as many students as possible, virtually irrespective of qualifications.

The key to national unity in Canada is not, and cannot ever be, everyone's becoming bilingual. No one would expect all the people of India, for example, to learn Tamil and Punjabi and Gujerati and the other fourteen major languages of that country. The solution is a recognition that we all are enriched by our various languages, heritages, and cultures and the existing rights to use them.

I was brought up English-speaking like, I suppose, sixty-five per cent of other Canadians, without absorbing French language or culture at my mother's knees. I have always been grateful, however, that at age twelve my parents sent my brother and me for what is now called total immersion in a French language school. We lived with a French family. We were the only non-French present. There was some strain for the first couple of months, but at the end of the academic year we came out speaking French, and that has been an enormous asset. One can adopt and enjoy and be greatly enriched by Canadian cultures other than one's own.

If we have blots on our history, let us recognize them. In one case, Canada has been less than generous in the past in the treatment of the Inuit and Indians, and I trust that their situation will be substantially improved. But let us also recognize our achievements. We Canadians have explored, settled, and partially developed a vast and rugged half-continent, becoming one of the richest and freest countries on earth.

We have been creative. In the 1837–67 period we pioneered together a new road to independence from imperial control through demonstrations and pressure and negotiated agreement. Much better than the wars that the Vietnamese and Algerians had to fight. We Canadians also pioneered what are now called regional policies, using fiscal, tariff, investment, and freight-rate measures to promote greater balance of development throughout a vast land. Now the world, in growing pressures for what is being called a New International Economic Order, is being urged to devise and implement regional development policies on an inter-continental scale, to increase investment and productivity in the Third World and to develop profitable export markets for them.

Canada also first proposed the idea of NATO for mutual security and invented the Commonwealth, which now comprises more than a billion people in almost all regions of the globe. More recently Canadians took the lead in developing associations of French-language universities and periodicals, non-governmental forerunners of a more recent inter-governmental association of Francophone countries for technical and cultural co-operation. We Canadians have also been among the most active supporters and innovators in the United Nations.

In my forty years as a practitioner in world politics, dealing with people of so many other nations, I always found being a Canadian an enormous advantage. Our national instincts and insights often have been priceless assets in dealing with other peoples and problems.

It would be tragic if Canada, far the most fortunate, and thus far, despite our errors and inadequacies, far the most successful of all plural political societies on earth, came apart at the seams. If we cannot make a go of it, what a shocking example to those less blessed than we.

It has been said that war is too serious to leave it to the generals. Certainly our country's unity is too important to leave it to party politicians. We must press them to serve us properly. We must be prepared to speak out frankly.

---

* ───────

Our Flag — Rooted in History
John Ross Matheson

On the day the new Maple Leaf flag was formally adopted, February 15, 1965, Prime Minister Pearson singled out John Matheson, a judge in Perth, Ontario, a World War II veteran, and at that time Pearson's Parliamentary assistant, at a special reception: "Here's the man who had more to do with it than any other." When the flag idea developed, Matheson had written to Pearson that any new design must be "judged by history" and not chosen on "passions of the moment". Sound heraldry from Canada's past should be fully considered, a subject dear to Matheson's heart. The Prime Minister urged him to become chairman of the all-party committee that would select a flag design for Parliamentary approval. Matheson refused, asking for ordinary membership so he could argue strongly for suitable designs and work behind the scenes to solve problems. Matheson also promoted into being the Order of Canada awards.

The minority government of Lester Pearson, elected in 1963, foresaw the possibility of the collapse of Confederation. Within Pearson's party caucus Quebec members reported regularly the terrifying growth of the forces of separatism. Pearson's first priority, the thrust of all his policy, was to save an endangered Canada.

Canada was in crisis. The depth of the national malaise should have been much more widely appreciated, but no prime minister can cry havoc from the House of Commons.

Among his several efforts to strengthen a sense of national consciousness was the creation of a new Canadian flag and, shortly following that, the Order of Canada.

No more eloquent plea was made for a new flag than by a great Canadian from Quebec, Réal Caouette, co-leader of the national Social Credit Party, which at that time held a considerable number of seats in the House of Commons. On June 10, 1964, Caouette spoke of keeping the symbols of either England or France in a new flag. Said Caouette, "When someone tries to impose the Union Jack as our emblem, we do not agree, no more than we would accept the emblem of France and the French . . . We are able to choose among ourselves an emblem for our own identity." He added, on September 8, 1964, "We are ready, we from Quebec, not as French-Canadians but as Canadians to approve any project for a distinctive Canadian flag." He was also proudly Royalist.

The Order of Canada was established with relative ease by order-in-council. The flag, however, by reason of prior commitments, needed to be brought to the floor of Parliament, where it engendered the most controversial debate since 1867.

After some 308 speeches and six months of acrimonious argument, a resolution was passed authorizing the government to recommend Canada's new flag to the Queen. The vote was taken at 2:00 a.m. Tuesday, December 15, 1964. Senate approval followed two days later. Her Majesty, as Queen of Canada, signed the Proclamation to take effect as of February 15, 1965. General Georges P. Vanier presided as Governor General over the impressive Flag Day Ceremonies. He prayed:

"Bless, O Merciful Father, this Flag and grant that this banner of our nationhood may proudly fly over a people devoted to the pursuit of righteousness, justice, and unity; whose faith and hope are grounded in Thee, who art the King of Kings and Lord of Lords."

Canada's flag is designed upon classic principles of vexillology or flag heraldry: simplicity of theme (the Maple Leaf), contrast in colours (white and scarlet), distinct proportions (2 x 1; 1/4 red, 1/2 white, 1/4 red), and precise colouration (a whitish white, a bright red between the reds of the Union Jack and the Stars and Stripes). Its purpose is communication. Its one message is *CANADA*.

The flag is the result of painstaking research into all significant Canadian symbolism since 1867. We discovered that in assigning yellow maple leaves on green to Ontario in 1868 and green leaves on yellow to Quebec, the College of Heralds had reserved the more dramatic *argent* and *gules* (white and red) for Canada. The guidon of the RCMP; the General Service Medal issued by Queen Victoria to the veterans of the first national army for the defence of Canada in the Fenian Raid and Wolseley Expedition (1866–70) and copied later in the Canada Medal ribbon in 1943; the Royal Military College Flag; the red leaf on white worn by Canada's athletes at Olympic contests since the Games in Saint Louis, Missouri, in 1904; and the authorized badge of the Royal Canadian Legion — all these demonstrate that in practice Canada's national colours were red and white. This was legally confirmed in the armorial language *argent* and *gules* employed in the blazon of the Arms for the Dominion proclaimed by George V on November 21, 1921.

World War I fixed the Maple Leaf in the public mind as Canada's distinct emblem. This device has been used to decorate each grave of Canada's overseas dead. The first recorded formal recommendation that the Maple Leaf symbol become Canada's flag came in 1919 from Major General Eugène Fiset, who later became Quebec's Lieutenant-Governor. On February 15, 1965, the flag was run up on flagpoles all over the world. It was recognized instantly as representing Canada.

To Canadians the Maple suggests the soil, the homeland of all Canada's children, whatever might have been their past differences or quarrels. It alludes to their land — vast, austere, awe-inspiring, and peaceful — indescribably beautiful and unspeakably dear.

6

*

Québécois and Canadian

My Two Worlds

Gérard Dion

Editor of *Industrial Relations* and professor emeritus, Laval University, Quebec; Dion has served on many industrial relations bodies and the Economic Council of Canada and has published widely.

Am I Canadian before being Québécois or Québécois before being Canadian? That is a poor way to put the problem, like asking a child whether he loves his father or his mother most.

I have always thought of myself as a French Canadian, living in Quebec, within the framework of Canada. That does not mean that I am as much at home in British Columbia as I am in Quebec (anyway, within Quebec I feel more at home in the city of Quebec than I do in Montreal); it is a question of degree and shading. Quebec and Canada are my country. I have no other. And they are my land because I was born here; my ancestors have lived here for more than 300 years, and I can find my descendants throughout the whole Canadian nation. They contributed to making this country.

I am a French Canadian nationalist in the sense that, belonging to an ethnic group possessing a particular and original culture, I nevertheless think this culture has a value that contributes to Canadian culture, and to all humanity, one that deserves to be protected and developed. Personally, it is through that culture that I can be myself most readily and in which it is easier for me to express myself. That does not hinder me in any way from participating in a Canadian culture, which shows that we Canadians from all of Canada have something in common that distinguishes us from the culture of the United States.

In order to maintain and develop this French Canadian culture, we need institutions in every area and at every level, including the political. And that is why the province of Quebec has its being and possesses a special role, not only with respect to the inhabitants of Quebec, where the heart of the French cultural expression exists, but also with respect to the whole of Canada.

I believe that far from being an obstacle to the maintenance and development of an ethnic group to which I belong, and its culture, the fact that Quebec belongs to Canada is really a protection against absorption into the great North American totality dominated by a different culture.

And, in one sense, it is because I want to be and to remain Québécois that I firmly wish to remain Canadian. This approach is not without its misunderstandings, its knocks, its difficulties, but it is still the most promising one for the future. Moreover, if one looks at the past and compares it with the present situation, with the enormous progress that has been made in every area, there is room, unless suicidal moves intervene, for optimism.

---------------- ✳ ----------------

Judgement From the Bench
Réjane Laberge-Colas

Judge with the Superior Court of Quebec; first Canadian woman to be appointed to a superior court; president–founder of Quebec Federation of Women.

When my paternal forefather, Robert Laberge, left France to embark for the far-away shores of North America, he was making a brave and heroic gesture by venturing into the unknown. That was in 1658. For more than 300 years his descendants have worked in the most diverse places and in every spot on the continent. From the first days of the emerging colony of New France, the people had to face severe weather, traps, and difficulties posed by nature, but their determination to be free men made them push even farther the frontiers of civilization and progress.

This unrelenting quest for new horizons, towards new conquests, did not end on the Plains of Abraham in 1760. On the contrary, the quest occurred also in the realm of the spirit, in intellectual knowledge, in the desire to wipe out ignorance, prejudice, and hate. The battle against the raw elements of nature changed into a fight against the destruction of a country left to us by worthy forefathers who had an insatiable thirst for liberty, hope, and the future.

They wanted their descendants to enjoy life wherever they were, free of restrictions, forearmed against insecurity, frustration, and mediocrity. We have come from proud men and women who built with their hands, intellect, and will, a young, dynamic, free, and powerful land.

I do not have the right to betray this ancestral tradition, to leave my children a heritage grown smaller in an atmosphere of prejudice, racism, and hate. Canada, from sea to sea, is my country, and must remain that of my children and their descendants. They must be able to see their fellow citizens as friends capable of working together in a communion of ideas to maintain a climate of freedom, security, and mutual respect.

That is why, with my husband, I have tried to make my children aware of being the inheritors of two civilizations and of two great cultures in which the entire citizenry of the country must participate, by working to develop a truly original culture that can henceforth be designated as Canadian.

It was also necessary to teach people how to preserve and develop the spiritual, political, and social freedoms that constitute an inviolable part of the common heritage, while insisting on safeguarding and extending the fundamental rights of all. We have encouraged them to bring their contribution to the development of a national community established on the basis of joint responsibility and regulated by the principles of justice.

One must recognize that such a task is not easy in the climate of dispute, claims, and fanaticism that we have known for already too long. It is a delicate task to want to rear children in an atmosphere of mutual acceptance, but we must not despair. Above all, we must try to instil in the younger generation the resolute will to work to put an end to rivalries based on issues of race, language, or religion, in order to participate in the mission that all

Canadians should pursue, that of ushering in an era of peace, collaboration, and federal agreement.

We should all aspire to develop together the civilizing contribution of Canada, to dedicate all our strength to the working out of a country totally absorbed in creating an atmosphere of harmony and social contentment, as well as to raising the standard of living, thanks to the economic and social co-operation of all parts of Canada.

---
*

Les Anglais — Not Homogenized
Lise Archambault-Scott

Québécois doctor in Montreal who has practised medicine also in Ontario.

I am French Canadian and was brought up in a bilingual part of Montreal. English and French pre-schoolers played together, but by age six we went our separate ways: different schools, different religions, different friends, different pastimes. I did not often think of *les Anglais* in my city, except when I happened to run into them: they were the loud teenagers in sneakers and white socks, the college athletes and their giggly cheerleader girlfriends, they were the stern businessmen guardians of the so-called WASP traditions as they appear to French Quebecers — money and supremacy.

In medical school, I decided to join the armed forces. I underwent basic training with medical students from all over Canada. Although our stay together lasted only two months, I did get a somewhat different view of *les Anglais*. In Montreal, I had encountered upper and middle class WASPs; during these two months, I met people of different ethnic backgrounds, religions, social classes. They all spoke English, but beyond the linguistic difference we had a lot in common. We talked a lot, we accomplished things together (not the least being that we survived the training!). Collaboration was easy, especially when it was aimed at defying the vigilant eye of the sergeant major.

We all went back home and it was only some years later that I moved to Ontario and entered the English community. We lived in Guelph for five years and in Elmira for one-and-a-half years. While my husband was studying to become a veterinarian, I worked as a physician at the student health services of the University of Waterloo. Living in Ontario has been an enriching experience. The reality of English Canada appeared to me. *Les Anglais* were not one homogeneous group but were formed of many ethnic communities: Guelph has a large Italian community; Kitchener is home to many Germans; in Elmira, I discovered the Mennonite culture.

I certainly missed the French environment, my large family, the *chansonniers*, but I gained sincere, caring friends, the music of Gordon Lightfoot, Mennonite food . . .

Most of the time, my contact with the people was rewarding. We were far from Quebec and far from the tension between French and English. My co-workers were as helpful as could be in easing my adaptation to the practice of medicine the English way. I had little problem being accepted by my patients: university students, not yet set in their ways, did not mind someone "different". They came from all over the country. I saw in them many of the same preoccupations, the same interests, the same hopes, and the same fears as in the students of the university I had left in Montreal not that long before.

I made many friends and felt welcome in their homes. I expected English people to be cold and unemotional. Although I did not meet many people who were as bubbly as the typical Québécois, most were very warm and friendly, under a more subdued and rational cover.

I am back in Quebec now and see with some sadness that the French and English continue to live parallel lives with very little positive interaction. I am very happy to be home, but I look back with nostalgia at what I left behind in Ontario.

Will there be a time when French- and English-speaking Canadians, without sacrificing their own identity, will be able to live together, communicate, and interact to the enrichment of every one? I hope everyone can have a valuable learning experience like mine.

The Other Side of the Schoolyard

André McNicoll

French Canadian free-lance journalist and sociologist from Ottawa and Montreal and now with the North-South Institute.

For almost as long as I can remember I have found inspiration and peace of mind in French and English literature. My first language was French. This was the language of my parents and most of our good neighbours in Ottawa's Lower Town. But from the time I was five years old I would sing and mumble (mostly the latter) in a strange language that I could hear on the radio, a big Electrohome encased in a glistening walnut cabinet, in front of which I would sit attentively for an hour or so before my mother put me to bed.

They were just noises to me, incomprehensible sounds that I would repeat over and over again, in some vague, childlike dream of being alone on a stage with a bright spotlight shining on me and an admiring public widely applauding the child prodigy.

One evening, when I was alone with my father in the little farmhouse we had moved to the year before in the village of Orléans, just outside of Ottawa, he asked me what on earth I was up to.

"I'm singing a song I heard on the radio," I explained.

"Ah, so you're learning English then," my father replied.

What a revelation! So that's what they called those sounds — English! With more resolve than ever I continued to repeat the meaningless sounds, determined to pronounce them perfectly, just like the wonderful singers on the radio. I was learning English.

By the time I was in grade school, and usually coming in first in French, my English was pretty good; good enough anyway to come to the rescue of Frère Donald, one of the Christian Brothers responsible for our education. Frère Donald, a ruddy-faced and cheerful man who reverently insisted on calling all the boys in the

153

school "vous", which we found very funny, was much better at playing softball during recess than he was at teaching his main subject, English.

His pronunciation was truly appalling; sometimes it was so awful no one would understand what he was saying and the giggling would rise from its normal murmur to an embarrassing symphonic level.

And so Frère Donald would ask me to help him out, and I would come to his rescue and show him how to pronounce big words like "neighbourhood". In fact, when I think back on it, neighbourhood was just about the first English word that I learned how to spell, pronounce, and understand. It's still one of my favourites.

We had to share the schoolyard with the boys from the English Catholic school. Although we were never formally forbidden to speak with them, which we wanted to do to practise the few words of our vocabulary, it was well understood that we had to stay clear of their side of the yard. Whenever any one of us wandered too close to the forbidden "English side", a dark frown would crease the faces of Frère Donald and the other black-robed Brothers, and we would quickly return to the "French side" wondering what those boys were really like whose shouts we could hear when they played softball and soccer. Since no one from the English side ever wandered over to our side, I assume they were under the same restrictions.

In the five years that I spent at École Ducharme in Eastview (it's called Vanier now) I cannot remember once ever getting close enough to the English side of the schoolyard to speak to anyone or even to see a face really close up. All I can remember are a lot of little boys dressed like me but with red hair and freckles. One of my best friends, Ronald Larabie, who claimed to have once talked with one of the red-haired boys, said they weren't English, they were Irish. I told him it didn't matter since they didn't speak French.

Things began to improve when I graduated and went on to Eastview High School (it has a new name now, École Secondaire André Laurendeau) and started formally to study French and English literature — as well, lo and behold, actually to talk with English-speaking persons.

Ah, how marvellous it was to discover François Villon, Pierre de Ronsard, and François de Malherbe. Then there was William Shakespeare, Francis Bacon, Edmund Spenser, and Christopher Marlowe. It was a new world, a world of letters and great thoughts, a world of beauty and reflection, of wisdom and serenity.

In the years ahead, including the several that I would spend at various universities, I continued to explore other realms of French and English literature, spending evenings and whole weekends sequestered with my books, compelled to read each of them from cover to cover, savouring every word. There was the poetry of William Wordsworth, John Keats, and Thomas Gray; the novels of John Steinbeck, Sinclair Lewis, and William Faulkner; and the plays of Oscar Wilde and Bernard Shaw. In French I buried myself in Albert Camus, Jean-Paul Sartre, Antoine de Saint-Exupéry, and later Marie-Claire Blais, Emile Nelligan, André Gide, and Jean Genet.

I have always managed to live and to work in both French and English cultures. Sometimes I immersed myself in English as I did when I lived in England to complete my post-graduate work and during the years of study spent in several English-language universities; sometimes in French, as was the case for the first twenty years of my life and seems again to be case now that I have returned to Eastern Canada after a sojourn on the West Coast. Having been able to penetrate so deeply into what I regard as the very origins of Canada's character has been of immense intellectual satisfaction to me.

Obviously, this type of cultural duality is not possible for everyone; it may not even be good for everyone. But it has permitted me to have an open mind about Canada; to be sensitive to the dynamics and the aspirations of both cultures; to realize the greatness that is possible in Canada simply in part because of its dual cultural heritage.

Perhaps then if we were less obsessed with the Gross National Product and more concerned with our cultural life, with our poets, painters, dancers, actors — the people who enrich our lives far beyond what is possible by the manufacturers of refrigerators and wipers for automobile headlights — the entire country would enjoy a delirious transformation in its experience.

There is no guarantee that a keener appreciation of our awesome linguistic gifts and heritage would moderate the tempestuous agitations of the few who think the Canadian experience a failure, but the sometimes spiteful regionalism that so plagues the country might well find its underpinnings yielding to a more uplifting vision of our destiny.

All of Us Are Free
Claudette Quinette

Recently moved with her family from Quebec to Regina, Saskatchewan.

It was when I left my native province of Quebec and moved to Saskatchewan six years ago that I discovered how different we Canadians are. I used to think that as a French Canadian I of course had a different culture, a different language than English Canadians. But to my amazement, when my husband and I and our children settled in the West I realized that Canadians in general seem to think differently in various parts of the country, and I started asking myself why. Is it because of our many different ethnic roots, spread over so many thousands of miles, some going back as far as time can tell, some of us to nearly four centuries while others merely to a single generation?

I also think Canada has become the freest country in the world. Freedom of speech is unheard of almost anywhere else. We only have to listen to politicians the likes of Western separatist Dick Culver and Quebec Premier René Lévesque, who would want nothing better than to break up Canada, to realize that freedom of speech in this country is sacred. If Mr. Culver was to speak about "separation" in his favourite country, the United States, which he wants to join with so much, he would probably be thrown in jail for "un-American activities". The same would be true for all other separatists in any other country.

But freedom of speech and all other freedoms Canadians enjoy are taken for granted. You would think that in being able to communicate so openly with each other we Canadians would know each other better. We know little about each other, and this is very sad. We seem to be so "regionalized" that we forget we are all Canadians. Whatever happened to being "Canadian"? We call ourselves Ontarians or Albertans or British Columbians or Quebecers or Newfoundlanders, but do we ever think of ourselves as Canadians?

I did not have any choice in picking the province I was born in, but I feel privileged to have known and lived in such a great culture and felt the warmth and joy of being a French Canadian and to have been part of a great city, my home town, Montreal. I live, however, in Saskatchewan, by choice. We travelled through Saskatchewan, we looked around us and saw the biggest sky we ever saw, and the clearest one, too. We had never seen such sunsets, and such land, so green in summer and like gold in the fall, the wildlife, the wild geese in the sky. We came back to Saskatchewan to stay, because life is good here, very good. I was quite pleasantly surprised, too, to find in Regina that there were schools that had a good French immersion programme. Now my youngest daughters have the same chance at being bilingual as my older children, who went to school in Quebec. If anyone feels that it is better elsewhere, or that other parts of the country are better treated than one's own, let that person go and live over there for a while; he'll find there are problems there, too. He might even find out that his problems were pretty small in the first place.

As great as our country is, it is not perfect, but we have to work towards keeping it as close to perfect as possible. We must get to know each other — and I *don't* mean sending our politicans out to meet other politicians. We must find out about each other ourselves by talking to each other as Canadians, for if we are not careful, we could lose it all.

Ontario Schooling En Français

Ray Chauvin

Sales executive in Montreal; formerly of Windsor, Ontario.

I was surprised and dismayed when I came to live in Quebec from Windsor, Ontario, and found that few people seemed to know that French elementary schools had continued in French Canadian settlements in Ontario since earliest times. The environment of my youth in Windsor and my education until my teens was entirely French. (French public high schools were not then available.) From secondary school on, my education was in English by choice (for I could have come to Quebec), but French continued to be the language of my home and church. My brother chose to continue secondary and college education in French by going to Quebec, where he now practises his profession. Some French Canadian areas of Ontario had even better French facilities than Windsor.

Unfortunately, well-publicized quarrels that took place just before Quebec's Referendum over the opening of new French high schools in Windsor and Penetanguishene, Ontario, caught the Quebec press's attention; by the same token the fact that these new schools are now in successful operation never seems to get a mention.

The language of my adult profession was and always has been English, for this was the language of the city of Windsor, but my early French education has been a valuable asset.

I am a Canadian, and always will be.

———————————— * ————————————

Why Canada Needs Quebec
Ian Macdonald

President of York University in Toronto.

To ask the question — Why does Canada need Quebec? — is itself a demonstration of the problem of unity peculiar to Canada, both in the past and in the present. In a family, when one member stands apart because of misunderstanding or disagreement, one does not ask, Why do we need him or her? Canada may be compared ideally to a family in which the various members retain a vital individuality of their own while they support and sustain one another for the good of the whole. It is a tragedy when the members of a family reject one member or allow him or her to reject the whole, for when one part falls away, the household is diminished, not just in size, but also in spirit and identity.

No family is without its problems; indeed, hardship and discord can help form familial character and distinction. Even when some family relationships become turbulent and painful, there is always the underlying truth that the conflicting members are inseparably related, one to the other, and that a complete emotional break, even when it seems most desirable, is never possible. Therefore, we should not ask Why does Canada need Quebec? because it is an unthinkable question. Rather, we should ask, What can every Canadian do to reaffirm the fact that Quebec is an essential and indispensable part of our nation, even though there may be a period of conflict and difficulty before wise compromises can be reached?

I believe that this reaffirmation is not as remote as it may seem, and that a radical change can be made as the cumulative result of small concessions on the part of individual Canadians. The future of Canada will not be found in the articles of constitutions but in the hearts and minds of men and women who believe that Canada can remain a happy place in which to work and to live.

One summer I was sitting beside an old gentleman at

a softball game in a small town in Ontario, and, in our conversation about life in different parts of the country, he said to me, "Well, I don't know much about Quebec, but I sure love Canada." Many of us simply do not know enough about other parts of the country, particularly Quebec, or, in some cases, we have strong views based on our sense of history or our personal attitude, which may or may not be in the best interests of the country.

If, like the gentleman at the softball game, we say we love Canada, the question is: Do we love it enough to accept the changes that are necessary and inevitable where Quebec and French Canada are concerned? Too many of us have tended to think of the so-called "Quebec problem" and to discuss it in terms of "we" and "they". How can we talk about "we" and "they" when "they" comprise 23 percent of our population where Quebec Francophones are concerned, or 27 percent where French Canadians are concerned? How can we think of a major portion of our country in terms of "others"?

If we love our country and want it to stay together, every Canadian, French- and English-speaking, must be prepared to make deliberate personal changes in attitude and behaviour. We must all learn more about all other parts of Canada. In addition, we should be using every possible channel of communication: businessman to businessman, union leader to union leader, teacher to teacher, clergyman to clergyman. Wherever organizations exist, they should be discussing new means of achieving national unity. In these times when the concept of the "global village" has taken hold of the popular imagination, Canadians should not have undue difficulty in thinking of their country as a community.

We cannot erase 200 years of history; instead, Canadians must take pride in and build upon our history. What we can do is to believe in ourselves, in our destiny, and in our future. It does us harm, then, to ask for reasons why Canada needs any one part of our nation. We must, instead, assume that all parts are irrevocably part of Canada. If we think far beyond the question of whether Canada needs its separate provinces, we shall be well on our way to a sense of nationhood.

---------------- * ----------------

Why Quebec Needs Canada
Philippe Garigue

Principal of Glendon College, Toronto, the first French-speaking public college in English-speaking Ontario; recent professor of sociology, University of Montreal.

It is my conviction, after more than twenty-five years of debate as to the future of Quebec, that an ever greater number of Quebecers are now accepting what a majority of other Canadians have already accepted: a clear differentiation between the claim for linguistic or cultural nationalism, and the claim for state sovereignty. The need for personal liberty and group development can be reconciled with the need for linguistic and cultural rights, without creating political boundaries that would separate Canada into different states.

   With the coming of the nuclear bomb, of multiple worldwide crises, of the migration of vast numbers of people across continents, the world is now a much less secure, and less nationalistically oriented, system. In fact, the feeling is spreading across the world that only through collaboration between countries and a lowering of barriers between them can world problems be solved. A major evolution has taken place; what is happening in Canada reflects world trends. Most Canadians have accepted the idea that each linguistic group should enjoy some cultural autonomy, while the English and French languages, because they are the founding languages of Canada, should coexist in the pluralistic political administration of the Canadian state.

   Canada is presently living what Europe discovered after World War II. While Asia and Africa, as well as some parts of the Americas, were discovering narrower national loyalties through decolonization, Europe was creating a new supra-national political identity. While decolonization created a proliferation of new states, Europe was reversing the trend and creating a new political structure out of nations. Because Canada has maintained a close identity with Europe, this gradually had an impact on our own perception of how to solve our problems. Around economic, social, as well as other questions, new solidarities have been gradually created which take over from the traditionally fragmented Canadian political mosaic.

The idea of a united Europe can be traced back to the Roman Empire. It took a thousand years for Europeans to go from the limited political units of the Middle Ages to the new wider political unity of today. We in Canada created our federal system a century ago, and we have no need to go through centuries of autonomous "national" units, again to unite into a large political system. This is well perceived by many Canadians, and even some of the leaders of the present government of Quebec speak of the day when there will be a "North American Common Market". Quebec depends too much on the rest of Canada ever to be able to solve by itself its economic or even its social problems. While separatism may speak of the obsolescence of the present Canadian federal system, and preach a narrower nationalism, the present government of Quebec is also well aware of the tremendous cost of independence on Quebec society. Therefore, while separatists are reluctant to accept the necessity of Canadian federalism, even the Parti Québécois sees the necessity of the integration of Quebec in a wider Canadian economic and political structure.

Quebec needs Canada because the aims of the Parti Québécois to achieve "self-development" through independence have reached their limits and have demonstrated the need for Quebec's integration into Canada. The various "thresholds of scale" required to develop industrial or commercial activities that are competitive in the modern world, are there to demonstrate the "harsh" limits set by resources and what a provincial government can do by itself. Various publications by the Quebec government have stressed this, and one of the most important among these, the Green Paper on Scientific Research, has pointed out that Quebec should forget about developing high technology research but concentrate instead on such traditional sectors as clothing, textiles and furniture-making, or hydroelectricity; that is to say, those elements best suited for the Canadian market. The message all these reports convey is the same: Quebec needs Canada, for otherwise it cannot cross the various levels of development or even maintain the standard of living of its population. This is valid in social as well as in economic affairs. The various activities that determine living conditions in Quebec are less and less set by what goes on in that province and more and more by what goes on in the totality of Canada. To make the government of Quebec totally responsible for everything that happens in Quebec is empty rhetoric, as can be readily proven by listing a few aspects of the situation:

• Since 1960, the Quebec population, far from growing more homogeneous, has become more pluralistic. While the proportion of French speakers is statistically rising, this is taking place within a greater ethnic differentiation. There is an ever larger proportion of French-speaking Quebecers who are not born in Quebec, and are of European, Middle Eastern, North African, or even Asian descent. Increased cultural pluralism is to be found (as well as the proposition that speaking French does not mean a single cultural identity). Being a French-speaking Quebecer has therefore ceased to be the foundation of an unitary political concept. In this Quebec is similar to the other provinces of Canada, where the English language has the same role.

• The decline in the birth rate in Quebec, from 30 per 1,000 in 1960 to less than 14 per 1,000 in 1980, is that of a society whose social characteristics and aspirations are more and more similar to the rest of Canada. Apart from having a different language, there are fewer and fewer social and cultural characteristics that separate French-speaking Quebecers from English-speaking Canadians in all the provinces.

• The sectional interests that exist in Quebec for political separatism are linked more and more to limited groups whose existence depends on their monopolistic position as speakers of French and as custodians of a newly created Quebec nationalism. To maintain that monopoly, they are willing to break their links with the other French-speaking groups in Canada. They perceive, as instruments of group power, French as a language and nationalism as an ideology. This has very little to do with the need of the various social categories that make up the population of Quebec.

• Quebec faces increasingly grave problems of sharply reduced job opportunities and decline in practically every major activity. This has resulted in a gradual "closing-down" of society, followed by a corrosive climate of disillusionment. Quebec needs the wider support of the rest of Canada if it is to restart its development.

Because it is possible today to create a federal system in which state sovereignty is separated from cultural and linguistic questions, it is also now no longer necessary to protect French-speaking Quebec by setting up the political limits of an independent state.

Indifference to linguistic values, or to cultural roots, the refusal to identify with one's kinship or local group, are signs not of a better world but of a mental sickness. We are members of our family, of our kinship group, of our local group, of our linguistic group, before we are members of wider communities. Yet, human beings are very different from the animals who remain seemingly forever classified by their family groups. While nations were created out of the evolution of linguistic systems, we are not limited by the language we speak. Today we can think political systems that can include linguistic and cultural differences and are new stages in the development of valid political solutions to human problems. Nationalism has its place in these new systems, but it will no longer be the absolute nationalism of the unilingual State.

Canada became in the eighteenth century a new experiment in the cohabitation of two peoples, of two groups who spoke different languages and had different cultures. We rewrote history in the nineteenth century so as to satisfy the need of the "two founding groups". Today, in the new social and political pluralism of Canada, in which bilingualism goes hand in hand with multiculturalism, we can open a new phase of federalism. In this new federalism, Quebec has its vital place. Furthermore it needs this new federalism to solve its growing problems and achieve the survival of French as a language and as a culture.

---⁂---

In Brief
Jean Drapeau

The colourful mayor of Montreal.

Drapeau to the editor, stating there was no need to write a contribution to *My Canada*: "Everybody *knows* I'm a Canadian."

---⁂---

Tribute to Roger Doucet
Serge Savard

The former captain and now general manager of the Montreal Canadiens hockey club reflects on Canada and his friend, the late Roger Doucet, who sang "O Canada" at Forum games.

Whenever I think of Roger Doucet and his great love for Canada, I remember the first time I came to Montreal. I arrived in Montreal at the age of sixteen from a very small town 500 miles away, to try to make a career as a professional hockey player. It was then that I began to be conscious of being truly Canadian.

For the first time in my life I began to form bonds of friendship with young people my own age from the four corners of our beautiful country, and it became necessary for me to learn to speak English. That allowed me, at the same time, to get to know my friends of the other culture better, and I quickly discovered that there was really no difference between us. We were exactly alike. Most of them, like me, came from small towns in their provinces and had exactly the same tastes. All of them, without exception, were, first and foremost, proud to be Canadian. That is exactly what I myself felt. After twenty years of my career, and my journeys, I feel it even more.

If it had been given to you, as it was to me, to live the moments of intense pride that I felt on the ice of the

Moscow stadium in September 1972, at the time of the first Canada versus the USSR series, when Paul Henderson finally assured us of victory with a few seconds to go in the eighth and final game, then you too would have experienced an unforgettable moment. A few seconds later, when they raised the Canadian flag and played "O Canada", indicating our victory over the Soviets, I could not hold back a few tears. I can attest to the fact that all my team-mates, without exception, had damp eyes also.

I am proud that I am Québécois and will remain so until death. Yes, I love Quebec, but I am, above all, Canadian, and will remain that also to the end of my days.

Roger Doucet was one of my best friends, and I admired him, not only for his golden voice but also for the way he loved Canada. Roger was really proud to be Canadian and he constantly proclaimed it. The last record of the late-lamented tenor, some months after his death, was entitled, "Let freedom live." It was once a tribute to his country, and at least once a week at home I played that record to hear Roger intone with his arresting voice, "Let's write the story of this great land where the time is right for building — across the plains and mountains, share your friendship. Believe in others. Let freedom live."

It is that word freedom that tells all and which makes us so proud of being Canadian. We are very lucky to have been born and to be living in the freest country in the world: freedom of speech; freedom to go where you want when you want; freedom to buy what you want; even freedom to live as you want, since we have four seasons, allowing us to sample the most beautiful and delicate gifts of the creator. Is there really anything lovelier than a fine summer's day? Anything more beautiful than a lovely spring or autumn day? Anything more beautiful than a fine winter's day?

I have been able to travel through the United States and practically the whole world. I liked many places, and I must say that the fact of being Canadian meant that everywhere, without exception, yes, even in the Soviet Union, 15,000 miles from Montreal, we were always received with open arms and everywhere showered with hospitality. That warmed our hearts. In spite of all that, I am always glad to return home to Canada.

I would like to close by mentioning that my wife Paulette and I try hard at all times to give our children — who already speak the two languages almost perfectly — the great love for Canada that we are so proud to possess. We are both of the opinion that Canada is the most beautiful country in the world; it is a rare privilege and a great honour to be Canadian, and we are proud of it!

———————————— ✳ ————————————

"I Stand With Canada"
Geraldine Doucet

Geraldine Doucet pays tribute to her husband, in whose place she frequently sings "O Canada" at the Montreal Forum.

This is how I will always remember the sincerity and simplicity of the gentle man we knew as "Mr. O Canada", Roger Doucet. Not long before he died Roger spoke of his great love:

"When I sing 'O Canada' I think always of a Canada with two coasts and the two great oceans. I think of the forests and the wheat fields and the mountains. And I think of the friends I have in every province. I am a proud Canadian. To sing 'O Canada' is to say hello to my country.

"I am patriotic in the sense of being Canadian. I am proud of being from Quebec and proud of my ancestors. But if there is a stand to be taken, I stand with Canada."

When Roger loved, he loved with pride, gentleness, and tenderness. He passed these characteristics on to me and our three sons and, I hope, to all those who came into contact with him or felt his sense of dedication.

---- ✳ ----

Alberta Student in Montreal

Kim Archer-Larson

Recent student at Bowness High School in Calgary, who participated in the Montreal–Calgary student exchange programme that encountered and solved language problems.

Horizons were broadened and new insights into French–English relations in Canada were gained during a student exchange between my Bowness High School in Calgary and Jeanne-Mance School in Montreal, arranged to help each student learn the other's language and culture.

For many of our fourteen- to sixteen-year-old Montreal French-speaking guests, it was their first visit outside Quebec. It was something of a shock to them, even though they had been warned in advance, actually to experience another part of Canada where almost no one could speak French.

Misunderstanding caused an unfortunate incident. Some Quebec students began smoking in our lunchroom as they were used to doing at their Montreal school, not aware of the strict no-smoking rules at Bowness. A few very rude Calgary boys booed them. Our guests were bewildered and hurt.

One host parent over-reacted and press reports of the incident went into headlines in Quebec and other parts of Canada. Shortly afterwards, students at Bowness tried to give a correct impression of our school to the press by signing up nearly every student and many parents on the People to People Petition for Canada Unity — a total of 1,500 — but, unfortunately, no reports of that were carried in Quebec or in the national press.

After the initial shock had faded somewhat, all the students were called together to decide what was to be done. The French students had only been in Calgary for a short while but several of the youngest wanted to go home right then, which hurt the feelings of their respective hosts. Then several of the older students, French and English, spoke up. The person we were hosting, the eldest of the French and also the most accomplished speaker of English, pointed out that leaving was not a solution at all and that if Quebecers ran back to Quebec whenever they were opposed they would end up stuck there forever. Others expressed the same view. Someone else said that the French kids shouldn't be so quick to judge all Westerners by the actions of a few.

The talk swung around to why anyone would act as the insulting students had. It was suggested that attitudes had been passed from generation to generation both in Quebec and the West. Here, some English-speaking Canadians see everything bad as coming from the East. Some have the misconception that in some way Easterners including Quebecers are responsible for tax increases and for a myriad of other government policies that are annoying to Westerners. In the East many Quebecers have come to blame English Canada for their problems, and especially for not allowing them to speak and live in the Quebec–French tradition. It was also decided that quite likely we English students would encounter the same sort of problems when we went to Montreal. This satisfied those who were most unhappy. An uneasy sort of truce was established. Although the incident remained in the foreground of some minds for quite a while, most of us just stored it up for future consideration and went on with the business at hand, that of making some new friends and learning all we could about and from these Canadians who were quite different from ourselves. In fact, until I was reminded of it the other day, I had forgotten the entire incident.

Then came my turn to go to Quebec. What I remember most about the exchange was learning what it was like to be an average person in Montreal. I had been to Montreal once before to visit my uncle but he lived in the suburbs and was English-speaking. I had sort of expected that Nicole, my billet, and the other students lived in the same kind of house and did the same kinds of things I did at home. I was surprised by the differences, most notably by Nicki's house. It took me a while to get used to the fact that she had lived her whole life in an apartment that was only one floor high and twenty feet wide, at the most. I had to get used to the fact that that was normal for the area she lived in and probably for a good number of Montrealers. I also had to get used to speaking French, or trying to at least, because in her neighbourhood unless you at least *tried* to speak French no one listened to you. I discovered this in several downtown stores as well. It was fun, if a little trying at times, learning the French words for things. Nicki had to laugh at my accent a lot but she was very patient as a rule and we learned a lot from her mother, who spoke even less English than I did French. She was always polite and patient as I tried to explain to her what I wanted, and she made a real effort to tell me things in English.

When I went to school with Nicki I only remember attending one class, her physics class. During that class I discovered that, if I listened carefully, I could understand what was being discussed. This was partly because I had already learned what they were learning and partly because of my increasing vocabulary. It was kind of fun once I got the hang of it.

I also enjoyed a "sugar-bush" party where I must have been the only English-speaker. Trips downtown to Place Ville Marie, and to the roller-drome, were interesting and fun, as was the trip through Westmount to look at the beautiful homes of famous or rich Montrealers. Another highlight of the exchange was a hockey game we got to see (the Canadiens won of course!).

Looking back on the exchange I'm glad we were given the chance to participate. It was nice to be able to show the students what life was like in Alberta. It was also good to learn what life was like in Montreal, especially since Quebec's separatist movement was so publicized at the time. We learned a lot about why Québécois felt as they did and about what they had to offer the rest of Canada. We also learned a little bit about how we could help them to feel more a part of Canada by learning their language and understanding their customs. We learned that it is not necessary to live as they do to appreciate them for what they are.

Nicki and I still write every Christmas, and if she or her friends ever come West again they know they are welcome at my house, just as I know I am welcome in theirs.

---- ✳ ----

Quebec Student in Alberta

Michèle Auclair

High-school student in Montreal who visited Calgary on the student exchange.

When I went as an exchange student to Calgary, I was fifteen years old. I lived in Montreal and attended the Jeanne-Mance Institute, and was chosen, with twenty-eight other young people from my school, both boys and girls, to take a trip to Western Canada.

For me and my parents it was a great adventure. Miss Doyon, organizer of the trip and an English teacher, was charming and conscientious. She collected material on Western Canada to help us picture this marvellous trip we would be making, including pertinent data concerning the young people in Calgary. After studying tastes and personalities, I chose Hilary Greene. I wrote to her and sent her my picture; by return mail she sent me hers.

Three long weeks to wait before the great departure. Finally the big day arrived. I left with a heavy heart, not knowing what was in store for me. On my arrival at Calgary airport Hilary and her father welcomed me with big smiles and sympathetic handshakes. After a few words and gestures I followed them, but, as I saw that they were nice, already my discomfort was going away.

We arrived at the house; the mother and little brother welcomed me warmly. In view of the late hour, they took me to my room, which I shared with Hilary.

After a good night's sleep in a pleasant little home it was breakfast time. Hilary's mother and father did their utmost to give me what I liked; it was at this point that I really began to enjoy myself. They offered me all kinds of things — jam, peanut butter, etc. There was a great parade of containers on the table. Everyone laughed good-naturedly, for we were having trouble making ourselves understood. But what a breakfast!

During my stay I visited the great city of Calgary, which

171

is growing daily. They took me to big restaurants, to the theatre, and for car rides to show me the great panorama of the city. What a trip! How many dreams come true! What a lovely family who made me feel so welcome!

To be sure there were some unhappy people among the French Canadians. Perhaps there were also some among the English Canadians. But in what country does one not find that? Certainly with some people racial prejudice dominates, but, the great majority of times, these are people who do not understand each other.

I must say that, after a painful leave-taking, I knew the chances were very small that I would see these friends again, but I was going home with great memories, more knowledgeable about customs. I hope that exchanges like this will continue. I hope that cities, provinces, and governments will share in them, for they enrich all who participate.

I, Michèle Auclair, and my parents, thank the Greene family of Calgary for having received me so well — a young Quebec girl who will never forget her wonderful trip.

---

* —

Twin-City Mayor

Andrew S. Brandt

Ontario Cabinet Minister and former mayor of Sarnia, Ontario, twin city of Trois-Rivières, Quebec.

I served as mayor of Sarnia during the days of the Quebec Referendum, and the thought kept occurring to me that although politicians were talking a great deal about a change for Canada, little was being heard from Canadians generally.

The very thought of a Canada without Quebec disturbed me greatly. This great county of ours was founded on the principle of two cultures and two official languages. Certainly we have our problems and our difficulties, but none of the magnitude that could not be resolved by people of common sense and goodwill.

The People to People Petition for Canadian Unity, which I personally delivered to Sarnia's twin city, Trois Rivières, contained more than 10,000 signatures representing people from every walk of life in my community. Their basic message was one of willingness to listen, compromise, understand, and work together in the framework of a changing and evolving, but nevertheless united, Canada.

I believe in this country and its future, but a Canada without Quebec will be less of a nation and a Quebec without Canada will be less of an entity as well. As we look around us in these troubled times, Canada remains a country of fairness and reason. It remains a country worthy of our efforts to build it and to develop it for the future generations of Canadians to follow.

———————————— ✳ ————————————

Twin-City Mayor
Gilles Beaudoin

Mayor of Trois-Rivières, Quebec, twin city of Sarnia, Ontario.

I have had the advantage of visiting most of the provinces that make up my land of Canada. On each occasion I returned home enriched by knowledge and experience of the citizens who form Canada.

Trois Rivières, of which I have had the privilege of being mayor for more than ten years, has played a very important role in the history of my country. Being the second city founded in North America, Trois Rivières has participated in the founding of several large regions of Canada, among them the Canadian West by Pierre Gaultier de Varennes, Sieur de la Vérendrye.

Today, several big problems are rousing the Canadian people, but it is said that it is during difficulties that one sees the strength of a people. Trois Rivières will soon be 300 years old. We extend to all Canadians the invitation to visit our city and take part in the celebrations that will emphasize the strength of character of the founders.

The freedom of our citizens throughout Canada and the quality of our life are the envy of most countries of the world.

For these reasons, I am proud to be a Canadian.

---------------------------- * ----------------------------

Two Languages — Asset or Threat?
Davidson Dunton

Former president of Carleton University in Ottawa and former chairman of the CBC; co-chairman with the late André Laurendeau of the Royal Commission on Bilingualism and Biculturalism, which studied French–English relations (1963–67) and made far-reaching recommendations. Dunton evaluates progress since the commission's work.

"Canada, without being fully conscious of the fact, is passing through the greatest crisis in its history." So stated the Royal Commission on Bilingualism and Biculturalism in its preliminary report in 1965 — and aspects of the crisis still remain.

We of the commission found that most French-speaking Canadians were becoming increasingly dissatisfied with their place in Canada; that separatism was growing in Quebec; that there were misunderstandings and unnecessary antagonisms on two sides; that major changes and accommodations were badly needed if the country was to remain whole.

Later we recommended changes we believed necessary to provide a basis for a sense of equal partnership between French- and English-speaking Canadians. These included: fuller recognition of French as an official language in the federal sphere; better opportunities for Francophones to work in the federal public service using their own language and keeping their culture; the full development of French as a working language in business and industry in Quebec; possibilities for education in their own language for francophones of other provinces where numbers warrant, similar to provisions for anglophones in Quebec; and adoption of French as an official language in New Brunswick and Ontario. We also thought there should be constitutional discussion taking into account the desire of many francophones to control many affairs of their own society.

Much has been done since the B & B report, but some misunderstandings, aggravations, and problems remain.

The federal Parliament, with all three major parties concurring, passed the Official Languages Act. The federal government took major steps to improve service to citizens in French where required and to increase the use of French and the number of francophones in the public service. Some of the efforts, unfortunately, were clumsy, and misapprehensions grew in some parts of the country. Great prominence was given to French-language training, but much less to the development of units in the service in which French would be a main language of work, as the commission recommended. Pitiable stories were spread about poor middle-aged public servants being *forced* to take French courses (and these free! in time off from work!).

Some people in English-speaking Canada got the idea that the federal public service was being made into a sort of French preserve. That, of course, was nonsense. Even today the proportion of francophones in upper ranges of the public service is well below their proportion of the total population. French is still in an unfairly subordinate position as a language of work in most areas. The bulk of jobs are still held by unilingual people. And it surely is not unreasonable to expect that for fairness and efficiency senior officers be able to read reports and understand submissions from subordinates and colleagues in the other language.

The pre-eminence of French as a working language in Quebec has been asserted strongly since the commission report, as is natural in a province that is more than eighty per cent francophone. Certain aspects of the Parti Québécois Language Charter appear overly severe and one hopes they will be modified in the future; but even with them the position of the anglophone minority in Quebec is in general actually better than that of francophone minorities in other provinces.

Major changes have occurred over the same time elsewhere. New Brunswick declared itself officially bilingual, has taken many steps to make this decision effective, and has provided wide facilities for education in French for its large Acadian minority (considerably larger in proportion than the anglophone minority in Quebec).

Ontario has steadfastly refused to make French an official provincial language, but has very substantially developed education for francophones. It has also moved, although slowly, in providing some government services and documents in French, and in provisions for some courts that can operate in French.

Manitoba has been found by the courts to have French as one of its official languages under the terms of its entry into Confederation, and is taking some steps to recognize the fact. It and other provinces have improved possibilities for education with French as a medium of instruction in some areas.

The proportion of high-school students studying French has, unfortunately, declined with looser programme requirements, but French immersion programmes in elementary schools have blossomed in many provinces in some cases beyond the ability of the educational system to meet the requests of English- and French-speaking parents.

In matters of language and education in general the balance of fairness between the anglophone and the francophone communities in Canada is much better than it was fifteen years ago, although all that is desirable has not been accomplished. Equity would be much more apparent, for example, if Ontario with the largest francophone minority outside of Quebec made the move, a move more dramatic than substantial, to accept French as an official language.

And the changes have been of no discernible harm to any groups, nor have they created any overly burdensome costs. A French sign in a federal park in the West hurts no one — but think of the delight of a visitor from Quebec who sees his language recognized.

Francophones do not expect to be served in French or to be able to use French wherever they go in the country. They know that huge areas are effectively unilingual, as are many parts of Quebec in reverse, but they appreciate the availability of French from national agencies.

A main expense for the federal government has been language training, and this is being reduced and has constituted a free educational benefit for a number of people. Provinces have been generously compensated by federal subsidies for minority education and second language teaching. And many people in other provinces forget that for generations Quebec maintained a full and excellent education system for its English minority without outside financial help.

It is in no way a matter of making Canada bilingual in the sense that nearly everyone would be expected to know the two official languages. Rather it is a question of "equilingualism" — of fairness between French- and English-speaking populations, taking into account diverse circumstances across the country.

Sometimes Canadians whose origins were in countries other than Great Britain and France say they feel demeaned by all the talk of two official languages and fair partnership between two groups. A number are, quite naturally, concerned about preserving their own languages and cultural heritages. But those concerns are of a different order. The commission was well aware of the concerns of other groups and appreciating their contribution to Canadian life. We recommended efforts to maintain other languages and cultures. But it saw the immediate peril to the country was in the relationship between the large English-speaking society, which such a multiplicity of cultural backgrounds and the smaller but more homogeneous one, centred in Quebec, which for reasons of history, concentration, and size is so important.

In short, it is not a question of the two founding peoples negotiating. It is a matter of two co-existing societies. History has willed Canadians a magnificent inheritance in its two main languages and two chief cultural streams, along with the valued contributions of others.

The legacy of duality offers special richness to the life of our country and strength to its place in the world; it also presents a continuing test to us, the inheritors. Can we develop and maintain over the long run mutually satisfying relations between the mass of Canadians who use English mostly in their daily lives and those who use French?

It is not easy. Francophones, a majority in what was Canada until nearly the middle of the past century, have become a decided minority in the larger Canada that has evolved. They have kept their strong majority position in their bastion of Quebec, but nearly a fifth of their number live elsewhere in the country. And anglophones in Quebec continue to outnumber the populations of several other provinces.

But it is not just numbers that matter. Practically all francophones have a strong sense of belonging to a distinct people, with its own language, history, and culture. In Quebec their society, complete in many ways, has been firmly established and operating for more than 300 years — well over three times as long as, for example a White society in Alberta. They are proud, with reason, of what they have done, what they are, and what they want to continue to be.

For a time in the spring of 1980 it appeared that Canada might well be on the verge of breaking up as the campaign for the Quebec Referendum opened. But on May 20, a majority of the people of the province — francophones by a slim margin — decided that they wanted to continue trying to work out their aspirations within Canada.

But the danger of a break is still alive. What can English-speaking Canadians do to guard against a renewed threat of a break? I believe we have to make manifest in real terms a belief that the partner francophone community, while not equal in numbers, has an equality in worth. We have to show respect for French language and culture — and fairness — by giving francophones outside Quebec language and education rights consistent with equitable rights for the English-speaking minority in Quebec. We must welcome francophones, while expecting them to keep their own language and culture, into national institutions, both public and private. We must accept that the majority in Quebec handles its own affairs to the greatest extent practicable within the limits of the real needs of the federal system.

The secret of success in a situation such as Canada's is that the majority be willing to make a strong effort to be fair to the minority. A majority has its own natural security; a minority tends to feel threatened unless it has firm assurances, and clear manifestations, of its acceptance.

In return, the majority should be able to expect loyalty on the part of the smaller group to the integrity of the whole country. The prospects of this loyalty now seem good, if we anglophones do our part.

Since May 20, 1980, the wave of extreme Quebec nationalism seems to have abated, and many francophones appear to have a new confidence in the place of their language and culture, in the possibilities of a full life as a people within Canada, and in accomplishing many things while remaining fully themselves in both public and private sectors. With that confidence should come a growing belief in a fair, productive, and honoured place in the Canada of tomorrow, and a readiness to participate fully in building a greater and better country.

The dangers to realizing Canada's great potential come not from outside but from what we Canadians think and feel about each other, whether we usually speak English or French. If we forge and maintain a fair and full partnership we can make one of the noblest countries of the world. I believe we will.

A State of Mind

Gilles Caouette

Radio talk-show host, Rouyn, Quebec; former political leader and son of the late Réal Caouette, MP and co-leader of the National Social Credit party.

When I was in politics, I had the pleasure of travelling all across Canada, from coast to coast. I have met true Canadians but I have also met narrow-minded people.

When I hear someone complaining because there is French or English on a Corn Flakes box, I feel sorry. Are these same people returning their Japanese TV because the operation manual is printed in French, English, German, and Spanish?

Being Canadian is a state of mind. I did not choose to be born in the northern part of Quebec from a Roman Catholic French family with white parents. Not a single one of us human beings has chosen his roots. Some have chosen to come to Canada, but that does not give them or give us who are Canadian-born any superiority nor inferiority. But together we certainly can keep building our country by respecting the rights of everyone.

So Much to Lose

Gordon Robertson

Chairman of the Institute for Research in Public Affairs in Ottawa and former clerk of the Privy Council and secretary to the Cabinet; a native of Alberta.

It is important for all of us, and especially for any in Quebec or the West who might wonder if Canada is worth maintaining, to appreciate how much works well in our federation and how greatly we have profited from its existence.

Each of our governments, federal and provincial, is based on the parliamentary, responsible system. In whole, it is one of the best democratic systems ever developed. The governments operate within a federal structure that gives great powers to the provincial units — powers to ensure effective expression of the differing characteristics and wishes of the great variety of peoples and tongues that is the nature of this gigantic country. With the marriage of federalism and the parliamentary system Canada has become one of the freest and most secure countries on earth. We have also become a community within which equality of opportunity, protection of rights, security against disability and ill-health, and provision for the individual from birth are among the best in the world.

What is incumbent on all Canadians is to ask whether our problems and discontents are really so serious that they should be allowed to make us incapable of the co-operation and compromise on which our success rests. Many Québécois are frustrated and resentful in the aftermath of patriation of the Constitution. There is no cause to think, however, that the lack of a formal veto on amendment will really impair Quebec's capacity to protect its vital interests within Canada. Other means can and will be found, if necessary. And as a part of Canada, Quebec will have the space, the economic strength, and the support of a great federation.

The solution to our basic problem was never really in constitutional change, desirable though some aspects of it may be. The vital changes are of another kind and are happening. The Canada of today is not the Canada of twenty years ago. "English Canada" is more understanding of Quebec's rights and interests than ever before and more generous toward the French fact that is so vital a part of Canada. It is more concerned to ensure that rights are protected and that discrimination should end. And Quebec is more French than ever before.

Consideration of the West's need for better representation in Ottawa is also under sympathetic consideration.

The twenty-first century may see a more prosperous world or it may well see a more difficult and dangerous one. Whichever it is, a strong, federal Canada will provide security and opportunity far beyond what would be possible for any part of Canada alone. No delay in the pace of change should lead us to risk the loss of the great achievement that is our federation. Patience, co-operation, compromise: these we will need. What we already have is too good to put at risk in frustration or in pessimism — or in the unrelenting pursuit by any group or region of its own interests and special concerns to the detriment of the whole of Canada.

Quebec's New Managers

Pierre Laurin

Executive with the Aluminium Company of Canada in Montreal; former director of the École des Hautes Études Commercial at the University of Montreal.

Canada represents for me an extended area for the expression of increasing power at a moment when Quebec francophones are expressing an unprecedented acclaim in their economic skills. Canada embodies the opportunity to work out, on a continent without borders, the stimulating expertise that we are developing daily in financial tools, transport organizations, and technology. I am thinking at the same time of this possibility of extending the Quebec market without crossing borders, as an economic springboard that gives entrance to the international scene.

I feel myself to be intensely Québécois and my identity is strongly rooted in my French Canadian culture. That is why I subscribe to the increasing march of Quebec towards control of the guaranteed political tools of our survival and unique development.

But my deepest bond with Quebec is a centrifugal force. Far from nourishing a defensive trend, it constitutes a force, a solid base, upon which I want to spread out and enrich myself by many encounters. I have the clear impression, in expressing these feelings, of reuniting a rising generation of Quebecers, imbued with a new assurance and a growing conviction that they are capable of competing in a healthy rivalry with anyone in Canada. Canada thus becomes a privileged arena for the expression of a new dynamism, of a push, an "opening up" made possible by a recently acquired cultural security and impregnated by the ever-vibrant spirit of the peaceful revolution.

To me, however, Canada is not only the cold territory of economic expression. The privileged relationship that the absence of borders brings gives the opportunity to weave further relationships that fundamentally reunite the human element across the land. Too often, indeed, Quebec francophones have felt themselves dominated by what was coming from elsewhere in Canada. The new self-confidence in Quebec brings Western encounters to a more equal footing, from which truly warm relations would necessarily be born. The relationships I have developed a little here and a little there across the country allow me to envision such a picture of Canada.

---------------------- ✳ ----------------------

Welcomed Everywhere
Gustav Gingras

Founder of the world-renowned Montreal Rehabilitation Institute, recent chancellor of the University of Prince Edward Island, and past president of the Canadian Medical Association; now resides in Monticello, Prince Edward Island.

My Canadian ancestry reaches back to the earliest days of French colonization. Most of my life's work has been in Quebec. Recently I retired to a seaside home on Prince Edward Island with my wife, a native Islander. My country is Canada.

Forty years of travel from the Atlantic to the Pacific and in more than thirty countries in the service of my profession and my speciality — the rehabilitation of disabled persons — have given me rich opportunities to meet and work with my fellow citizens everywhere. Never has my French Canadian background been a barrier to my activities and to my making friends in English Canada. This has not changed today as I travel across our land to secure and assure aid for our disabled fellow citizens. Possibly I am even better received than when I was president of the Canadian Medical Association. This, in spite of the Referendum, in spite of Western alienation, and in spite of "Common Canadian Complaints", a well-known national endemic disease. I have been and I am still welcomed in Edmonton or Halifax as warmly as I am in Montreal or Quebec.

It was my privilege to attend the needs of the wounded, shattered, and sick Canadian servicemen during the battles of World War II as a young medical officer, fresh out of the medical school of the Université de Montreal. No barriers of race, language, creed, politics, or colour ever divided my colleagues and me. Our unique and common links were to succour our brothers in arms, stop the spread of tyranny, and serve our country. In modern times new young Canadian heroes have emerged. They are soldiers of peace; to name only one — Terry Fox!

No doubt my profession and my knowledge of English were helpful resources. After the war, the late Professor Wilder Penfield of the Montreal Neurological Institute, one of the world's greatest neurosurgeons, urged me to enter the field of rehabilitation. Penfield was responsible for early experimental studies demonstrating that children who learn two or more languages early in life develop a higher level of intellectual capability than those who do not.

We are indeed privileged in Canada to enjoy a dual-language country. It is for me a source of great satisfaction to note that French immersion courses are springing up rapidly in the early grades of schools in all parts of English Canada. I am fully aware also of the large number of parents in Quebec who are anxious for their children to become proficient in English.

Quebec no more is behind other provinces in the field of education. Young men and women of Quebec emerge from first-class universities, colleges, and schools with superb professional, technical, and artistic training in all areas of human endeavours. They have pride and confidence in their capabilities and their province. Their ideal is to succeed. They will.

Belonging to Canada, they will find great benefits, as I have, to working in other parts of our great country and from giving to and gaining from other Canadians.

Excellence and goodwill are respected all over the world. It is also a law of life, as well as a common observation in biology, that diversity provides strength. This is a truth that holds for a nation, too.

If I had to face a new beginning, if I were in a position to make a free choice to live and work in any country in the whole world, without hesitation it would be Canada.

7

✳---

Native Perceptions

---------------- * ----------------

Me, a Canadian?

Alootook Ipellie

Editor of *Inuit Today*; author and artist from Baffin Island and
Ottawa.

Where I grew up there was no such place as Canada. I
knew no Canada. I had never heard of it. My elders never
mentioned Canada because they did not know Canada
existed either. Later in life, I found out that I had been
born in Canada, raised in Canada, and lived in Canada.
Why did I not know about this place? Had the existence
of Canada been censored in our land? I found the answers
to these questions soon enough.

I was born in a small hunting camp on Baffin Island
where my elders lived off the land. They had never heard
anything about the outside world. Survival was a daily
preoccupation when food was scarce, and they travelled
from one hunting camp to the next in search of game.
The Arctic was a hard land to live on but it was part of
their lives and the only place they knew how to exist in.
The land and the animals were sacred to them. Even if
someone had told them they could lead easier lives in
the cities and towns south of their land, they simply could
not have survived there, or for a very short time only.
Their upbringing had taught them to follow the traditions
of their ancestors, and that was the only real life they
knew. In earlier times, Canada did not exist for their
ancestors although they walked on it every day.

I was brought up in the tradition of our ancestors. I
suffered the hard days along with my elders when the
hunters from our camp did not bring back any animals
after being away for days at a time. And when food became plentiful, I rejoiced with my elders. We suffered
when there was a lack of food and rejoiced when there
was plenty of food. Life went on like this in our part of
the world from day to day, week to week, month to
month, and year to year. Food meant survival. The land
provided the food and this land happened to be Canada.

When I was about eight years old, I went to school for the first time. I did not know a word of English then. Our teacher was a Qallunaaq (White) who spoke no Inuktitut, my mother tongue. She was more alien to me than I was to her. She had been sent to our land to teach and tell us about a whole new world we didn't know about. She taught us the language she spoke, and soon after that first year of school I heard her say the word "Canada" for the very first time. She then explained to us the history of Canada and how it began.

One thing I didn't understand at first was when she told me I was a resident of Canada and that I was a Canadian. Me, a Canadian? As long as I could remember I had been brought up as an Inuk first and foremost, and here was this teacher telling me otherwise. When she explained that I was an Inuk as well as a Canadian, I relaxed.

As I grew up and learned more about Canada and what it stood for, I became proud to be called a Canadian. Canada, I found out, respected my freedom to express myself through speech and civil liberties. This was important to me then and is today.

Canada is one of the few countries in the world that can say it has living in it a group of people who, through sheer determination and will to live, have survived for thousands of years on a land that tried to starve them out during its many fierce winters and brought them face to face with death and the possibility of extinction almost every day. Their survival speaks of hearts of steel.

The history of the Inuit is so long it surpasses human memory, although we do have some idea of where they came from. As the original people of Canada, they are in one sense "hosts" to all the nationalities who have settled in Canada and become Canadian citizens. Since Canada respects the cultural heritage of the Inuit and the freedom they enjoy, to live as they please, the Inuit have accepted the invitation to be called Canadians. By choosing to accept one another and live side by side, both benefit. Brother to brother, they are stronger today.

Without this sense of belonging to one another, we cannot hope to have a strong Canada.

Indian Voice

Jean Folster

Magistrate of Norway House, Manitoba; twice elected chief of the Norway House Band of Indians, a Cree tribe; first woman chief in Manitoba.

I am proud that Canada is my birthplace. I cherish this land of freedom where I find peace and sweet contentment and the knowledge that it will always be my home. It is a place where all of us have freedom of choice in religion, speech, and language. It is where other people who are less fortunate have come to start a new beginning. It gives one a deep, heartfelt feeling that we, as Canadians, live harmoniously with people from other countries as brothers and sisters.

It also gives me great pleasure to know that Canada has a lot of heroes both in the past and present. People such as Joe Keeper, an Indian from Norway House who ran a marathon in Sweden in the early 1900s. Iona Weenusk, who died in a plane crash with other Indian students twelve years ago, and Terry Fox, a young White person who stole the hearts of many Canadians. He taught us that nothing is impossible. Even though we never saw Terry in Manitoba, there will always be a special place in our hearts for him, along with the others.

Progress is a very good thing but it also saddens one's heart and mind that pollution is slowly destroying our once wealthy land. It was once the basis of an Indian's livelihood where we obtained food for our families, food that was very nourishing to an Indian person. But I guess we cannot always have both as progress heightens.

But there are many problems, and we should not avoid them. In the past, Indian children who have left their homes have been adopted by families all over Canada and outside of Canada. I think it is time that Indian people look after our own kind. It is better that we keep our children in our reserves. It's about time we have a say in the future of our own children. I speak from knowledge. I am a grandmother with four daughters and four sons, fifteen grandchildren, and two great-grandchildren.

I am doing something myself. I belong to a group of Indian grandmothers who have started to take action. When an Indian child is forced to leave his home, we immediately meet the child and investigate the situation. The child is first placed in a good Indian home. Then we go back and meet the parents and try to help them improve their situation so that the child can go back to its own family. Last year, nearly fifty children went back to their own homes through our group.

I believe that we Indians, as well as other Canadians, must always solve our problems within the borders of Canada. No matter what happens, Canada will always be cherished in my heart.

A Métis States His Case

Don McIvor

President of the Manitoba Métis Federation.

I am a Canadian first and a Métis second. Some of my people get angry at me for saying this. But if everybody isn't a Canadian first, we cannot keep the country together. It is just damn foolishness to think that the Métis or any of the different racial groups could prosper if Canada broke up into a lot of little countries.

Being Canadian is the one thing we all have in common. If we only think of our own ethnic background, we can't have a country, and if we don't have unity in Canada, we won't be able to keep our freedom. We have to work together, whether we like it or not. But we don't all have to be the same to get along in the world.

I am damn proud of being a Métis. I have worked all my life to encourage the culture of my people and I will fight for their needs as I have for many years. Most Métis have Indian and French backgrounds. My ancestors are Indian and Scottish. They hunted buffalo and trapped beavers on the Indian side, traded furs on the Scottish side, and as Métis people were great canoe paddlers and guides.

Nobody should be taught discrimination against another race. I say, take a man or woman at face value. Each race in Canada must tell others about its ways and traditions. Part of the trouble in Canada is a lack of knowledge and appreciation of each other. Even a new Cabinet Minister in my own province did not know what a Métis was. He learned fast. If each racial group works hard at telling its own story, there will be more understanding, less prejudice, less injustice.

Canada lets everyone keep his traditions. We never have to lose our ethnic identity. That's a great privilege, a helluva lot better than most countries allow. I have learned that all of us are the same under the skin. We are humans. I carry on the Métis traditions but I get along okay in White society, although sometimes my people are rejected by both Whites and Indians. I tell my people that we have to get off our butts to help ourselves instead of always depending on the government. In the North, where most Métis live, there are lots of forests, lots of wood. We should try to forest it, make lumber, build and heat our own houses from it, and sell our extra products. There are lots of lakes for fishing and room for trapping, so we shouldn't need welfare if we can use our resources.

I learned about education the hard way. I stopped at grade four; I didn't think schooling was necessary. As a result, I have had to work very hard for thirty-six years. Now I tell my children and their friends that they must keep going to school if they want to have a better life.

My goal is to help all my people raise their standard of living and to do it in co-operation with all other races. What a great country Canada is where we have a chance to do this.

———————————— * ————————————

The Land Is Alive
Oliver Brass

A Cree, and twice a member of the Band Council of the Pee-peekisis Reserve in Saskatchewan, Oliver Brass is an assistant professor at the Saskatchewan Indian Federated College, University of Regina, a pastor, and director of Native Ministries for the Free Methodist Church in Canada.

Canada is a land intertwined with my soul. The land and I belong to each other. My ancient forebears' spirits lovingly haunt the forests, the rivers, and the plains. Their ancient flesh has long since been reunited with the land and today provides nourishment for my body and encouragement for my soul.

The land is alive. Sometimes as I lie on my back by a forest lake or on a lonely prairie hill, time and space become transcended and I feel total union with the ancient land and all my ancestral family. I was born here. I wish to die here and become once again one with the land.

Canada is also a political entity of nineteenth-century vintage. As a state founded upon democratic ideals, it has provided me with opportunities to fulfil a good deal of my human potential. I am a Canadian both by birth and by choice. I've been to other countries of the world; this is the best one. Socially, politically, economically, spiritually, and professionally, Canada has afforded me opportunities limited only by my ideas and exertion. I would gladly give my life for Canada as did both my grandfathers.

As I traverse Canada in all directions, I have discovered that I feel a deep brotherhood with all Canadians — all kinds and shapes, the left and the right, the urban and the rural, the good, the bad, and the ugly. My people all. I am proud.

Tributes to Chief Dan George

Chief Dan George

Following are tributes to the late Chief Dan George of British
Columbia, along with a few of his own personal statements
about Canada. Deeply respected by his people and other Canadians, he was an author and actor appearing in films and on
television here and in the U.S.

From *The Globe and Mail*, Toronto, in an editorial, September 24, 1981:
One man alone could never hope to erase the image of
the North American Indian that was shaped in the rip-
roaring rubbish of early Hollywood westerns. There were
just too many references to forked tongues and scalpings,
too many whooping encirclements of wagon trains, too
many timely arrivals by the U.S. Cavalry.

And yet, the soft, husky voice and compelling, simple
wisdom of Chief Dan George dissolved much of it. He
died quietly in a Vancouver hospital yesterday — it was
characteristic of him to go gently — having done much
to educate us all on the philosophy and capabilities of
Indians.

He would then turn around and try to persuade his
Indian brothers to change their thinking. He did not want
to dwell in the past. He told them the Indian would never
return to campfire and forest because "that which he
seeks is no longer there."

From *Jean Folster*, twice chieftan, Cree Tribe, Norway
House, Manitoba:
Chief Dan George . . . reminded me of my very old and
very respected grandfather when he was alive. There was
something awesome, majestic, and intelligent about both
men when they talked about the past, present and the
future.

In Chief Dan George, one could feel the very presence
of love, warmth and understanding by just looking at
him and hearing him speak. . . . He set a great example

for the Indian community and gave us pride in ourselves. He sought love not violence, effort not hate.

From *Don McIvor*, Manitoba Métis leader:
Chief Dan George taught us to revive and revere our Indian traditions and made us proud of having Indian ancestry.

From radio station CJOR, which on the morning of Chief Dan George's death in Vancouver presented the text of a radio talk given some years earlier by the chief:
Regardless of colour, race, creed, or religion, we are all brothers here on this earth. That means integration should work, and with integration working, both sides, we should meet each other half-way. That is the problem today of our children — integration. The culture of the white people is just as different between the Indian and the White man as it is between the Chinese and the Scotch. Their cultures are different in the same way, and a lot of our children are not used to this kind of life. They have their own way of living and their own way of talking, and so on. Integration makes it kind of hard for them until they become used to it and then they'll all be brothers, regardless of race or colour. One of these days every person in Canada will be a Canadian.

Chief Dan George on the occasion of the campaign of the People to People Petition for Canadian Unity:
I call on all of my peoples and all the peoples of British Columbia and of Canada to reach out a hand of friendship to the people of Quebec by signing this petition to make us a better Canadian family.

8

---*---

The Oppressed Find a Home

Heaven Was the Word for Canada
Martin Luther King Jr.

The late leader of modern Blacks in the United States once spoke on the CBC about the significance of Canada for slaves in the pre-Civil War U.S. and about their secret code words.

Deep in our history of struggle for freedom, Canada was the North Star. The Negro slave, denied education, dehumanized, imprisoned on cruel plantations, knew that far to the North a land existed where a fugitive slave, if he survived the horrors of the war, could find freedom. The legendary *underground railroad* started in the south and ended in Canada. Our spirituals . . . were often codes. We sang of "heaven" that awaited us, and the slave masters listened in innocence, not realizing that . . . Heaven was the word for Canada and the Negro sang of the hope that his escape on the underground railroad would carry him there. One of our spirituals, "Follow the Drinking Gourd", in its disguised lyrics contained directions for escape. The gourd was the big dipper and the North Star to which its handle pointed gave the celestial map that directed flight [at night] to the Canadian border. (From "Conscience for Change", by Martin Luther King Jr., published by CBC Enterprises, 1967.)

Grandson of a Slave
George F. McCurdy

Executive director of the Nova Scotia Human Rights Commission and former labour leader; a sixth-generation Black in North America, descended from American slaves.

My maternal grandmother, Susan Holton, was born a slave in Kentucky. She was only fifteen months old when her family, including mother and brother, arrived in Cincinnatti, Ohio, just before the start of the U.S. Civil War. For the price of one dollar they received their family "Deed of Emancipation", which was obtainable in Ohio by that time. Together, in 1858, the family quickly travelled along the middle-western line of the famous Underground Railway, taken from secret hiding place to hiding place at night, leading from Cincinnatti to Amherstburg, Ontario, Canada, and freedom!

I can, vicariously, feel the pain, suffering, and humiliation of that dehumanizing system of slavery, in the frame of reference of a third-generation descendant not that far removed from an evil slave system designed to reduce a person to a thing and rob Black men and women of their self-respect and self-esteem.

My family's carefully preserved "Deed of Emancipation", signed in the year of escape, has motivated a long-standing family covenant to exercise fully the rights of Canadian citizenship and resist strenuously prejudice, discrimination, or second-class citizenship:

". . . In consideration of One Dollar to me paid by the said Susan Holton for herself and for her said children, the receipt of which I do hereby acknowledge and for divers other good causes and considerations to me thereunto moving. I do hereby emancipate set free and discharge from all and every claim whatever of servitude and slavery the said Susan Holton and her said two children — free persons and as such entitled to all the rights, privileges and immunities of free persons of colour, in the United States, and elsewhere, and as that any and every child or children that may hereafter be born of the body of the said Susan Holton and Laura Dorcas Holton."

Slavery was also a sad chapter in early Canadian history over a 200-year period. Slavery was first recorded in New France in 1628, only twenty years after that settlement was founded and only nine years after the first Africans were landed as slaves in Virginia in 1619. Matthew De Costa was the first Black person to come to Canada, with the DeMont expedition that founded Port Royal, Nova Scotia, in 1605.

Although the British Empire was still committed to

maintain the institution of slavery, American slaves and freed men joined the British forces against the U.S. Colonial Rebellion, because of the desire to leave the condition of slavery and the pervasive perception of the British as committed to the cause of freeing the American slave. Hundreds of American slaves, property of the United Empire Loyalists who had to leave the States after the Rebellion, were, however, *not* granted their freedom upon arrival in Canada.

The transition to freedom was first discernible in 1828 when the Executive Council of Lower Canada issued a statement that invited fugitive slaves to Canada in defiance of the U.S.: "The state of slavery is not recognized by the law of Canada, nor does the law admit that any man can be the property of another. Every slave, therefore, who comes into the Province is immediately free whether he has been brought in by violence or entered of his own accord."

The Imperial Act of London's Parliament in 1833 technically brought slavery to an end in Canada, and in the rest of the British Empire.

So, in reality, society has been conditioned to think of Blacks as slaves, and our greatest struggle has been against the myth of inferiority, which has been difficult for us, for racism has been buried deep in our country's customs, institutions, and psyche, producing a tendency towards prejudice and discrimination.

Black Canadians have, in spite of the historic barriers, helped build this nation, dreamed its dreams, contributed to its greatness, and felt the weight of its failures. Observably, Black men and women have achieved in politics, law, education, medicine, religion, and business. Black Canadians can relate to the poignant statement attributed to Arthur Haley, author of *Roots*: "The evolution from slaves into a family with education, dignity, and freedom symbolizes the sheer drama of America. We need to tell this story."

Direct responsibility for the enforcement and administration of human rights legislation, as executive director of the Nova Scotia Human Rights Commission, and promotion of the national human rights goals of freedom, justice, and equality of opportunity for all Canadians, seems a fitting role for me, a sixth-generation Black Canadian who has been close to the tough cutting edge of Canadian life.

✳

The Mennonite Covenant

Walter E. Kroeker

A Mennonite farmer and entrepreneur from Winnipeg and Winkler, Manitoba.

It was a cold winter afternoon. I remember it well, though more than two-score years have since passed. We were comfortably ensconced in the living-room of my wife's parental home, an oak log crackling in the oil-drum heater, the conversation desultory and lagging.

Apropos of nothing in particular, my father-in-law exclaimed, "Walter, I am a better Canadian than you are!" The unqualified assertion commanded full attention. I was, after all, a second-generation Manitoba-born citizen; he had but recently attained naturalization and still conversed with me in German, if not by necessity, certainly by preference. After a dramatic pause he continued, "I *chose* Canada to be my home, you are a Canadian simply by accident of birth!"

It was a new concept for me, and we debated it at length that day. We talked about flag-waving patriotism, about conscientious upbuilding of our nation, and the difference between them. We argued the concept of a national family and cultural distinctives. By the time we ended the discussion I had been taught by this wise and insightful recent immigrant a good basic course in the elements of Canadian citizenship.

My Mennonite grandparents settled in Manitoba in 1876. They came from the Southern Ukraine, where the religious freedom promised to their forebears by the Empress Catherine was suddenly denied them. Canada, eager for settlers, gave them the covenants they sought to practise their beliefs freely. The destination on the prairie frontier was thought by these new immigrants to be but another wayfarers' pause in the seemingly endless quest for a permanent home that began in mid-sixteenth century for the Anabaptist Christian followers of Menno Simons. But the wayfarers' pause did indeed become a permanent home.

Canada has been good to our people. Promises were scrupulously honoured. The Mennonites for their part contributed to their new homeland in their pioneer development of frontier land, in agricultural innovations, increasing flocks and herds, feeding many with the abundance from their fields, raising sons and daughters trained to a sound work ethic, a sturdy independence of outlook and action, to give rather than receive, to build rather than destroy.

The Mennonites are but one of the many religious–ethnic groups from various parts of the world that have found in Canada a true homeland. All in their own distinctive way have immeasurably enriched this uniquely multicultural nation. Many have not found, nor even searched for, the words explicitly to express the appreciation and love that lie deep in their hearts. But their lives and their actions are more eloquent than words. The great majority have brought to Canada a willingness to work with others in making our democratic processes more meaningful and more effective. The understanding tolerance of other Canadians has permitted and even encouraged these groups to retain the distinctives of tradition, language, and culture; the interaction and interplay of many diverse cultures has greatly enriched our society.

One of Canada's great strengths, then, has been the melding of its many dissimilar cultures into a nation. Certainly we have our problems. We do not always behave as a nation should. Few nations do. But as we continue to live by the principle that citizenship — being a good *Canadian* — is not the privileged accident of birthplace but an achievement of constructive goodwill, we can proceed with confidence and assurance to the great future of our nation.

German POW Returns

Ed Billet

A German who fell in love with Canada while a Prisoner of War here, eventually settling in Thorold, Ontario.

When I look back over my life I realize more and more that my feelings about Canada may differ from those of others.

I was born in England of a French father and a German mother. When my father died my mother moved back to her native Germany, where I experienced the Depression of the 1920s, followed by an extended decade of Nazi supremacy, during which things changed at a frightening speed. Individual freedom was exchanged for a certain affluence, Christianity for Teutonism.

When I was drafted into Hitler's army in 1938 and my ailing mother lost her sole bread-winner, the German war machine was getting ready for its thrust across Europe. The prevailing atmosphere in Germany was fright, excitement, and national chauvinism. Although I was engulfed by the first two feelings, I experienced no patriotism, as I still felt estranged in a country that was not mine by birth; but by the same token, I also had lost all emotional ties to England, where I was born.

The war that followed a year later took me from Holland, Belgium, and France to the Balkan countries, Crete and, towards the end of 1941, to the North African desert. By that time I had served with an anti-tank unit and the ski troopers and was finally posted to the Africa Corps. Each transfer was preceded by an early promotion; my military skill was recognized, yet I was not considered fully the Prussian-type soldier that appealed to my superiors. I was different. On December 23, 1941, I was slightly wounded in battle and taken prisoner south of Benghasi. After spending months in the transit camps of Alexandria, Cairo, Palestine, Suez, and South Africa, I was among the thousands of POW's who reached Canada in the summer of 1942.

My first impression of Canada was awe — awe for the vastness of the land and its abundance of natural products and resources. As a soldier I had come to know not only Central Europe but also the Middle East and North and South Africa; but I had never experienced sheer boundlessness blessed with untold natural richness. As time went by, the environment of my past shrank within my memory and the environment to which I was exposed made its indelible imprints on my mind. When I was finally able to exchange my base camp for a lumber camp in North-western Ontario and my dream of roaming the vast open spaces of God's country came true, a feeling of belonging began to grow inside of me until it became a bond between me and the country that now held me captive in more than one way.

The year 1944 saw the end of the war drawing near; sooner or later we would be sent home. I had met a Canadian girl in one of the neighbouring lumber camps with whom I had a secret relationship. I tried to stay behind and escaped, but was picked up by the RCMP.

In the fall of 1946 I was sent to England and in 1947 back to Germany. I recall travelling by train from Bremerhafen to my home near Cologne, passing the ghostly ruins of bombed-out cities and looking into the resigned faces of the hungry and the homeless. When I reached the village where we had lived before the war, I found that our house had been completely destroyed and that my mother was dead. I felt lonely beyond words and my mind went back to the days I had to spend in Canada, which in spite of incarceration had been so rich in adventure and had opened in my heart a loyalty to the country I had first perceived in awe.

I worked for the British Military Police in Germany as an interpreter and married in 1949. But all along I dreamed about Canada and tried to return. Finally, in 1951, my wife and I were among the first Germans who were able to immigrate.

We arrived in Niagara Falls with five dollars in our pockets but with the treasures of enthusiasm and perseverance. We were flexible and willing to do any work offered to us. I became a rough carpenter, a labourer, a sales clerk, and broadened my education by studying electronics at Radio College of Canada. I then put my acquired knowledge to use in the maintenance of radio and television receivers and later on worked in the industry. I retired in 1968 to devote my time to free-lance writing.

In the meantime, we had purchased land and together with a native Canadian had pioneered a subdivision by building its first two houses. We still live in one of them, although we have built and sold another one since.

My wife and I have travelled extensively and because of her family ties to Germany return there for visits often. It was during these visits that I fully realized what Canada meant to me, especially when we went to East Germany where most of my wife's family live. I was always seized by a feeling of apprehension when we crossed the heavily guarded border that separates East Germany from the Free World and isolates a country dominated by Soviet Communism, engulfed in grey despondency and oppressed by a relentless military dictatorship. But if West Germany was free and affluent in comparison, it bore for me the stigma of smallness with its population cramped into an area that did not allow them enough breathing space, creating an atmosphere filled with morbid ambition and ill will towards one another. I missed the wide open spaces and the imperturbable character so typical of Canadians. Needless to say, I was always glad to go home again.

Canada gave me fulfilment; I was able to achieve what I strove for and I still see unlimited opportunities for those who set goals and persevere. It also means security. But these gifts are worthless without an environment in which one can cultivate friendship, harmony, and goodwill and, thus, find peace and happiness. Canada gave me access to all these when it became my homeland.

Escape to Freedom
"Mr. X"

A young Chinese storekeeper living south-west of Saskatoon, Saskatchewan, who escaped from China at age fourteen. His name is not used, to protect his family in China.

The train from my home in Canton, China, got me four hours closer to Hong Kong and freedom. I hid my fear. I was only fourteen years old and trying to leave the world of Chairman Mao and everyday propaganda. Like my school friends, I did not believe it any more. The world we saw daily was too different from Communist ideas. My young cousin tried to escape three times. Each time he was caught and brought back. All his hair was shaved off and he was forced to clean streets in public disgrace. He had a bad time. Others had worse.

I slipped off the train 60 miles from the border and hid. For two nights I walked, hiding in the daylight. I swam over a river to Hong Kong. Not long afterwards I came to Canada as an immigrant. I knew nothing of Canada; no information or news about the rest of the world had been told us in China.

No one would believe the difference between two worlds, the life of a boy in China a few years ago and life in Canada. When I was nine yers old, I stole three carrots and was sent to a very bad jail for two days. There were nine people in our home; the only food for one month for one person was ten kilograms of rice, three ounces of cooking oil, eight ounces of sugar, eight ounces of meat, and no candies. During the 1961 famine we ate bamboo shoots ground with rice. I was lucky to get one new shirt a year. My Dad in China still wears a fifteen-year-old winter coat covered with patches.

The biggest problem was pressure all the time to believe the government's ideas and to fit into its plans. Five days a week I went to school from 8:00 to 12:00 in the morning. The equivalent of one day each week we were taught Communist ideas. Every student then worked at a job from 1:00 to 4:00 in the afternoon. We were then forced to study at school from 7:00 to 10:00 p.m. or attend evening meetings for propaganda or correction of bad students. Once I watched TV in a community hall instead of attending evening study. For the next three days sheets of paper were put on the walls and all of the class had to write on these papers what was wrong with me. Then I had to pick up garbage in the schoolyard for a long time.

My father and working people were forced to go to propaganda meetings nearly every night. No one could leave China without a permit, which was impossible to get. No one could go to another city or into the countryside from the city without a permit. If a farmer went to a city and was caught, he would go to jail.

The government decides where you go to school, where you work, and what you think. My cousin was sent to the country to work on a farm. Her food coupons would be stopped if she refused. The government owns all the houses renting cheaply, but in most Canton homes nine people lived in 200 square feet.

There was no way to save money. It was hard to get extra work and extra money could not be spent without a ration card. Doctors, dentists, and hospitals were, however, not expensive.

The top people were well off. Big shots had cars. Each person was forced to join a commune in the city or country, which held meetings every night so the government could control what everyone does and thinks.

I left China before the Cultural Revolution started. My sister, who stayed behind, was forced to join a youth gang for ten years. They travelled free on trains, visited towns and villages, attacking everything, robbing food and arms, fighting other gangs — no school, no learning, and no working. It was a terrible time, almost destroying China, until Mao died. Now things are better — but not good. No one is allowed to leave the country or travel, but food and work are better, and there is less propaganda.

In China there is always pressure to believe Communist ideas. You cannot say what you believe is wrong, except to closest friends or family. This is the worst thing. An eleven-year-old school friend wrote "Kill Mao" on the bathroom wall of our school and was sent to jail for two years. A middle-aged lady, a friend of the family, wrote "Kill Mao" on the wall of a public toilet in Canton and was arrested. A court was held in the street and crowds came. The policeman said she had written words in the bathroom. The crowds chanted "Go to jail" and the judge complied, sending her there for twenty years.

In Canada I work hard at what I choose. I save money. Now I own a small business. My children go to school at regular hours. Schools in Canada encourage them to say what they think. Nights, weekends, and holidays, my children are with the family, without pressures on them. We are no longer afraid to say what we think. All of my family are happy to be Canadian.

---

* ───────

Boat People

Three of thousands of Indo-Chinese refugees who came to the west speak of finding safety in Canada.

The place is cold but the people are warm.

Tu Tu Mac (Chinese)

We found some difficulties in our adaptation in the Canadian society. These difficulties, we believe, are mainly due to cultural differences. We found that Canadians are generous, open, and helpful. While the weather here is a bit severe to us, our main problem is with employment.

Khamtanh Phouthonephackdy (Laotian)

As soon as I arrived here I found that Canada is a country full of human feelings. I hope that these feelings will warm up the hearts of the wandering souls everywhere in the world and give them a ray of hope. Thank you, Canada.

Tran dinh Thu (Vietnamese)

No Longer Sad

Monica Paulse

A student at Tupper Secondary School in Vancouver, British Columbia, who came to Canada from Cape Town, South Africa.

I was too young at the time to know enough to ask why my parents were doing what thousands of others had already done. They were leaving their home, friends, and work, the three most important elements in any person's life. I vaguely remember the journey across the vast Atlantic. When we finally arrived, we were poor and homeless, but for the first time we were free. I remember that my father's eyes weren't sad anymore. He came to Canada to give his children a chance, that special chance that he had not been able to have. I don't know what it is like to live in a country of political and racial violence, and as long as I am in Canada, because of my father's decision I will not have my school, work, and social activities chosen for me.

My feelings for Canada are the same as my father's — enthusiastic and optimistic. I feel this way because my future is as a Canadian citizen, with the rights of a Canadian citizen assured. Through education I have learned about Canada politically. Canada might not be a world leader but I feel more secure living in a country that will not be the cause of war or violence.

---
*

Ocenzurowano (Censored)

Paul Ciechanowski

Of Squamish, British Columbia; a Polish Canadian student in pre-medicine at the University of British Columbia and a contemporary and classical pianist.

I recently received a letter from a favourite cousin in Poland. I recognized immediately the wanton invasion of privacy common to so many such letters we have received over the years — the stapled closing of a letter after it has been opened; the loud label "OCENZURO-WANO" (Censored).

I could predict the contents of her letter; since it passed the censor, it would be carefully structured with a backbone of forced expression, downright lies that were as important to the hope of her letter passing the censor as was the postage stamp. As usual, there was no mention of the current Polish problems, incarcerations, the riots, the food shortages, the effects of the military regime, a force the rest of the world understands.

For the first time in my life I seriously juxtaposed our separate lives in my mind and compared the freedoms, the opportunities, the sociological atmosphere we each experience from day to day.

Nearing my twenties, I am just beginning really to appreciate and understand what it is to be a Canadian: The more I contemplate these differences in our lives, the more I realize that I am proud to be a citizen of this land, genuinely proud.

I thought of the opportunities I am granted. In Canada I am only limited by my own capabilities and ambition. Whether I decide to be a carpenter, poet, doctor, or musician, the choice is in my hands and my fate or future depends on the work I invest in it. Though not totally deprived of choice, my cousin is relatively restricted in her endeavours. It is more than just a lack of opportunity. It is a lack of freedom.

I did not understand the real meaning of freedom until

recently. My cousin's letters represent a stark contrast to the freedom of expression I have for so long taken for granted. The world is mine, it seems. I am in control. Now if only there were only some way I could share with her at least a spoonful of my freedom, the lack of which she must refrain from complaining about in her letters.

In the course of our letters, my cousin and I often discuss various aspects of popular music, an art form of which we are mutually fond. In doing so, our individual contributions become unbalanced, for I have so much to tell and so much to brag about. Canada is becoming world renowned for its vibrant talented musicianship. Each year more and more young Canadian musicians advertise to the world our "large slab of land" above the U.S. (as many see us). Canadian bands such as "Doug and the Slugs", "Loverboy", "Brian Adams", have made the headlines in American and world markets.

I am also pleased that Western Canadians are beginning to follow Quebec music, which seemed difficult before because the lyrics were in French. Now the superb melodies are attracting listeners and the French words are becoming understood.

Our own music is giving many young Canadians like myself a Canadian identity and an appreciation of music that my cousin may never have a chance to develop.

I am fortunate to have been able to make these comparisons, for it has helped me achieve a personal, honest love for my country — and a love for my Canada. Now I can only hope and pray that my cousin, too, will one day live in a free country, a paradise like mine.

On this beautiful summer day as I write, I look out of my window to Mount Garibaldi, a majestic edifice, a perpetually snow-capped prima donna rising above the other peaks in contrast to the stark rock and green billowing ranges below. At the other window, the striking blue of our thirty-mile, mountain-ranged fiord, Howe Sound, stretches the imagination in another direction to the Pacific Ocean. Canada.

Girl From the Azores

Maria Franco

A Portuguese Canadian student at John Oliver Secondary School in Vancouver.

A better way of life! This is the reason many immigrants turn to Canada. This is the reason my parents came to Canada. The living standards are better and people have a chance of obtaining greater satisfaction from life. In the Azores, Portugal, we lived a life of poverty. We owned nothing but the clothes we wore and the food we grew. Even the land we farmed was not ours. We lived in a village with a population of less than 500 people. The only cars we saw were cabs from the distant city. True, we managed and no one died of starvation, but my parents wanted more for their children. So we came to the land of opportunity, Canada.

The immigrant soon realizes Canada has disadvantages as well as advantages. The main problem we have, of course, was communicating. We did not know English. We also realized that we had to work just as hard as previously. In the Old World, Canada and the United States are referred to as a haven from poverty, lack of work, and the lack of better opportunities. But cold facts and reality soon moderate these dreams.

Even though we were disillusioned with some aspects of Canadian life, in others we found happiness and contentment. We had access to many parks, stores, and friends. In the Azores, public transit is costly and does not run daily. Here, however, we can use the bus any time at an affordable cost. Here we also have the time to enjoy a pleasant afternoon, go on picnics, or just visit friends. I even have a driver's licence, which would have been impossible in the Azores. Also, I can now strive to accomplish a lifetime dream of becoming a lawyer. Back in the Azores, education is costly and there is only one university. In Canada, a person can be anything he or she desires to be. The tradition that women "belong in the kitchen" is still an integral part of many European societies.

Canada means that I can worship as I wish. Also, the Canadian system of government is much more stable than that of the Azores. In Canada a person can vote as she wishes and speak freely about political leaders. In the Azores, as well as the mother country of Portugal, one finds governments being overthrown.

I mentioned freedom of speech. Yes, I think this basic right is very important in my appreciation of Canada and in my evaluation of her meaning to me.

---

* ---

No. 1 Treatment

José Venturelli

Assistant professor at the McMaster University Medical Centre in Hamilton, Ontario, a member of the Medical Network of Amnesty International, and a refugee from Chile.

Ingred and Federico Luchsinger were in love and decided to marry. They lived in Chile. A bloody military coup occurred just about that time in September 1973.

One month after the marriage, Ingrid was kidnapped by the secret Chilean police from the hospital where she worked as a doctor. She disappeared, as was the routine in that country, and for more than three months she was taken to secret places of torture and detention. Her husband, Federico, flew to Canada and asked for political asylum.

Once here, with relatives already living in Ontario and with the support of hundreds of Canadians and many human rights organizations, he initiated a national and world-wide compaign on behalf of his wife. This pressure ended with her release by the Chilean military junta. She arrived in Canada in March 1975. The Luchsingers settled down in Hamilton, Ontario.

They had, however, only received a temporary permit to remain in the country and were facing a most upsetting threat of deportation. Thousands of Canadians again came to their support. Letters and petitions were sent to the government, finally obtaining satisfaction. Federico, thirty-nine, and Ingrid, thirty-three, now live in Mississauga, Ontario, with their two daughters, Camila, five, and Josima, six months. Ingrid is a microbiologist at the Mississauga Hospital, and Federico continues to work at Stelco in Hamilton. They continue to be concerned with human rights in different parts of the world, and with good reason. Throughout the 1970s and early 1980s more than 12,000 people arrived in Canada from Latin America.

"Canadians have shown to us that justice and freedom are deeply rooted in this country," Ingrid and Federico told me. "We have finally found peace and stability and a reassuring sense of social respect. We are thankful to all those who have helped us."

In my travels in Europe and Latin America with Amnesty International, I have visited many refugee camps. I can report, without qualification, that Canada's treatment of the refugee is second to none in the world.

As a member of the Medical Network of Amnesty, I am specifically interested in the problems of torture, this revolting political tool used by dictatorial governments around the world. The fact that Canada is trying to develop a centre for the treatment, rehabilitation, and prevention of torture tells you a great deal about the degree of respect for human lives that exists in this country.

Having come from a part of the world where dictatorships and repression have attained a massive level, I can paraphrase a French saying that was in vogue shortly after World War II. "Freedom is to hear some noises at your door at six o'clock in the morning, wake up, say to yourself, 'It's the paperboy,' and go back to sleep."

9
---*---
Food, Clothing, and Shelter

H.E. English

Professor of economics and international affairs at Carleton University in Ottawa; Canadian delegate to the Pacific Co-operation Conference.

In the case of Canada, our problems arise out of affluence; our quarrels are essentially related to varying views on how to share that affluence.

---------------------------------- ✳ ----------------------------------

First, the Land
Robert Blair

President of NOVA Corporation in Calgary, Alberta.

For me, Canada is first the land itself. Of the northern one-quarter of the globe, we "own" one-quarter and thus one-sixteenth of the earth for just over twenty-million people — nearly all of the inhabitable land from Great Britain west to Russia.

So, Canada has this immense terrain under foot and fresh and salt water in one jurisdiction. Cropland, grazing land, orchards, good bush, and useless but lovely bush, and so everything wild or cultivatable a person would ever dream of sharing as to what is nowadays called "land use".

Canada is northern. Vigorous climate and daylight change within each year. It is therefore our nature as inhabitants to strive harder, to relax more rowdily, to drink more, grumble more about government and, mainly, to each choose our own way. We shouldn't overlook the significance of our northernness: we are just placed a long, long ways from easy warmth and soft natural living. Imagine Canada's latitude boundaries as if they were in the Southern Hemisphere. Such a country would be beyond the remote southern ends of Africa, Australia,

New Zealand, and South America — on the edge of Antarctica.

No wonder, therefore, that maybe three-quarters of Canada is, and maybe always will be, occupied only by "native" people as a permanent, generation-to-generation residence, something worth thinking about.

Then, we have the people. Most of the original immigrants were looking for gain from work, and they made a good choice here. As long as that is the main social objective, our further development shouldn't go wrong. You can't, however, count on laying onto this peculiar geography every luxury or sophistication popular in Western or Eastern Europe or the United States; the land isn't entirely fit for that. Fragments of other cultures help, but a national will of Canada has to be custom created. Any individual should be welcomed to come here, or to stay here, for the admission price of recognizing that this place is different and has to act differently. That way we would also keep the admission accessible, which is good because one thing we need is a lot more people to justify retention of the size of land we are claiming as Canada.

Not that the management of Canada needs to be either crude or materialistic. Excellent transportation and communication systems have been started, and mineral and agricultural production wealth provide the basis to trade with and learn from every part of civilization. Already we can afford to use and even originate pieces of culture and the finest sciences and arts. Also, turn a Northerner loose as trader or farmer and you get a productive kind of pirate, as Scottish, Normandy, Ukrainian, and like individuals have shown throughout history.

Having a northern home is favourable to getting around internationally. It makes the people more desirous of frequent travel.

We Canadians don't have to forego anything fine in life; we just have to work out how to keep the home base as safe and attractive as possible and use it for the best. That boils down, for my short list, to land use as a skill, individual freedom as a feature, and public assistance for the dependents as a necessity. To provide the public assistance, we tend somewhat to the left in public policy. There's nowhere across Canada where our old may find year-round summer or the poor kids get by on bananas. The North demands an extra degree of state responsibility for shelter, heat, and nourishment of some of its people, anywhere north of 45 degrees; observe Scandinavia or the North-western United States as parallels.

However, this North is also so big it can only be handled properly by using the latent energy within individuals building their own lives, with freedom for enterprise, the ultimate human energy source, better than oil or anything. There never has been a successful Northern civilization created by government fiat or compulsion.

Along this line, Canada will always need higher than usual taxes for public support and those in turn require more entrepreneurs of all kinds with scope enough to pay the darn taxes, with enough work freedom to keep up their enthusiasm. There occurs our hope of national survival and prosperity. You don't help state funds by adding public officials at one hundred per cent expense and taxing back thirty per cent of their pay.

It is very challenging to comment on one's own country. The feelings I've summarized come forward as socio-economic because that's our main issue. One could daydream that a grandchild given such an assignment in 2020 might emphasize that generation's arts and philanthropy towards the Southern world, but I doubt if we can be in that position that fast.

I'd guess that, given our geography and sparse population, we're going to have a developing country for a long time yet. That affords us lots of room to love it, laugh at it, and work at it, which is all just fine, because how better can you approach whatever is good?

I would guess that feelings like these are recognized across our West, Northern Ontario, rural Quebec, and on the Atlantic side. They do get missed in our largest cities sometimes, which tend to be more like bigger, foreign metropolises.

If Canada will make it, it will be by deserving to keep the land. Maybe it's time for Westerners or Northerners to take the lead about this. The land is what Canada is really about.

---------------------------------- ✳ ----------------------------------

Integration — Strength of Our Economy
André Raynauld

President of the Canadian Economics Association and former chairman of the Economic Council of Canada; professor of economics at the Université de Montreal.

A political system of the federal type involves the existence of at least two orders of government — that of the member state of the federation, and that of the state constituted by the federation. In such a system, citizens are subject to dual jurisdiction. The very nature of the system means the sovereignty of the federation's members is shared. This sharing of jurisdiction is based on the principle that member states are entrusted with control over matters falling within their borders or that spill over their borders only slightly, while the federal authority, on the contrary, is charged with co-ordination, interaction, and unification of the country as a whole.

A federal system is adopted when the populations involved wish to preserve a certain autonomy, culture, and history of their own while simultaneously choosing to live with others in a common homeland. When union is chosen over complete independence, it is because the interests and feelings that draw people together are stronger than the differences that separate them.

Such is the case with Canada. This country owes its past and future to the vision of the two great peoples, strong and proud, who agreed to form a nation and territory. They gave the provincial governments jurisdiction over their internal affairs and the federal government jurisdiction over what could be called their foreign affairs in relation to each other as well as other countries.

Were the provinces independent countries, they would be obliged, much as they are today, to establish the most harmonious relations possible among themselves; they would have to decide on a common or separate monetary system; they would have to develop an open or protectionist trade policy, which would either favour or discourage inter-provincial trade as well as trade with the rest of the world; they would envisage common infrastructures for rail, air, and sea transport. What would the difference be between such a hypothetical situation and the present? If the provinces were independent, the rules of the game would be based on the economic or military power of each of the provinces, whereas under the present system they are established through the arbitration of the federal government. The choice of complete sovereignty is one based on economic power; the federal solution, while recognizing economic power, tempers it by bringing political power into play, drawing on the sense of solidarity and of sharing that shapes the actions of compatriots as opposed to neighbours.

The most obvious example of this federal arbitration at the moment is the establishment of a Canadian oil price that is lower than that sought by Alberta or other provinces but higher than the price consumers want to pay. In the 1950s, the federal government imposed an oil price higher than the world price on consumers living west of the "Borden line", in order to foster the development of the Alberta oil fields. Today, many conflicting interests persist but the situation has been reversed.

The will to live together within one country cannot be reduced solely to a question of interest, but it is helpful to recall from time to time that our belonging to Canada, whatever the province we come from, is not only our guarantee of freedom and growth but also the promise of a better future. There are two sets of reasons for this: reasons related to *economic efficiency*, and reasons related to the *sharing or redistribution of resources*.

A country is an economic territory within which the mobility of production factors and goods and services makes it possible to benefit from trade gains, specialization, and scale. Both by definition and by experience, we know that mobility is more restricted with the outside world, however open the policies of the government in power may be. No province alone, therefore, would reap these full production and trade benefits. Consequently, the system of economic union under which we live produces a higher standard of living for the population as a whole.

When there is free trade between various regions in Canada, regions or provinces can specialize at little extra cost in the production of goods for which they are most suited by virtue of the natural resources within their area and other advantages they may enjoy. The larger the economic territory in which businesses operate — such as all of Canada — the more they can reduce their average costs of each item produced by spreading their fixed costs, such as the cost of a production plant, over a larger volume of production. Furthermore, the ability of capital and worker to move around freely assures that shortages in some regions can be taken care of by surpluses in another. Monetary union, involving the adoption and use of a single currency throughout the country, significantly reduces transaction costs and currency exchange risks; it also frees the provinces from balance of payment constraints. Finally, the legal system, legislation, and the institutional framework, if not unified, are at least harmonized so that the mobility referred to may be real, concrete, and effective.

It would be long and tedious to go into many statistical indicators to prove it, but the Canadian economy is now a firmly integrated system. A close interdependence exists today among the various regions of the country. There are large population shifts; in one year recently, some 16,000 people from Quebec moved to Alberta, where the economic picture was kinder. The exchange of agricultural, energy, mining, and manufactured products between Canadian regions, as well as financial, professional, and technical services, is of great importance, though in varying degrees for each province. Because the resources of the different regions are both rich and diversified, the country as a whole enjoys remarkable balance, protecting it to some extent from the hazards of unforeseen circumstances and structural changes. Our economic recessions would be more severe without it.

The federal system not only expands the economic territory of the provinces and allows a surplus for the benefit of the population as a whole, but it also engineers massive resource transfers from the have to the have-not provinces. The principle of sharing riches in Canada is present everywhere; it is even inherent in the notion of arbitration referred to earlier. Obviously federal policies do not affect all regions in the same way. Even a standardized family allowance plan most benefits the provinces with the highest birth rate. What about agricultural, transport, and housing policies? If these effects, direct or indirect, deliberate or off-chance, are so marked, the federal government must be concerned with the consequences of its policies, for it has the power to build or to destroy the future of any part of the country.

It is therefore not surprising that the Canadian government has, as a rule, chosen to follow a policy of assuring regional balance by using its powers of intervention in the interest of equality and sharing. The system of equalization payments is perhaps the best-known example of the principle of redistribution of wealth. It is based on the idea that people are entitled to public services of equal quality, whatever the province they live in.

For some years, the provincial economic accounts prepared by Statistics Canada have made it possible to identify the source of all federal taxes and the initial destination of all federal expenditures. A net fiscal balance can thus be established for each province — that is, the difference between taxes paid to the federal government and federal expenditures made in each province. Whatever the basis of comparison, the transfers of fiscal resources are enormous and allow a more equitable redistribution among the provinces. Generally speaking, Alberta, Ontario, and British Columbia paid more in total taxes in 1979 than they received in federal expenditures, whereas all the other provinces benefited from a surplus of funds. The amounts in question were of the order of ten billion dollars — a considerable amount.

In short, although Canadians may have many more important reasons for their attachment to their country, economic considerations alone should encourage them to maintain this attachment.

————————————— * —————————————

Energy Is Our Future

J. Peter Gordon

Chairman and chief executive officer of Stelco Inc., Hamilton, Ontario.

There is no question in my mind that Canada stands on the threshold of a future of immense economic potential. Our nation has an abundance of the three elements that are essential to the functioning of any society — food, fresh water, and energy. We are a major producer of commodities such as iron ore, potash, gold, silver, nickel, zinc, and copper as well as strategic minerals such as cobalt and tungsten. We are also the world's second largest producer and leading exporter of pulp and paper.

In addition to its vast natural resources, Canada has also built over the years a relatively diversified industrial and manufacturing base. While considerable segments of our secondary manufacturing infrastructure are not competitive in the world market place for a number of reasons, not the least of which is the reality of a small, widely dispersed population occupying the second largest land area on earth, we do have a number of industrial success stories. We can, for example, certainly be classified as being world competitive in nuclear technology, aerospace, telecommunications, optical fibres, and steelmaking. Our steel industry enjoys a world-wide reputation for efficiency and technological innovativeness, and an added source of pride is the fact that it is one of the very few major Canadian industries that is almost totally domestically owned.

Yet, the ability of our country to realize the immense economic potential represented by all these resources is being placed in jeopardy by a staggering array of seemingly chronic economic problems and an unparalleled degree of constitutional conflict and discord. This has brought about not only a loss of confidence on the part of the international investment community and our major trading partners in our ability to manage our affairs but also, more alarmingly, a diminishment in our national self-confidence and sense of purpose.

It is essential that we, as a nation, rediscover a pride in being Canadians. In order to achieve this we must find a cause or a challenge, something that will restore that sense of nationhood and national self-esteem without which no society can prosper or, indeed, survive. I believe that just such a challenge exists within our own borders: the very real opportunity for Canada to achieve a position of world leadership in the development, transportation, and management of energy. While there might well be a number of nations that may have more proven reserves of a particular kind of energy, I cannot think of one that can match us in sheer diversity of resources and, consequently, in the number of development options open to us.

The distribution pattern of these energy resources meets, as well, the requirement that our national challenge be one that every region of our country can participate in and contribute towards. Western Canada has conventional oil and gas, heavy oil and tar sands deposits, uranium, coal, and hydro power. Ontario has coal, uranium, and hydro power and is also in the forefront of efforts to develop technology that will permit the widespread use of hydrogen as a fuel. Quebec has the vast hydro potential represented by James Bay. The Maritimes have coal, hydro, and tidal power, and offshore oil and gas, while the vast energy potential of our Arctic regions has barely been scratched.

This will be a monumental undertaking, but I cannot believe that it is beyond the capability of a people who have woven together a unique cultural mosaic; built, against all the laws of constitutional logic, a nation from east to west on a continent where the geo-economic pull is so clearly north to south; and preserved their cultural heritage and independence while sharing a 4,000-mile long border with the most powerful nation on earth.

That is the challenge and that is the opportunity facing Canadians today.

---------------------------------- ❊ ----------------------------------

Labour Viewpoint

Art Coulter

Until recently, executive secretary of the Manitoba Federation of Labour; currently volunteer worker with the Board of St. Boniface Hospital, the Blue Cross, Winnipeg Business Development Council, and various co-operative labour and management councils.

You couldn't find a steady job anywhere in mid-Depression Winnipeg, 1935, when I graduated from Daniel McIntyre Collegiate Institute. Some of my chums went to a government work camp at Clear Lake where for ten dollars a month they sawed, hacked, and dug through the bush to build Clear Lake National Park. Many of them sent the money home where even at the CPR shops their fathers only worked a few days a month. Families stuck together through those tough times. Looking back, I see there was a good spirit. I realize that we didn't "feel" deprived.

I decided to stay in town and hustle for odd jobs, delivering ice cream for Palm Dairies one summer, painting, and paper hanging, and finally, two years later, doing fairly steady work washing cars at Western Canada Motors, for twenty-five cents an hour.

I wanted to do better, so I started turning up every morning at the office of the Canada Malting Company at seven, letting them know that I wanted to work for them (they payed better — forty five cents per hour). Then I would rush downtown to start my washing job at 8:00 a.m.

After a month of this routine I was hired by the Malting Company. Two years later, the company was organized by United Brewery, Flour, Cereal and Soft Drink Workers of America and I was a founding member. At our first union meeting they appointed me to represent the local at the Winnipeg District Trades and Labour Council, and a new career began for me. Our first contract at Canada Malt raised the wages to sixty-two-and-a-half cents an hour.

When I think about my own experience, three special things make me appreciate being a Canadian: I can join a labour union of my choice, I can organize others into a union so they can join together to express their individual needs, and I can belong to or help organize a political party that I believe will represent the interests of labour. I equally appreciate Canada as giving every citizen the right to form companies and to support any political party.

I have always felt that business and labour have a common interest in the success of a company and the economy; otherwise there would be no profits to bargain over in order to improve labour's standard of living.

I also appreciate the freedom Canada has given me to participate in voluntary organizations helping the underprivileged and disadvantaged and serving on boards and city councils.

My work over many years has proved to me that the secret of getting things done is to bring people together from opposite and different sides, encouraging them to co-operate with an honest and realistic attitude.

The best things in Canada have been built that way. This is the Canadian spirit, but it needs us all working at it.

---------- ✳ ----------

Living Beside the U.S.A.
Ralph K. Cowan

Director of the Institute of Canadian–American Studies at the University of Windsor, Ontario.

I live in Canada directly south of the U.S. border. Indeed, my home city of Windsor, Ontario, seems almost surrounded by the giant American industrial complex of Detroit, Michigan. I am a graduate both of U.S. and Canadian universities. I have worked in industry on both sides of the border and have taught in the universities of each country. I have deep roots in both countries. I have seen the best and the worst of the two nations and remain intensely Canadian.

My economic studies and experience, reinforced by the fact of a 4,000-mile common border with the largest industrial nation on earth, compel me, however, to accept the reality of Canada's unchangeable geographic position. Our destiny is inextricably tied to a close working relationship with the U.S. We could not defend ourselves against attack without U.S. help. Our economy is comparable to the movement of water in a bay that is attached to a huge lake representative of the U.S. economy. When the water in the lake goes up and down, so does the water level of the bay, i.e., our economy.

Canada's culture is a marriage of many elements — French, English, Scottish, Irish, Ukrainian, Native Indian, etc. — with a high input of U.S. creativity — not all of it desirable — through literature, technology, movies, TV, sports such as baseball and football, and so on.

This has been a two-way street. Canadians have contributed greatly to U.S. culture from movie stars of old such as Mary Pickford and Raymond Massey to today's performers Anne Murray and Robert Goulet; to economists such as John Kenneth Galbraith, university presidents such as Wallace Sterling of Stanford and Harold Shapiro of Michigan, hockey players, scientists, and leading figures in many U.S. fields of work. Canadian goods and raw material also find their biggest market by far in the U.S. and U.S. goods and services have their largest market in Canada. And as every Canadian knows, massive numbers of us winter in the southern states while huge numbers of Americans summer in Canada's cooler climate. Accepting these realities — and learning to work positively with them to the advantage of both nations — is not, for me, a threat to Canadian identity.

Canada's political and legal systems; our growing numbers of scientists, doctors, athletes, writers, and educators who shine on the world stage; the greatness of our beautiful land mass with its open spaces and vast resources; the growing fact of Canada as an independent nation in world associations; our historical roots; our family and organizational intertwining from ocean to ocean — all these have increased, not lessened, the sense of Canadian identity in my lifetime.

The Canadian concept will continue to grow, I believe, in spite of temporary conflicts and in spite of a shrinking continent and a compacting world brought on by rapid communication through news, computerized information, and ease of travel. Why? Because we all need a source of identity, a place we call home.

Canadian identity, to me, is not antagonistic to other nations and peoples but is, rather, a base from which to plan and act in our own interest in co-operation with all other countries and peoples with whom we have a vital common concern — the future security of a world order, the spread of freedom and of legal and economic justice, and the maintenance and development of civilization itself.

My work convinces me that we should point our future planning towards the creation of a North American economy, including Canada, the U.S., Mexico, and other Latin American states, within a world trading system. It is the only practical future and requires a strong Canada with all its resources maintained together to improve the effectiveness and the advantages of trade with others.

Western Europe's Common Market is an experimental pattern of immense value for us. Also, the combining of the automobile industries of Canada and the U.S. have shown that the system can work, in spite of ups and downs.

Whenever the opportunity exists, the movement of goods and services north and south needs encouragement. *Ideally*, Canadians should be able to buy and sell in the markets that offer the best combination of price and quality, regardless of where the products are made. And capital and technology should move freely in response to market forces.

Movement to a North American economy cannot succeed overnight. In Europe, co-ordinating the various industrial changes from country to country to achieve a common market was carefully planned over a period of years in such a way that those nations and industries most seriously hurt by one particular change would have time to adjust to new products, new jobs, and new trading roles.

I worry when too much effort, most often by governments, is spent in trying to create a totally Canadian economy. In its extreme such an approach attempts to be self-sufficient, looking inward and thus heading us back to increased living costs and a kind of stone age mentality.

Every growing industrial nation has needed outside capital. When the U.S. became independent in 1776, most of its industries were owned by English, French, and other European sources of money. In time, internal growth of wealth led to U.S. supremacy in ownership at home. Our direction can be the same. I am hopeful for Canada's future. We have so much in our favour with resources, land, capital, and skilled manpower. We can find new products, new trading patterns, new economic approaches in which we can excel.

The world I am talking about is one in which no one country or one city is the hub of the universe but rather is connected with all other parts of the world. Within this context we can be fully Canadian and world citizens at the same time, a programme that will bring us to our full potential as a nation, if we but accept and work at it.

--------------------------------- ✳ ---------------------------------

Labour Pioneer
Neil Reimer

National director of the Energy and Chemical Workers Union and a founding vice-president of the Canadian Labour Congress; of Edmonton, Alberta.

I will never forget first setting foot on the land that is Canada. The Reimer family disembarked at Quebec City in 1927 as immigrants from the Ukraine. We knew we would never go back to the oppression the Stalin regime represented.

My Uncle Isaac remained in the Ukraine. He and his

wife were later exiled to Siberia for eleven years. They were finally allowed to come back to "normal life" when they received a letter from Russia's premier stating that the late Stalin had sent him and his wife to a Siberian labour camp without cause. My uncle's experience may very well be an indication of what could have been in store for us had we remained in the Ukraine. About forty years after our arrival, Uncle Isaac, by then more than sixty-five years old, was able to come to Canada to make a new home. Yet he still has a deep sympathetic and compassionate feeling for the country he left. He never became bitter.

When we first arrived in Canada we knew very little about the country and its people. We knew that it was large, that there was land available, that it had cold winters and beautiful autumns, and that there was political and cultural freedom. But that was enough, for we were determined to make this land our new home no matter what was in store for us. Saskatchewan was hard to pronounce and we had never heard of Glidden or Madison, where we eventually settled on a farm.

It was exciting to plough new soil. When the horses pulled the breaking plough that turned over the sod it demonstrated a traumatic change. The grass that fed the buffalo and other animals was turned down. The rich gumbo soil was turned up ready to feed people inside and outside our borders.

During the Depression in Saskatchewan many people helped each other and worked together in order to get through the ordeal and deal with an extremely adverse economy. They constructed a society that was to become the flagship for social change in Canada. Saskatchewan is today a province in which people have a fierce pride in Canada and their community, for adversity was turned into success. Where else but in Canada could anyone have the experience of being part of moulding a new society?

I came out of the College of Agriculture at the University of Saskatchewan to work for the world's first Co-operative Refinery, where we soon formed a union. As this enterprise was viable it became the centre-piece for many more co-operative endeavours. Just imagine, farmers and workers owning their own means of production and distribution!

I was then asked to join the Oil Workers International Union as a staff representative in 1951, becoming the Canadian director in 1955. The next year we formed the Canadian Labour Congress. It was a merger between the Trades and Labour Congress and the Canadian Congress of Labour. I am proud to have been a founding vice-president, a position I held for eighteen years.

Within my union, 1955 was an eventful year. Through the merger of the Oil Workers International Union and the Gas, Coke and Chemical Workers Union, the Oil, Chemical and Atomic Workers International Union was formed. The founding convention chose me as its first Canadian director. For many years we worked closely with our American colleagues but the time had come in 1980 to "Canadianize" our Union. We got our complete autonomy that year, and both the Americans and Canadians were convinced it was right. In so doing we then merged with the Canadian Chemical Workers and Quebec Federation of Labour affiliates to form the Energy and Chemical Workers Union. I am proud to be the national director of this union, a position I have held since the union's inception.

Back in 1956 the Chemical and Atomic Workers International union called for a political realignment. From that day forward we all worked hard to build a new political party. The Canadian Labour Congress took the initiative. In 1960 the New Democratic Party was formed. This new party is very much part of the Canadian fabric today.

The very worthwhile collective bargaining achievements of the Energy and Chemical Workers Union would fill a book. A book could also be written about the social contributions of the union and its predecessors. Yet progress often appears to be slow, and the evolutionary process for change that has become a Canadian trademark somewhat caters to that perception. However, someone has said, "The art of progress is to preserve order amid change and to preserve change amid order." Things can be done in Canada if you get into the action.

The people of Canada do have values. Perhaps they

are practised so freely that they are taken for granted. No one is sent to a Baffin Island "Labour Camp" for insisting on human rights. Recently I read an article that a person was shot in Guatemala for registering a new social democratic political party. It has not happened in Canada. A free trade union does exist in Canada. The comfortable will often be upset with change, but change is possible.

A country is measured by the quality of its people and I love Canada. My wife, daughter, son, and son-in-law feel the same way. Most people in it care. It is a land where one can dream and work to make the dream come true.

✳

Christmas in Adversity
Robert Lowery

Journalist in Thompson, Manitoba.

We have had quite a Christmas up in this Northern Manitoba mining community of Thompson, Manitoba. Like so many other places on the continent and elsewhere in the world, we have been in the midst of a lengthy industrial lay-off. The effects are compounded when it happens to be a one-industry town.

At Christmas 1982, we were at the mid-point of a three-month shutdown, involving more than 2,000 nickel miners, smelter, and refinery workers, as well as Inco Limited staff people. For many, it was the first taste of adversity.

The remarkable thing was the way the community of about 15,000 stood together and tried to make the most of the situation. There seemed to be a almost total absence of bitterness and blame.

Just before the Inco complex shut down on November 1, 1982, the 1,580 members of the United Steelworkers

Union broke with tradition and voted in favour of a four-day work week, which ran for six months starting in February. The federal government provided unemployment insurance payments to help cover pay lost on the fifth day.

This work-sharing arrangement was followed by a one month's paid vacation shut-down starting July 8. After that, Inco reopened fortunately on a regular shift basis.

During the shut-down, more than 300 extremely useful jobs were created, thanks to a lot of inspired local initiative backed by the federal and provincial governments. Much needed — and otherwise probably unaffordable — improvements were made to the schools, hospital, ski chalet, church, etc. There were fifty projects in all.

Scores of mine workers used their free time to brighten up and remodel their homes under the watchful eye of their wives, who, of course, they claim are far tougher to satisfy than any Inco foreman!

One of the most common sights during those days was to see families coming home with loads of wood they'd just cut from the surrounding bush and wooded country around Thompson. An estimated seventy per cent of the homes are totally or partially heated by wood burning stoves.

In this setting, Christmas had fresh meaning. There were more than 1,500 people out singing carols for an hour on a bitter cold Advent Sunday afternoon. Afterwards, the local service clubs invited them indoors, where they consumed close to 1,800 hot dogs and 123 gallons of hot chocolate.

One of the job creation crews and their families put together a giant Christmas wreath fifty feet in diameter, a feat they are trying to have written into the Guiness Book of Records as the biggest ever.

Another special thing about Christmas that year was the number of people from the South — including my sister, Gertrude — who travelled to the North to spend Christmas with us.

Underneath the activity and the celebrating, there was a lot of hard thinking going on. Many said they were sorting out their true values. Despite all the concerns and fears for the future, people here approached the new year with gratitude and growing faith. With such a spirit, Canada can meet the challenges ahead.

————————————————— ✳ —————————————————

Farming Shapes the Nation

Glenn Flaten

Saskatchewan farmer and president of the Canadian Federation of Agriculture.

Agriculture — commercial agriculture — has played a central role in the shaping of Canada as we know it today, indeed in making it possible. It was the railways that finally bound Canada together. The settlement of the West for the production of grain for export was, in turn, what the building of the transcontinental railway was all about.

The basic need for food made farming, of necessity, the foundation of settlement throughout Canada. As a Prairie farmer in this still very new country, the consciousness of Western settlement is bred in my bones. My father, a Norwegian immigrant, came, as did thousands of other men and women from Europe and the U.S., to pioneer development in Western Canada, largely in response to the lure of free land and new opportunities in a new land. Three of his sons are still farming today in Saskatchewan.

Canada's climate is a harsh one for agriculture; survival depended upon an entrepreneurial ability to incorporate, and indeed to create, new technology, as well as to take high risks. These abilities have served Canadian agriculture well. At the same time, the need to develop new varieties and new technologies that would permit the very survival of Canadian and especially Prairie agriculture made the role of agricultural research, led by the government of Canada, a matter of life and death. There has always been a strong central government role in the development of Canadian agriculture.

Long transportation distances with their high costs, the uncertainties of export markets and crop yields, and the need to sell competitively — all these have also made their contribution to the shaping of our farming attitudes and institutions and the search for protection against exploitation and intolerable insecurity. The Canada Grains Commission, the Canadian Wheat Board, and the Crows Nest Pass Statutory Grain Freight Rates are all examples of Canadian government initiatives in the Prairie grains industry that have shaped this country in major ways, for the needs of their time, and all for the better.

There is drama piled on drama in the Canadian farming story, which can only be hinted at in these few words. The result to date is a strong agriculture, responding to new scientific and technological challenges, exporting forty per cent of what it produces (four per cent of the world's wheat, three-and-a-half per cent of its feed grains) and a major factor in Canada's balance of trade.

Canadian farmers have been able, to a large extent, to offset the difficulties of weather and international markets by adopting new technology fostered by strong research programmes, a steady growth in the size of farms to incorporate the use of modern mechanization, by educational programmes to keep updated on new developments in the use of herbicides and pesticides, livestock feeding programmes, soil management, environment controls, and by the use of sound marketing structures for the benefit of producers and consumers.

What has also emerged is an agriculture with highly developed market institutions of many kinds — federal and provincial — designed to put order, efficiency, and some degree of security into the production and marketing process. Evolving from this is a uniquely Canadian, government-assisted and monitored but most often producer directed, system of federal and provincial market agencies, shaped by the complexities of Canada's federal–provincial jurisdictional requirements. Here, as elsewhere, the challenge is to combine the strength and value of our intense regional identities and loyalties, with the final strength, purpose, and commanding identity that only a unified Canada can provide.

Driven by the circumstances of pioneering and the need

for mutual self-help, Canadian farmers need to work together through their farm organizations to adopt a reasoned, rational approach to problem-solving and their responsibilities in dealing with governments.

We also need a willingness on the part of the federal and provincial governments to work together for the development of sound agriculture policies for this vital industry. Because we rely on the export market as an important outlet for part of our production, we require a concerted effort on behalf of all producers and governments to co-ordinate our efforts for the benefit of our farmers and to play our role in feeding the needy of the world. Changing world trading patterns will require determination and co-operation if we are to develop our markets to greatest advantage.

I believe that we have great opportunities for agricultural production in Canada, as I believe we have great opportunities for the country as a whole. The success of our industry will depend upon our ability to work together for the good of all. This requires that one take a broad perspective of our industry, to see the needs of farmers in all parts of Canada, to rise above the limits of provincialism, and to return to the concept of help thy neighbour, or at least to have some concern for him. We have one of the greatest countries in the world. I am very proud to say that I am a Canadian. Working together and co-operation were important elements in developing this country. They will be important elements in solving some of the problems that now face us as farmers, as citizens, as provinces, and as a country.

---
*

Towards the Global Village

Larkin Kerwin

President of the National Research Council of Canada, member of the Science Council of Canada, professor and former Rector, Laval University, Quebec.

There was a time when even the most recent scientific and technological developments could be placed at the service of the individual or of the small community. Each person could have a radio, each house a telephone, every village its artifical ice-rink, every city its modern hospital, every region its university resources. In many of these cases a network was involved, that of the telephone company or of the source of medical instrumentation. But even these networks were frequently of limited extent, and in general the technical apparatus had a certain personal identification: You had "your" electric typewriter, the town had "its" radio station.

Today all of this is still true, increasingly so, in fact. Our standard of living and our comfort are buttressed by an increasing variety of products that serve our needs or whims at the level of the individual. We can all have pocket computers of a capacity that was available only in a large, expensive installation just fifteen years ago. Individual homes have audio-visual reproduction systems whose quality rivals that of the best concert halls. Everything points to an ever-increasing application of technology to personal needs.

Now, however, a new dimension is being added to the human technological adventure: the exploitation for the common good of installations so huge that even on the scale of an entire nation only one or two may be envisaged.

The nature of this dimension is illustrated by several projects. The James Bay hydro-electric installation in Quebec with its appurtenant distribution networks integrates a large part of North-eastern North America in so far as electrical energy is concerned. Only a vast, common endeavour enables us to install and maintain the satellites that ensure many of our communications across the continent. In all of Canada there is only one source of meson radiation for cancer therapy, and its duplication — which would be enormously expensive — is improbable.

This new dimension will take on greater importance during the balance of the twentieth century. The era of megaprojects has arrived.

The megaprojects, which are being undertaken in many parts of the world, have been made necessary by several factors. The increasing need for energy is pushing us towards the exploitation of "difficult" sources: oil and tar sands, fusion, solar energy. This requires resources on a national or even international scale. The village is out of the race. The energy must be transported: oil pipelines, gas distribution systems, electrical networks at the megavolt level — all of these must also be constructed on national scale to be economically viable. The development of electronic information and entertainment networks for access by the individual requires vast data banks of information, literature, entertainment, as well as other networks involving several technologies — microwaves, fibre optics, lasers. Such projects require the resources of an entire nation.

With its twenty-five million inhabitants, its natural resources, its universities and laboratories, its small technology-based secondary industry, Canada possesses, but only just, the necessary dimension for megaprojects, at least for the medium term. We can therefore look for breakthroughs in several fields: energy, deep-sea mineral mining, the development of the Arctic, important increases in food production, the restructuring of cities, the assembling an distribution of information, and important advances in medicine and agriculture through the use of biogenetics.

Such projects, however — and similar ones will be developing in other countries — will be brought to fruition only if two conditions are met. The first is that a suitable programme of research and development be undertaken. We shall soon have to devote two-and-a-half per cent of our Gross National Product to well-planned R & D programmes. The second condition is that a very close collaboration must exist between the various governments, industry, institutions, and agencies of the country. We shall not succeed with megaprojects using only the human and other resources of one province or one region of Canada.

The fact is that even Canada as a whole will not be sufficient for the task in the long term. Farther into the future it will fall to international consortiums to develop the major global projects. This has already begun, for example in space engineering, fusion development, and the eradication of certain illnesses. Europe has organized itself into a single economic community for certain purposes. It is improbable that Canada would have obtained its large telescope had she not allied herself with France for its development; our space programme would be minimal had we not entered into agreements with the United States.

The space shuttle remote manipulator, or CANADARM, is a current, highly successful example. Canada's $100-million contribution to the Space Transportation System was developed through active co-operation between the National Research Council of Canada and a group of Canadian companies for which the Canadian company SPAR Aerospace, was the prime contractor. The agreement with NASA in the U.S. gives Canada not only a first-class ticket on the shuttle but also leaves Canadian industry with a solid competitive edge in space-age robotics and has led to hundreds of jobs.

The world is progressing, as Teilhard de Chardin explained; the future holds even greater intellectual and spiritual adventures for us, in ever-improving circumstances. We shall eventually overcome the grievous problems that afflict mankind on a global scale. The prerequisite is that we unite and collaborate. The Global Village comes closer. So much the better.

10

*

Peacekeepers, Freedom Keepers

---------------------------------- * ----------------------------------

Incident in Istanbul

Sid Wheelock

Of Victoria, British Columbia; a Nova Scotian Rhodes scholar, veteran of World War II naval services, and long-time Canadian representative on the World Bank.

I was in Istanbul, Turkey, for the first time on business some years ago. After lunch one Friday (the Moslem day of rest), I realized that I had a free afternoon. The sun was shining, the whole city was sparkling, and I had yet to explore it. In the courtyard of my hotel, taxi-cabs were waiting, and I asked in a loud voice, "Anyone here speak English?" One driver held up his hand and after talking with him for a moment, I knew that his command of English was good.

I told him that I had three hours to spare and had seen nothing in the city. I asked him to drive me around and show me the interesting spots. This he did, giving me a fascinating and informative afternoon and bringing me back to the hotel at five.

When I asked how much I owed him, he said, "Nothing at all." I protested, saying that this was the way he earned his living, that I had enjoyed the afternoon immensely, and that surely he couldn't afford not to be paid for his work.

He then told me that he had been in the Turkish Army in the Korean War of 1950–53 and had fought beside a Canadian brigade. At one point, he had been pinned down by enemy fire, and three Canadian soldiers, risking their lives, pulled him back to safety. He had promised himself at that time that any Canadian who got into his cab after he returned to Istanbul would be his guest.

---- * ----

At the Ready
Philippe Bernier

Long-time mayor of Drummondville, Quebec, recently retired;
flew fifty-two Missions over Germany with the Royal Canadian
Air Force in World War II.

As a Canadian, I am proud of the country I consider the
most beautiful in the world.

I have had the opportunity to visit the major cities of
the ten provinces, and I am convinced that our young
Canada is a land rich in physical and human resources,
with a promising future.

That is why I voluntarily served my country during
World War II and why I would not hesitate to risk my
life for it again.

---- * ----

Our Military Tradition
George F.G. Stanley

Eminent Canadian military historian associated with the his-
tory department of Mount Allison University, New Brunswick,
World War II veteran, and the now fully bilingual Lieutenant-
Governor of the province of New Brunswick.

Canada has never been a militaristic nation. You could
say that Canadians are not a military people. We have
never engaged in acquisitive warfare; we have never fought
to expand our territorial frontiers; and we have never
taken up arms in order to extract economic privileges or
trade concessions from other countries.

Although Canada's past has not been stained by military aggression this does not mean Canada has had no
military history, or that Canadians have scorned the military virtues of courage, comradeship, discipline, and self-
sacrifice. On the contrary, Canadians of all origins —

French, British, Native Peoples, and others — have fought in wars in North America, Africa, Europe, and Asia. They fought in defence of their country when it was called New France; they fought in defence of British North America in 1775 and 1812; they fought to preserve unity in their own country in 1837 and in 1885; they afforded assistance to British troops in South Africa in 1899; they participated in the two World Wars in Europe in 1914 and 1939; they joined the forces of the United Nations in Korea in 1950. In all of these actions, Canadians, as soldiers and sailors, played a notable, creditable, and distinguished role. They proved themselves capable of great effort, skilful improvisation, and conspicuous gallantry.

During our early history, responsibility for Canadian defence rested in large measure with the regular troops of our mother countries, France and Great Britain. Canadians were enrolled in companies of militia that served actively wherever and whenever they were required to do so. In early encounters with warriors of the Iroquois Confederacy and the Anglo-Americans of the Thirteen Colonies, and later during the Seven Years War, which ended in 1763, Canadian militia and colonial regulars were in the forefront of battle and on the lines of communication. Every Canadian schoolboy is familiar with the name of the French commander, the Marquis de Montcalm, but few of them know the names of Louis Coulon de Villiers and Charles Deschamps de Boishébert.

When Canada was ceded by France to Great Britain, there was little change in the military policy that had existed during the *ancien regime* in Canada. The British authorities continued to enrol Canadians in the local militia or in the colonial regular regiments. The successful defence of Canada during the War of 1812 against the United States was due in large measure to the efforts of these Canadian soldiers. Memorable as were the services of British regular officers such as Sir Isaac Brock, Sir Gordon Drummond, and Sir John Sherbrooke, equally important were those of Canadians Charles de Salaberry, "Red George" MacDonell, the Shawnee Indian, Tecumseh, and even the sixteen-year-old John Richardson.

In the mid-nineteenth century, the traditional militia

system underwent a complete change. The old compulsory militia was replaced by a new volunteer militia. Many of the Canadian militia regiments of the present day were formed at this time. When the provinces of Canada with New Brunswick and Nova Scotia formed the federal union of Canada in 1867, responsibility for military affairs rested with the central government, and when the first federal Militia Act was passed by Parliament, it confirmed the volunteer principle as the basis of the Canadian military system. The old *levée-en-masse* was retained in the act as a reminder to Canadians that defence of their country was an obligation of citizenship, but it has never been invoked.

Following a combined British–Canadian expedition to Red River in 1870, undertaken to ensure the peaceful entry of Manitoba into Confederation, the Imperial government withdrew all British regulars from Canada, leaving the defence of the country on land entirely in the hands of the Canadian authorities. The outcome was an increase in the number of militia units and the establishment of a military college at Kingston, Ontario, to train officer cadets, and the recruitment of a small force of regulars to serve as an instructional cadre for the citizen soldiers. That is why the force sent to the north-west in 1885 to assert federal authority over the rebellious Métis and Indians in Saskatchewan was composed entirely of militia units from Manitoba, Ontario, Quebec, and Nova Scotia. Only at sea did the British continue to provide Canada with protection, British vessels being based at Halifax and Esquimalt, BC. Ultimately, these bases also became a Canadian responsibility, and in 1910 Canada set about building her own naval force.

On August 4, 1914, war broke out in Europe. Within the space of a few weeks, the greater part of Europe became involved in a war that lasted four years and three months, changed the political face of Europe and Canada, and gave a new direction to world history. Not as a result of her own political decision, but as an integral part of the British Empire, Canada found herself at war with Germany and Austria. Canadians generally believed that the Franco–British–Russian cause was just and flocked to join the expeditionary force that the Department of

Militia and Defence mobilized to send overseas. Some volunteers feared the fighting might be over before they could get into it. But apart from enthusiasm, Canadians had little with which to fight: a small Permanent Force numbering about 3,000 men, and a non-permanent volunteer militia of 55,000. Our naval forces were no better. They consisted of two obsolete ships-of-war. The remarkable thing was that, inspired by the inward conviction that they were fighting for justice or by a desire to adventure, 650,000 Canadians, approximately one-tenth of Canada's total population at the time, joined the armed forces between 1914 and 1918 as soldiers, sailors, and airmen. Some 66,661 of them gave up their lives. From the many battles Canadians emerged with the reputation of being the best shock troops in Europe.

The 1914–18 war was largely an army affair as far as Canada was concerned. The Royal Canadian Navy's activities were limited to checking vessels entering Canadian ports, directing movements of shipping, controlling wireless stations, and patrolling for submarines: necessary tasks, but not eye catching. Because Canada had no air force, Canadians entered the Royal Flying Corps (later the Royal Air Force), where they achieved special distinction as fighter pilots. W.A. Bishop and Raymond Collishaw were among the most notable, in terms of personal victories, among the pilots of every nationality, German as well as Allied. On the home front, Canadian men and women turned their efforts towards expanding production in the fields and in the factories. The export of grain, beef, and pork increased enormously. More surprising, however, was the output of shells, fuses, and aircraft engines. It was an indication of the fact that Canada was changing from an agricultural society to a largely industrial one.

Our country had entered the war in Europe as a self-governing British colony; it emerged virtually an independent nation. Not only did Canada sign the Treaty of Versailles, it also became a member of the League of Nations. A few years later, following the Imperial Conference of 1926, the term British Empire was dropped in favour of British Commonwealth of Nations. In 1931, by the Statute of Westminster, the Imperial Parliament in

London gave up its right to legislate for Canada or any of the dominions, except at the request of the government of the dominion concerned. Finally, when war broke out in Europe in 1939, Canada's participation was the result of a deliberate decision by Canadian Parliament. The day when Canada was automatically bound by a British declaration of war had passed.

When the peace treaty was signed in 1919, we were again content with a minuscule Permanent Force and a small non-permanent volunteer militia. Military conscription, imposed in 1917 to make up for the heavy casualties of the earlier war years, had proven politically divisive. In September 1939, Canada once again found herself at war with Germany — not the old imperial Germany, but a new Germany, militarized, aggressive, and menacing. This second World War lasted just short of six years. In no previous conflict had Canadians ever been called upon to serve in so many different lands or in so many different roles. What an outpouring of courage, will, grim determination, skill, and self-sacrifice followed on the part of men who, only a few short years, even months before, had been driving tractors, teaching school, clerking in stores, or engaged in any one of a dozen other trades and professions in civilian life. And on land they were led not by British but by their own Canadian commanders. Andrew McNaughton, Harry Crerar, Victor Allard, Guy Simonds, and Paul Bernatchy are the best known among them. All told, more than a million Canadians served in World War II, virtually all of them volunteers. In all, 41,700 were killed. Slaughter is not glorious; but self-sacrifice is.

The members of Canada's armed forces today are no different from those who served our country in previous generations. They are inspired by the same ideals. They, too, are volunteers, not conscripts. They serve because they want to do so, not because they have to. The number of regulars has been considerably increased. Now they provide the bulk of Canada's defence force, the militia having been diminished in numbers and their role being that of acting as a reserve force to back up the regulars.

Only once since World War II have Canada's men and women seen active service in war. Between 1950 and

1953, some 22,000 Canadians served in the United Nations Force in Korea in what was euphemistically called a "police action" against the North Koreans and their Chinese allies. Canadians have frequently been engaged in what is known as peace-keeping operations. In 1954, Canada was asked by the United Nations Organization to contribute men to truce commissions in Vietnam, Laos, and Cambodia. Two years later, Canada assisted in the organization of the United Nations Emergency Force to patrol the frontiers of Israel and Egypt. Until 1959, this force was commanded by Canadian general officer E.L.M. Burns. Subsequently, Canadians served in Kashmir and in the Congo, and since 1964 they have helped keep Greeks and Turks in Cyprus from grappling with each other. This task of "keeping the peace" is neither dramatic nor colourful. It demands the very special qualities of patience, discipline, perseverance, and calm endurance of provocation. It has, however, brought prestige to Canada and demonstrated our capacity for organization and adaptability, and our sincere desire to co-operate with other nations in stalling if not preventing bloody encounters that could lead to a major war. The fact is that "international police" are as essential to the world's well-being as national police are to the well-being of any national society, particularly when those international police have no political or religious axes to grind and are free of imperialist ambitions.

Within the confines of Canada's frontiers, our armed forces stand on guard in defence of our native land. Canada's air and marine forces patrol our coast and conduct search and rescue operations on land and sea. Our soldiers give assistance in civil emergencies such as floods, fires, mud slides, and earthquakes. Our army engineers build bridges, roads, and airfields in Canada's northland, and our navy divers combat serious oil spill problems at sea. Canadian servicemen help train the reserves, students, and cadets. In brief, in times of peace, our armed forces personnel are employed in a variety of ways, never forgetting, however, that their first responsibility is to protect Canadian civilians in the event of invasion, insurrection, or outbreaks of terrorism.

It is no secret that our men on duty in North America, Europe, and Asia are inadequately equipped; they have to make do with vintage aircraft, ships, and military hardware which they do, all the while remaining individually and collectively among the best in the world from the standpoint of morale and professionalism. Some of the old guard may deplore the passing of the old-style uniforms, forgetting that neither the colour nor the cut of the uniform makes the serviceman. Rather it is his or her sense of dedication to the ideal of public service, his or her willingness to undertake the tasks assigned without regard to the constraints and limitations imposed by politics. In the case of Canada, perhaps it is his or her realization that members of the Canadian armed services, drawn as they are from all parts of Canada, are an example to the rest of the country of what Canadian unity really means.

Now for our consciences, the arms are fair,
When the intent for bearing them is just.

(William Shakespeare, Henry IV, Part 1

---------------- ✳ ----------------

Clearing Misunderstandings

Jules Daigle

City Councillor in Dorval, Quebec; veteran of World War II battles in Western Europe and member of the post-war Canadian forces and the Royal Canadian Legion.

My memory goes back to my first two weeks in England during World War II. As a young French Canadian volunteer army officer, I had been sent over in December 1941 to join a Canadian artillery regiment. It was made up of volunteers from Vancouver, Regina, and Winnipeg. To my sorrow, the other officers were reluctant to speak to me at first because I was a francophone. I worked hard at my tasks and within a month I was fully accepted. I am glad all that has changed in the post-war Canadian army, which I know well.

As I travelled across Canada with the Legion's Unity Campaign in 1979, I found some of the misunderstandings of World War II still present. Most French Canadians I knew in Quebec before the war had a strong loyalty to Canada but not to Great Britain. Our origins lay in France from whom we had been cut off for 400 years. When England declared war on Germany in 1939, the general feeling in Quebec, rightly or wrongly, was that it was England's war. In English-speaking Canada where most had roots in Britain, there was instant appreciation of the need to join the battle.

I found that the attitude of Quebecers changed a lot when the United States entered the war. Then it did become more their war, a war of concern to all North Americans. These are emotional situations, problems of concept and background, and I want to speak about it now and try to clear up the misunderstandings.

I long ago faced the choice of where to place my loyalty — to England, to France, to Quebec alone, or to Canada. I chose Canada, and I know more than ever that I made the right decision. I can maintain my French Canadian cultural identity and language while being part of a great, larger nation.

Quebec separatism divided my family like so many others, for a while. Before Quebec's 1980 Referendum, one of my daughters was for Canada, another for separatism. Now we are closer together. It has become apparent to many French Canadians that the drive for separatism has isolated French Canada from the rest of the continent.

Ancestors on one side of my family came from Normandy in France and on the other side were granted by the king of France Le Seignory de Rouville at Mont St. Hilaire, south of Montreal. I am proud to be a Canadian and a Québécois. That is why I joined a parade of Canadian Legionnaires to be present at the Place Ville Marie Square in Montreal to welcome those Canadians from other provinces who brought to Quebec nearly a million signatures on the Peoples Unity Petition, April 11, 1980, one month before the Referendum.

---- * ----

Sustaining the Veterans

Bob McChesney

Insurance man from Kirkland Lake, Ontario; a Canadian Air Force veteran of World War II, past Dominion president of the Royal Canadian Legion, and chairman of its Canadian Unity Committee.

Canada is a unique land, and Canadians a unique people. We have come a long way in our short history from a primitive colony to a recognized and respected nation. It has not been an easy road to maturity.

As Dominion president of the Royal Canadian Legion, I had the opportunity to meet with veterans' organizations around the world. None has a better record of honouring or caring for their ex-servicemen and service women than Canada, and none has a better record of extending help to the other veteran organizations of the Commonwealth. Canadians willingly shoulder the cost of generous disability pensions and treatment facilities for those veterans and their dependents still paying the price for wartime service to their country.

Canada not only honours these financial commitments but also assists other Commonwealth veterans that fought at our side. Canada is recognized as having the greatest Veteran's Charter in the world, thanks to the meaningful presentations made to the government on behalf of veterans by the Royal Canadian Legion, and thanks to the responsible attitudes of Canadians serving in all the political parties.

Perhaps my most personal experience of the respect other nations hold for Canada was when I was asked, as Dominion president of the Legion, to travel to Holland to act as godfather at the christening of Prince Floris, son of Princess Margriet of the Netherlands. Princess Margriet was born in Ottawa during the war, and she and the Netherlands Royal Family treasured their connection with Canada's servicemen and service women who courageously fought for and successfully regained their country's freedom in 1944.

Is it any wonder I am so very proud of my Canada?

Interdependent World

George Ignatieff

Chancellor of the University of Toronto and former senior diplomat in the Canadian foreign service.*

We need to reassess Canada's role in light of the far-reaching changes going on in the world. Two main forces are in contention. On the one hand, there is a renewed militarization of the cold war between Canada's two superpower neighbours, the U.S. and the U.S.S.R. The competition involves acceleration of the arms race, access to sources of energy and other raw materials, and intervention in local conflicts with the inherent risk of escalation.

On the other hand, there is the growing interdependence of nations, arising from the impact of the technological revolution, especially affecting communications, computer control systems, and aerospace. While all of us are aware of the marvels of the space shuttle, we are also made aware through the media of the growing gap between the have and have-not countries. The latter group includes an overwhelming majority of the world's countries; their demands for a new deal or a more equitable system of managing the world economy, therefore, cannot be ignored. This is the main issue of the North–South dialogue.

Canada, as a founding member of the United Nations and its network of world organizations and as a founding member of the collective security arrangements under NATO, has an important role to play as a bridge builder. Important differences exist between the U.S. and its European partners in NATO over strategy — both military and political. The gap between the industrially advanced

*From material prepared for *Spectrum*, a publication of the Canadian Imperial Bank of Commerce.

North and the economically developing nations of the South is widening. The meetings of the seven main economic powers of the North held recently in Ottawa imposed heavy responsibilities on Canada, especially at a time when some of the nations are stepping up expenditures on arms and cutting their economic aid.

World expenditures on arms at the current rate of more than $500-billion a year are incompatible with significant contributions to improve the rate of economic development and productivity in the South. The paradox of the arms race is that any weapons system developed by any nation will result in the development of a similar system by others, thus eroding even the limited stability of reciprocal deterrence and diminishing the security of all. This is the main reason that Canada should push its proposal of a "Strategy of Suffocation" to put restraints on the technological impulses to accelerate the arms race.

Another paradox of the arms race is that nuclear weapons are unusable, except at the risk of destroying the very civilization we are trying to defend. This paradox tends to diminish the influence of the superpowers that have become muscle-bound through overkill capacity, in favour of countries that exercise their influence through control of natural resources and technology, contributing to increasing productivity.

Here is Canada's chance, provided we can maintain political and economic unity within a federal system, to use our comparative advantage in trade and technology to pursue objectives through world efforts such as peace keeping and strengthening world order and stability; maintenance of the balance of power in NATO at the lowest level of military confrontation that is possible; protection of the environment from pollution; and improved resource management, especially of non-renewable natural resources.

In pursuit of our destiny, Canadians are approaching an important crossroads. Let us be sure that we read the signs aright and choose the direction to interdependence and greater stability, rather than accepting the inevitability of drifting towards war.

Man of the "Van Doos"

G.A. Turcot

Lieutenant-General (R), of Magog, Quebec; commander of Quebec's renowned Royal 22nd Regiment during World War II, and a post-war general in Canada's armed services.

When I look back on my life and remember my happy childhood and youth and the thirty-six years of service in the army, I can sit back with happy memories. Very early in my military career I was offered the opportunity to serve with what to me was the best regiment in the world, the Royal 22nd Regiment. I sailed with it to England in 1939 and stayed with it throughout the war.

Fulfilment of one of my early ambitions was realized when I had the honour to become this regiment's commanding officer in the last year of the war, leading it triumphantly through the streets of Quebec on our return home in 1945.

We must always remember all the brave soldiers who never returned home and gave their lives for our liberty. I can assure you they were magnificent in action and now rest in the field of honour. Lest we forget.

Unlike today when so many things seem to divide Canadians, the war brought us together, to an extent, I believe, never seen before or since. By the end of the war, every serviceman could be proud of his country's contribution to the war effort. For most Canadians, the war opened up new horizons in terms of travelling both in Canada and remote parts overseas. When they came home, they realized what a beautiful country they lived in.

For me it was also the beginning of a period of travel. I had the privilege to get to know the character, the points of view, and the way of life of people who in many ways were different from me but who also were proud to be Canadians. I am very fortunate in that I have good friends from coast to coast. The regrettable aspect of that is that our country is so large, you don't get to see farflung friends very often. Indeed, I am quite sure the greatest impediment to unity in Canada is the vastness of the country and the fact that the traffic on our continent is mostly north and south.

Coming from a family whose origin traces back some eleven generations to the days of the founding of Quebec City in 1608, I have often wondered if my ancestors ever truly appreciated the potential of their new country. During my years as Commander of NATO's Mobile Forces, travelling extensively throughout Europe, and as commander of Mobile Command, which covers all of Canada, my conviction was further strengthened that while there is a great deal of beauty in the world, Canada certainly enjoys a great share of it.

It is therefore very important that we should continue to defend our country and guard our freedom as our fathers and grandfathers did before us. Let us not rely on neighbours and friends to protect our rights and liberty or even attempt to do it on a regional basis. Let us accept the burden and do our share. It is surely worth the sacrifice to pay the cost of our defence and to ensure that our children and grandchildren will also enjoy our great country in liberty.

A Lasting Bond

Marion Dewar

Mayor of Ottawa.

I see our country blessed with an abundance of God's natural resources. We are striving to create an effective and lasting human bond within our borders and this we will do. The strength of our unity will be reflected in our ability to contribute more to the well-being of our brothers and sisters throughout the world, a necessary building block of peace in any home, city, or wider community of humankind.

11

---*---

Dignity and Freedom

---- ✳ ----

My Rights
Andrea Till

High-school student, Oromocto, New Brunswick.

Canada's democratic government gives me, one in about 25 million, with the same chance to "get my finger in the pie" — in other words, to be a part of my country's government. I can help elect members of the Parliament and the Prime Minister. I can even run for and be elected to one of these key positions. In a dictatorship, the people have almost no say in their country's destiny.

To me, the freedoms of our country are very important. For instance, in some countries people are not free to go to a church and worship God. I also have freedom of expression. I can write to government with my opinions and give newspapers a piece of my mind. I am also free to travel in and out of Canada without complications.

---- ✳ ----

Change by Dialogue
A.J. de Grandpré

Chairman and chief executive officer of Bell Canada Enterprises, Inc., Montreal.

Canadians are respected and appreciated throughout the world. An outside observer often perceives better than we do the significant accomplishments of our young society, in all areas. Among these, the evolution of our political and social system shows a characteristic that contrasts strongly with the universal experience of history and arouses interest and admiration: here in Canada, tensions and conflicts do not follow the path of physical violence and repression but rather that of conciliation and democratic compromise. We do have revolutions — quiet ones! In fact, the laws of the country tend more and more to frustrate all inclination towards "tyranny by the majority". In many respects, what happens in our country can be looked upon as a model; not only does our society endorse broad humanitarian and democratic principles, as do many other societies, but it also institutionalizes them, holds them up as collective standard of behaviour and, in large measure, succeeds in putting them into practice.

Of this, we have reason to be proud. Such results are certainly not achieved without effort and prove we know how to compromise with divergent opinions, interests, and ideals. In fact, this art of compromise is terribly demanding and calls for an individual and collective maturity difficult to attain and, ultimately, never acquired. We are speaking here of a delicate balance that requires constant attention, for otherwise it will be upset.

In a word, it is often very tempting to spare ourselves exhausting democratic debates and wranglings, accentuated by the complexity of our institutions and ideological pluralism, to seek comfortable unanimity "among like-minded people". Most Canadians, however, feel that this road leads to impoverishment, whether this withdrawal into one's shell rests on ethnic background, culture, religion, ideology, social standing, economic stratum, political allegiance, or other secure haven.

No doubt there are some who regret the drabness, the lack of spark in a liberal society such as ours where, nowadays, too little seems to be undertaken with genuine enthusiasm and a spirit of challenge. If it is true that we seem to be going through a phase of rather bitter self-criticism, this does not mean that we will not get our second wind and the determination that served us so well in the past to unite our efforts in order to develop this country to the full extent of its possibilities. Our society surely has the necessary resilience and depth to develop strong leaders in all areas of the social, economic, and political structure.

In a pluralistic society, blessed with democratic institutions, *de facto* and *de jure*, there is no need to fear a strong leadership. On the contrary: the liberal society, because it is based on the exercise of all freedoms, in mutual tolerance and pre-eminence of the common good, calls for an enlightened and morally strong leadership capable of uniting citizens above and beyond their differences in the pursuit of similar objectives.

Our country has come a long way. One need only visit other countries to realize our remarkable success: we have built a society that is free, tolerant, peace-loving, open, and generous; a productive and competitive society that has reached, over many years, an advanced stage of development and an enviable standard of living; a political society that was able to meet many challenges and which has undertaken to build, not without difficulty but nevertheless in an orderly way, its unity amidst diversity. The project is exhilarating.

In a way, Canada is a laboratory, a privileged place for the emergence of a political society of the future, which will have mastered, at home and in its best interest, the art of interdependent living. This interdependence, we sense and indeed we know, will be evidenced more and more in relationships between countries. The Canadian experience, bold and demanding, is in a way exemplary. It is therefore a responsibility and, indeed, an object of legitimate pride.

---------------------------------- * ----------------------------------

The Hope and the Promise

John Ross Matheson

A judge in Perth, Ontario; was badly wounded in World War II and has been a Member of Parliament and worked with many service organizations.

I was born in the month of the battle of Passchendaele of dreadful World War I memory, November 1917. I have lived since through war and rumours of war, but depletion of resources, pollution, man's greed, and pre-disposition to barbarism notwithstanding, there is abundant evidence to be seen of human progress. Optimism was once described as a form of courage. Courageous Leonard Brockington repeatedly affirmed that Canada was the world's greatest experiment in human brotherhood. Could this actually be so?

That Canadians among all people are favoured is not disputed. Where, for a start, is such treasure of real estate occupied by so few? But Canada's greatest worth is not resources but people. This we are beginning to discover.

Myrna Kostash writes that the first generation of Ukrainian Canadians are the great-grandchildren of serfs and the grandchildren of poor peasants. The candour of this writer, her bitter-sweet recollections of family, encourages readers to examine their own immigrant beginnings. Almost universally one finds memory of some injustice or degradation, some bitterness, some recollection of despair. What is ultimately important is that a kind Providence brought us to this place of hope and promise.

My ancestry was of "the Clearances", victims of the disaster of Culloden in Scotland. In retrospect, once the grieving was over the exile proved to be a great blessing. My father's father was born in Scotland's Isle of Skye and emigrated with poor crofter parents from a patch of highland soil. The family were hereditary tenants of an hereditary landlord, obligated both in rent and service, a form of serfdom. My grandfather perfected English at McGill University and entered the ministry — a massive improvement in status from servitude to profession in a single generation. But this was Canada where anything was possible.

Earlier ancestors, United Empire Loyalists, were cleared from their homes twice, first from the highland Scottish glens and short years later from the valley of the Mohawk in New York with their Tory Dutch and Palatine neighbours and Iroquois allies at the time of the American Revolution against Great Britain. After seven years of bitter fighting and defeat they were rewarded with conditional title to small parcels of swamp and bush in Canada. In convenient military settlement they constituted a ring of militia to withstand the U.S. invasion that was to come.

All our Canadian beginnings were full of harsh suffering and adversity. It has made us what we are. It is what we have in common. For too long we have nursed our sensitivities and wrath respecting the past. Canada's future must never be held hostage to the past.

Actually we, the oppressed, have done rather well for ourselves in this great icy land! All our people may point to some past or present sorrow or shame — the Indian and Inuit, the French, the Jews, the Germans, the Irish, the Japanese, the British. The most uncomplaining of the exploited were the Chinese coolies who built our railroads. Though we have had restrictive laws, such as those against the Chinese in the nineteenth century, these have been corrected. We have managed to make it through every hardship and adversity. Now can we make it through together in affluence?

Abroad, Canada is perceived as a refuge from tyranny, oppression, and hopelessness. We are thought to be a nation intent upon building an ever more humane and compassionate society, a homeland where all people are invited to lay their gifts upon the country's altar. We are believed to possess an exemplary model of federalism, a federal structure that has survived and has evolved over an enduring period of time. And lately we ourselves have been preoccupied with making it better.

The Bill of Rights, bequeathed to us first by John Diefenbaker, was a sort of benediction expressing that sense of morality and fair play common to us all. We proclaim today that Canada is a large room with equal shelter and concern for all her children. But true brotherhood does not come in a week's wishing or in a new Bill of Rights.

The universal vices — envy, greed, and hatred — upon which I do not choose to dilate, are the root causes of our real problems. As Pogo remarked, we have discovered the enemy; it is ourselves. Our priority should be to turn this hatred unto love. Recent years have been decisive. Refugees from Hungary, Indo-China, and Latin America remind us of our treasures, peace, order, and good government, a democracy that is truly the light of many minds, the work of many hands, the love of many hearts.

In 1980, through the Quebec Referendum, we made a fateful decision that Canada, that our land, wide open, fruitful, is best. We must press on now towards making it "a better country". The spirit to do it is there.

Overseas, preparing for battle, we discovered that we

loved one another. After the bloody ordeal on the Dieppe beaches, elements of Les Fusiliers Mount-Royal were rounded up for "special treatment" by German Intelligence officers. These prisoners were offered generous chocolate rations, which they would have devoured like ravenous wolves had they not noticed that no rations were forthcoming to those who were English speaking. They refused to accept the chocolate. Better that they all be shackled together!

This is not the winter of despair but the spring of hope! This is the very best of times, the present, the time to plant, to build, to bind up. With hope we await the promise, believing in the reconciling mercy of the Creator and in the goodness of his creation, the human race, our race.

May this dream of brotherhood be fulfilled.

---- ✳ ----

Mission Unfolding
Ron D. Johnstone

For many years a United Church minister on the Prairies; now ministering in Victoria, British Columbia.

I cannot think of Canada without recalling my earliest memory of the church back on the Prairies during the dirty thirties. The church was the focal point of many communities and gave Canada much of its character. It was the one institution that gave hope when there seemed to be no hope; that gave direction when there was mainly bewilderment as people struggled to survive the driving winds and swirling dust. Much of social life was within the church; the fellowship of fowl suppers, programmes for youth, the annual picnic and summer camps. There were no songs on radio or TV. These things did not exist. The one place where you could sing was in the sanctuary of God.

The war years of 1939–45 were years of service, as many Red Cross parcels came from the hands of the church women at work. The church was one institution that gave hope amidst the war and was the sole comforter for people when delivered a telegram they hated to receive. The war ended with the bang of the atomic bomb and the church struggled to find itself and speak to people in the new age of power and increased transportation and communication. But the church was divided in itself into competing denominations, structures, and purpose.

The church today still struggles with the same questions, but has found a few answers in its being the servant of God, as it has become the eyes to the blind, comforter to the lonely, legs for the paraplegic, joy for the shut-ins. It has become more than ever the voice of God in a world community as Christian denominations, Sikh, Muslim, Buddhist, Baha'i, Jews, Nestorians, and others sit down together at a common table to discuss religion and world peace.

The church of God (no matter what name you call him by) is a disturbing force, a challenging force, a unifying force, and a loving force. Religious differences and divisions matter less in today's society than they did twenty or more years ago. May God's blessings be upon the church as "the Canadian experiment in world community" grows to maturity.

---

*

People Are the Reason

J.N. MacNeil

Native of Cape Breton and Roman Catholic Archbishop of Edmonton; has served his church in Nova Scotia and Saint John, New Brunswick.

Canada is my home. Anywhere in Canada I feel at home.

It has been my privilege to have been born and lived in Nova Scotia, to have lived in New Brunswick, and to live now in Alberta. Which do I prefer? All three of them!

They are complementary areas of this one country. Each has a uniqueness within a common Canadian reality.

Innumerable times I have crossed this country and worked with and visited many friends in many places. Always I feel at home. I have lived outside Canada for some years and I have travelled extensively on many occasions. Each return has made me appreciate even better my country and my countrymen.

Why? Without a doubt, I enjoy, immensely, our magnificent scenery, the oceans, the woods and trails, the snow and ice, the big skies, the vastness. We are truly blessed by the Lord! But the people are the real reason why I like Canada. We are a people proud of our racial and cultural roots and just as proud of our common Canadian identity, a people who have the best of two worlds — the world of tradition and history and the world of the present and future. This is a land where people of Highland Scottish origin are very much at home in Cape Breton revelling in the best of their Scottish heritage, at the same time an integral part of a new and vibrant Canadian people. The same may be said for the first settlers, the French, and the latest, the boat people from Vietnam.

Canada is a country of an almost infinite number and variety of communities. I refer not only to cultural communities, towns, and villages, but also to the communities of various religious persuasions, of business, labour, health care, Native Peoples, education, fraternal organizations, social and welfare organizations, professional groups, civil servants, artists, sports, media. These provide precious and personal links between Canadians forged by free association through multi-levelled groupings.

Canada to me means a country where people are comfortable with each other. It means a people who help one another live in freedom, love, and service. Canada means a people who appreciate God's great goodness to them; a people of deep moral and ethical principles; of great respect for the worth and freedom of others. This is my home.

---------------- * ----------------

Many Freedoms

James M. Brady

Of Charlottetown, Prince Edward Island; founding secretary of the PEI Public Service Association Union.

In terms of labour relations, I have been asked, what does Canada mean to you? After about a decade and a half of working in Canadian provincial public sector labour relations, that seemingly innocuous but sweeping question gives me pause. It calls for some reflection and self-examination. It conjures up a parade of past experiences — both positive and negative — together with present happenings and future aspirations.

The question, too, evokes a procession of nationalistic word images. They troop by as if aroused by a fanfare of patriotic trumpets at dawn. Words such as freedom, equality, democracy, loyalty, honour, unity, security, credibility, tenacity, tolerance, participation, persistence, and patience swing marching through the mind in full battle array, ready for action.

But of all these soldierly semantic symbols, I believe Canada means most to me in terms of freedom. Here in this country we have fought for and won many freedoms: the freedom to speak, organize, associate, petition, criticize, consult, negotiate, experiment, and advance to new and expanding liberties.

These are the rudiments on which most employer–employee relations structures are being built in Canada. Many of these freedoms are newly gained in public employment. Both in the federal service and in most provinces they are the legacy of the 1960s and 1970s. They have not been won without fight. And pockets of resistance still exist, particularly among the craggy peaks of collective bargaining. Whatever the problems, however, we can look for solutions shaped in a forum of freedom within our Canadian democracy.

Or can we? Are these freedoms already safe in consolidated territory? Should we now push on without so much as a backward glance at the hard-won landmarks behind us? Are our defences secure? If not, how do we defend these gains in the freedoms of our workplace? I suggest that there are three key factors to which we must direct our continuing attention: *participation*, *persistence*, and *patience*.

Effective participation is a particular problem on the worker's side of the employer–employee relations coin. For example, it would be exceptional rather than normal for managers to take the initiative in the activities of works' councils, consulting committees, or other joint assemblies. Instead, it usually falls on worker representatives to call meetings, prepare agendas, and lead discussions. Without the push and participation of employees, joint discussions and mutual problem-solving sessions — with their associated freedoms — soon disappear and are forgotten.

Persistence and patience also nurture our democratic freedoms, especially in the public sector. Early in this century two English social reformers, Sidney and Beatrice Webb, observed a trend and coined its description in the phrase, "the inevitability of gradualness". What could more graphically illustrate the process and progress of achieving legislative changes, such as those setting out the rules and regulations of labour relations? Anyone who has pierced the protective and often puzzling web of government bureaucracy rarely has done so without testing his capacity for tenacity and tolerance. These two qualities are, indeed, essential to success in holding and securing the scope of freedoms we have gained.

In addition, let us learn from the lessons of others in the pursuit and protection freedom. Let us note well the evils of suppression as well as the benefits of expression. And let us always be vigilant!

---------------------------------- ❋ ----------------------------------

Basic Values
James M. Courtright

Director of estate planning for Queen's University in Kingston, Ontario, where he previously was vice president; in his youth a world-ranking javelin thrower and later an executive with Shell Canada.

My roots in North America go back to 1663. I was raised in a typical Canadian household where family solidarity and parental concern for the children were paramount. We knew we were loved. In our community, schooling was available to all. Sports and a host of extracurricular and neighbourhood activities were part of life. We were taught the importance of work, thrift, patience, and perseverance, of sharing with one another. We were taught that happiness does not depend on affluence. We learned that in Canada there is respect for authority, that rights imply duties, that liberty is different from licence, that initiative and diligence are avenues to progress. The lessons of those times ring in my ears and still have application.

Canada, fortunately, has been modest and reasonable in expressing its democratic views to the world. Our credibility has been established. The education, management and technical skills, and investment capital of our people are appreciated abroad. Canadian know-how and advice are frequently sought by other countries.

We are a democratic nation. Yet over recorded world history, government of peoples has most often been authoritarian and is, in most cases, even to this day. The norm is autocracy or dictatorship. *The real revolutionary societies — those that change things in human history — are the democracies of the western world*. They have dared to be different, to allow freedom of choice, and to discipline themselves through laws arrived at in open discussion rather than imposed from above by individuals or a tightly knit clique.

Our society is pluralistic. By that I mean it manifests a great variety of races and of collective human endeavours. This is a good thing. It brings much important information and different points of view to the fore. But it raises a question. Who speaks for the common good?

Today, special interest groups abound and can be dangerous. They are usually unwilling to admit that any good can have a higher priority than their special cause. They are often unable or choose not to compromise intelligently for a workable consensus, and media reporting gives them undue attention. The public often receives a partial picture of an important issue to the detriment of the general welfare. Real freedom is more likely to prevail when we have well-balanced, up-to-date information.

Canada's history also tells us that a democratic nation requires wise leadership with an understanding of what is both needed and workable — a healthy degree of pragmatism. Equally important, our financial structure must not collapse. When will we all learn that the size of the pie is limited?

My hope and prayer is that Canada, uniquely blessed, will not become an autocratic nation at home and will not grow narrow, self-centred, or pompous abroad. Our prime role as Canadian citizens, I believe, is to be good stewards of the country that has been entrusted to us — to be true to ourselves.

--- ✳ ---

Barriers Removed

Gilbert Finn

President of Moncton University, New Brunswick; insurance company executive and well-known Acadian.

We are living in an industrialized country where with a sense of belonging we must transcend regionalism, cultures, and language, without losing sight of these essential parts of a nationhood.

Our language, customs, songs, dances, and folklore are riches that have been left to us by our ancestors, and these must be conserved. The fishermen of Cape Breton and the Western farmers certainly do not have the same habits, customs, or language, but each group reflects its own natural environment from the diverse regions of the country.

We must, nevertheless, rise above the natural frontiers that separate us and go far beyond those often built by man himself. In order fully to enjoy our freedom and our nationality, it is essential that we are able to feel at home everywhere in Canada. If we all wish to be Canadians from "sea to sea" and to have that gut feeling of identity, long-expressed desires must become realities. Throughout the country, we must speak to each other and each one of us must learn to be more conciliatory.

There are barriers to be taken down, but in a spirit of close collaboration our children could, if we give them the chance and the means, live tomorrow in great areas garnished with lakes, forests, mountains, prairies, towns, and countryside; a busy life — a life of liberty and peace.

———————————— ✳ ————————————

Rooted in Justice

Samuel Freedman

Chief Justice of the Manitoba Supreme Court.

I have never sought to keep secret my affection for Canada. It was not, I regret to say, the land of my birth. That regret is genuine. I was born in Russia, a circumstance that fills me with no pride but which I simply record as a fact. Our family left Russia when I was about three-and-a-half years old, so, fortunately, my memories are all Canadian. Indeed, I take my Russian origin on the basis of information and belief.

In assessing the land of my adoption, I must guard against a double danger. One is the danger of romanticizing on the theme, of yielding to uncritical, fulsome praise. So let me acknowledge at once that Canada has had its blemishes, its hours of shortened vision, its mistakes, and its fools. That is to say, it is human. And the other danger is of adopting the cynicism of the worldly wise cynic, to play the role of the perpetual fault-finder, the eternal kicker, the person who regards everything Canadian as necessarily inferior simply because it is Canadian. I find no allure whatever in this kind of inverted patriotism.

Many are the reasons for which Canada may legitimately be esteemed. I will refer only to three, knowing full well that other reasons, no less pertinent or valid than mine, will emerge from the contributions of others who are parties to this project.

First, we have made a commitment in favour of democracy rooted in freedom. We are a free society. In such a society the state exists for man, not man for the state. Deeply cherished are the fundamental freedoms — freedom of speech, the press, assembly, conscience. The free society believes that life has an ethical basis and that nothing counts for more than the dignity of human personality. The unfree state has the pagan outlook on life and believes, in the words of an American educator, that man simply eats, drinks, sleeps, dies, and goes down into the ditch, man and beast alike.

Second, we believe in the rule of law. That means something different from law and order. The latter phrase conjures up memories of Bull Connor and the truncheons and mace and the fire hoses and the dogs — indeed the whole apparatus of official repression. The rule of law is something else. In its best, ideal form it implies a government of laws and not of men; it rests on the concept of equal justice for all; it aspires to that higher morality in which law and justice will be one; and it recognizes that the courtroom, no less than Parliament itself, remains a citadel and a sanctuary of our democratic faith.

So, within the framework of a society committed to democracy rooted in freedom and functioning under the protection of the rule of law, Canadians have been given the opportunity of living their lives both freely and creatively. In responding to that challenge Canadians have evolved the concept of multiculturalism, which brings me to the third of my reasons for holding Canada in high esteem.

Within our country two major groups and several minor groups are still learning the lesson of living together as Canadians. The problem is frequently made more difficult by counsels of extremism coming from two different quarters: from those who speak the language of group exclusiveness or separatism, and from those who would impose conformity to a fixed pattern. In an earlier day, the price that members of a minority group were expected to pay for Canadianism was their own disappearance as a recognizable group, a disappearance effected by bleaching themselves of their ethnic heritage and background. A more enlightened sociological attitude exists today in the form of multiculturalism.

I would set two pre-conditions to the right to practise multiculturalism: the first, one political allegiance only, namely to Canada; and the second, participation in the corporate life of one's surroundings, not withdrawal therefrom. But over and above what I would call these shared interests exists room for minority cultural concerns. And out of the interplay of group with group, each contributing something of its special heritage to the common treasury of Canadian citizenship, can come reciprocal stimulations and enrichments making for a healthier and more vibrant society.

12

*

Yesterday, Today, and Tomorrow

Memories and Dreams
Jean B. Forest

Chancellor emeritus of the University of Alberta, founding member of the Alberta Human Rights Commission, and recipient of numerous awards for services to her community, her church, and her country.

For me, Canada is first and foremost my country, my home, my native land: not just a place to be, but also a point of departure and happy return, and not just in a physical sense but emotionally and spiritually as well. For me Canada holds the security of a sense of belonging, and she is never more inviting, more beautiful, more precious, than when I have just returned from a stay on foreign soil.

For me Canada is an immense collection of memories, memories of:

- A rambling farm home where I was born and raised and the fertile fields of the Swan River valley, Manitoba.
- The worried look of a father as he gauged the potential impact of an approaching hail storm on ripening crops of wheat.
- The sound of sleigh-bells and the frosty crunch of trodden snow.
- The smell of buffalo robes and a freshly cut Christmas tree.
- The challenge of learning in a one-room schoolhouse, at Oakhurst and Minitonas, and of teaching in two others, at Rosa, Pine River, and Barkham, La Salle — all in Manitoba, and all long gone.
- A church wedding in the midst of a Prairie Blizzard.
- A first glimpse of post-World War II Edmonton from the winding approaches of the old Dawson Bridge (still crossed daily, thirty-five years later).
- An exciting motorbike trek through the Rockies near Jasper.
- Summers of sunning, swimming, and sailing with seven

kids and a good-natured husband, "Rock", on Point Alison, Lake Wabamun.

- Winters of wiping noses and tying ski boots for the same kids at Marmot Basin, Jasper, and sharing with Rock their thrill in conquering the slopes and later the peaks.
- Celebrating Canada's Centennial — all nine of us — with a cross-country tour (including visits to Parliament and Expo) in a renovated school bus that blew up and burned at Matapedia, Quebec.
- Celebrating, with thanksgiving, the recovery of a badly burned Rock and the safe return home of all, thanks to Air Canada, and the help of many Eastern Canadians.
- Returning years later to Gaspé to finish that ill-fated trip and finding many of Rock's long-lost French Canadian cousins.
- Memories of many other visits across Canada: setting down in a tiny float plane on fog-bound Barkley Sound on Vancouver Island. Putting in at Fort St. James, BC, and travelling up to Takla Lake by river boat.
- Watching from Hay River, NWT, a tug with her barges in tow set out for the mighty Mackenzie and the Beaufort Sea.
- Climbing Signal Hill, Newfoundland, with Rock remembering "The Gates" from his navy days in World War II.

Memories, many memories, both happy and bittersweet. But Canada is so much more than yesterday's memories. Canada is also as thrilling today, a sight to behold in all her seasons:

- The startling beauty of her lacy new leaves and first spring flowers.
- The brilliant blue of her sunlit lakes and summer streams.
- The golden glory of her September grain fields.
- The riot of colour in her autumn hardwoods.
- The magnificent splendour of her snow-capped mountains and frosty plains.

Most of all, Canada is a fascinating future, an exciting challenge for all — to strive, to spin, to weave one's hopes and dreams into the fabric of her many tomorrows:

- Exciting tomorrows, discovered by a dynamic people alive to the possibilities of a challenging world.
- Creative tomorrows come true for an inspired people stretching to reach new heights in knowledge and truth.
- Resourceful tomorrows made real by an industrious people working together with differing talents and skills.
- Peaceful tomorrows made possible by a freedom-loving people — native and newcomer alike — living together in new-found harmony and understanding.
- Giving tomorrows, made good by a kindly people, blessed with abundance and sharing their bounty with their less fortunate friends at home and abroad.
- Happy tomorrows, made glad by the laughter of young and old alike living in love and harmony within the hearts and the homes of the nation.

Together these many tomorrows could make of Canada the hope of the world. "I stand on guard for thee!"

✳

Appendix

More than 1,000,000 Canadians and 1,000 Civic Councils from nine provinces and two territories signed this Petition, which was presented to the people of Quebec in public just before their Referendum of May 1980.

PETITION COMMITTEE
CHAIRMAN AND CO-CHAIRMAN
James MacNutt, P.E.I.
G. Keith Cowan, B.C.

URGENT - YOU CAN HELP UNITE CANADA - PLEASE STUDY AND SIGN

PEOPLE TO PEOPLE PETITION FOR CANADIAN UNITY

"IN A SPIRIT OF UNDERSTANDING AND TO BETTER MEET THE ONGOING NEEDS AND HOPES OF ALL OUR PEOPLES, WE THE UNDERSIGNED FROM BRITISH COLUMBIA TO NEWFOUNDLAND INVITE QUEBECOIS MEMBERS OF OUR CANADIAN FAMILY TO REMAIN CANADIAN AND TO CONTINUE BUILDING WITH US THIS MAGNIFICENT CANADA."

HONORARY CHAIRMEN

Newfoundland: Dr. G.A. Frecker, O.C. Chancellor, Memorial University.

Nova Scotia: Hon. Victor de B. Oland, Lieutenant Governor - 1968-73.

Prince Edward Island: Dr. Gustave Gingras, C.C. F.R.C.P. (c). Past President C.M.A. and Chancellor, University of Prince Edward Island.

New Brunswick: Hon. Hugh John Flemming, Premier, 1952-60; **Martin J. Légère,** O.C., General Manager, Federation of Acadian Credit Unions.

Ontario: John Fisher, O.C. "Mr. Canada."

Manitoba: Sylvia Burka, World Speed Skating Champion, 1976-77, Canadian Female Athlete of the Year, 1977.

Saskatchewan: Hon. Dr. Stephen Worobetz, Lieutenant Governor - 1970-76.

Alberta: Mrs. Jean B. Forest, Chancellor-Elect, University of Alberta.

Northwest Territories & Yukon: W. Grant Hinchey, Vice President N.W.T. Chamber of Commerce.

British Columbia: Mrs. Norma Sharpe, B.C. Chairman, Canada Week Committee;
Chief Dan George.

FULL TEXT
TO OUR FELLOW CANADIANS OF QUEBEC AND TO ALL CANADIAN POLITICAL LEADERS

We the undersigned are Canadians of good will from many faiths, many ethnic and language backgrounds and every part of the country.

Our petition comes from hearts and heads that care about Canada. It began among ordinary citizens in Charlottetown, P.E.I., where Confederation itself was conceived. For we are convinced that the voices of ordinary Canadians must reach to each other across the often diverse claims of political parties and the often angry postures of many voices in T.V., radio and the press.

Decisions about the future of Canada which will vitally affect not only ourselves, but the well-being of our children and the generations which follow should not be made without weighing the massive good will and faith which we believe lies unexpressed among the vast majority of Canadians.

We fully recognize that when Canada was formed 110 years ago the two cultural groups who agreed to Confederation, also agreed to accept each other's rights, dignities and symbols of parenthood. We recognize and regret that these rights and dignities have sometimes been neglected or offended. Yet we earnestly believe that our short history has been a valuable learning experience of great achievements and many growing pains from which we can together shape those challenges which will ensure a better future. By keeping together our huge natural resources which abound in Canada from coast to coast and our skilled and energetic human resources which have already brought prosperity, by world comparison, to most Canadians, we are certain that we can best meet the future needs of our still neglected areas and peoples.

We also believe that we can give hope to a watching world badly endangered by divisions, the consequences of which we cannot escape, by demonstrating that different peoples can solve their problems in mutual respect and to mutual advantage while living within a common border.

We believe, too, that the concepts we jointly cherish of the dignity of the individual person, freedoms of speech, religion and the press and the right to democratically change a government are unifying forces and are best preserved in a unity which will also protect minorities in all provinces.

We then, the undersigned, reach across to Quebecois members of our family to ask with full hearts and clear heads that you choose overwhelmingly to remain with us and continue to build together a more magnificent Canada. To all Canadians, this is a call for rededication to Canada's future.

We further urge our Provincial and Federal political leaders to heed our concerns and resolve national issues in a fair and workable way which will ensure a united future and more fully meet the ongoing needs and aspirations of Canadians in all parts of the land.